L.C. no. 48-6188

ordered 4-9-54

HEIRS APPARENT

HEIRS APPARENT

The Vice Presidents of the United States

Klyde Young
&
Lamar Middleton

PRENTICE-HALL, INC.

New York

CONTENTS

CHAPTER I

John Adams

IN THE EARLY YEARS of the eighteenth century in this
country, when our elders dressed better and regarded a mug
of ale at night as a solemn duty, a restive few men lived in the
several urban communities of the British Colonies. But most
families lived on farms, the farms adjoining the villages and, with
the help of the conventionally large brood of children and, at
times, a small village industry, there was a living of sorts to be
had. But life was undeniably precarious.

One such farm was located at Braintree, Massachusetts, the
property of the Adamses, and it had been in the possession of
that family for four generations. In intelligence and industry,
its members were more than a cut above their neighbors. In 1640,
the American founder of the Adams clan, Henry, was awarded
a land grant on condition that he "do build a house and cultivate
said grant of land." He did more than that: he "cultivated" a
family of twelve children. He prospered better than most on the
stony, unrewarding soil of Massachusetts where farmers rejoiced
when, along the seaboard, storms washed seaweed, which served
as fertilizer, over the land.

As a progenitor, his son Joseph was almost as prolific as the
father. Joseph begat eleven heirs, one of whom, John, was to be
the father of the John Adams of American history.

The father of that Adams had attended Harvard College and,
indeed, by 1732, forty-nine young men of the Braintree area had
been subjected to the seat of learning—somewhat rudimentary
then—founded by the New England carpenter, John Harvard;
to those who had the means, Harvard was the one and only col-

lege to attend. He was duly graduated and, in 1734, he married a pretty Worcester girl, Suzanne. After a year Suzanne came to bed with child, in the homely locution of the day, and there was born to her a son, John. His father remarked that he was a chubby boy "serious of mien from birth," and those who knew him later added the observation that he was "serious of mien to his death." The date of the birth of that Adams, who was to become first Vice-President and later President of the infant United States of America, was October 19, 1735.

George Washington was then three and one-half years old; Thomas Jefferson was not to be born for eight years; John's cousin, Samuel Adams, who was to wield much influence over him, was a lad of twelve; and Benjamin Franklin, a printer and one of the liveliest citizens of Philadelphia, was twenty-nine. On the other side of the Atlantic, King George II of Britain was confronted with a hostile Parliament, Europe was in the turmoil of the War of the Polish Succession, and that of the Austrian Succession was looming on the horizon.

Because his father needed help as soon as possible—he was not only a farmer but also a cordwainer, a village selectman, and a militia officer—John was promptly subjected to the three R's; in adult years he protested wryly that "when hardly out of petticoats I started to school." His first teacher was one Mrs. Belcher, who sought to make him digest Latin and Greek at an age when today most boys would have progressed no farther than the multiplication tables. With an acute eye for turning a penny, the pupil took Mrs. Belcher's corn to the mill, for which she paid him three coppers a trip, and earnestly advised him to hoard that munificent sum and use it to buy land.

The young Adams had a schoolmate at Mrs. Belcher's class, John Hancock, who was also to be with him later at Harvard. Some years later, Adams defended Hancock on a charge of smuggling wines into the country, and succeeded in obtaining an acquittal although the evidence was overwhelming against his client. For all of that, Hancock and Adams were never cordial, and Hancock once wrote that Adams was "a pecunious student, vain and vaunting."

In those colonial days, young men went to college early, if they went at all. There were no schools corresponding to the secondary classes of today, and at the age of fifteen the young Adams entered Harvard. There is virtually nothing recorded of his college days other than suggestions that he was unhappy at Cambridge. He once wrote that he would always be a "country boy" and that he had found it difficult to adjust himself to a "select school for gentlemen"; apparently, he felt confined, and missed roaming through the woods at Braintree. So uncomfortable was he that he soon left school. He had his father's permission but his parent insisted, since the son was uninterested in Harvard, that he do something constructive and productive.

The future President was put to work digging ditches on the ancestral farm.

The young Adams soon discovered, however, that digging ditches at Braintree was even more distasteful than the confinements of Harvard. His father consented to his return to Cambridge but warned that there was a limit to his patience. Adams went back to Cambridge, unhappy over his inability to make decisions and chafing also at the domination of his father—a relationship about which he complained often in later life.

Despite his determination to resume his education, the young man never became an intrinsic part of the Harvard student body. In his years of young manhood, the first Vice-President was undeniably something of a prig. In his last year at Harvard, two students were expelled for "indignant and personal insults" to an instructor, which shocked Adams, and he was appalled also when during Commencement Week he learned that "students indulged in gambling, rioting and all kinds of dissipation. Many entertained their friends in their quarters and served them punch," he recorded in horror, and "many even indulged in the practice of addressing the female sex."

But his straight-laced conduct and toeing the mark paid divi-

3

dends. He was graduated as fifth highest in his class. He had had no pleasant, fraternal life at college, and had left no mark as a leader in any undergraduate activity, but he had been an assiduous grind, a lonely youth who had returned to school rather than continue digging ditches.

Adams returned to the Braintree farm where, with the aid of the Congregational parson, he found a teaching post. Then as now teachers were wretchedly paid, and part of his stipend came in the "privilege" of boarding, a week at a time, in the homes of his pupils. When he began teaching, the twenty-year-old Adams was described by a colleague as "haughty of mien, vain and arrogant"; had there been a psychologist in his day, his finding probably would have been that the young schoolmaster had been employing arrogance to hide an acute inferiority complex.

Adams' parents had hoped that John, once out of Harvard, would turn to the ministry; both father and mother were staunch Congregationalists and, while clergymen were paid almost as miserably as teachers, the older Adamses felt that luster would be added to their name if the son became a country preacher; moreover, his selection of subjects at Cambridge had prepared him for the ministry.

Pressure was increasingly exercised on the young teacher by his parents. To determine his own feelings, he took long walks through the Braintree woods. He wondered unhappily whether he could accept the tenets of Calvinism in their entirety; and he speculated also whether he might not make a better physician or surgeon. In this period of self-doubt and anguish, he journeyed to Boston to survey the opportunities for medical study. The more he inquired into that field, the more he felt he was unsuited to become a physician; but at the same time, he felt increasingly that he was unfitted to become a man of the cloth.

In the end, he decided upon the law. It was a historic decision, both for himself and the future United States.

These were the days of the French and Indian War. While the young Washington was in the West, campaigning with General

Edward Braddock, Adams studied law under a Mr. Putnam and later under the eminent Gridley. He was only a fair student but he persevered. By 1758, he believed he was sufficiently prepared to hang out his shingle at Braintree. He was soon admitted to the bar, along with Josiah Quincy, who was to become a leading pamphleteer in that pre-Revolutionary period, and the two young men celebrated their success by drinking punch at Stone's Tavern in Braintree.

He lost his initial two cases—more cause for the chronically worrying Adams to entertain gnawing doubts of his abilities. He noted despondently, in his diary at this period, that "I am not destined for the Law"—a remark that in retrospect seems somewhat bizarre. He appears to have been cajoled out of his monetary despairs by the pretty wife of one Dr. Sabil, although for a time he neglected his practice to devote hours to discussing Ovid's *Art of Love* with the lady. At this period he read widely in fields unrelated to the law which, at least, resulted in an increased vocabulary. How much use that was to the young Adams might seem open to question, since he utilized it chiefly for acidulous criticism of virtually everyone with whom he came in contact—his women acquaintances included.

In 1761, his father died and John, the eldest son, then twenty-six, became the head of the family. Life was now a degree more earnest, and his mind turned to politics as a means of advancement. He cottoned up to the armchair politicians in the twelve taverns in Braintree, most of them young men whom Adams had openly criticized as wastrels in other years (he had assailed them as "men of vile and filthy dispositions"); and he was perhaps more surprised than anyone when he succeeded in getting his brother appointed a deputy sheriff. But it was a lesson in practical politics.

But apparently, in 1763, he suffered another lapse from grace since he noted in his diary that he neglected his practice because of a prepossession with young women. In self-horror, he confessed that he "dallied with the ladies," and that he was "amorous," but he was careful to qualify this damning indictment by writing that he was not a seducer and that "no virgin or matron ever had cause to blush at the sight of me."

One of the young women with whom he was "prepossessed" was Abigail Smith, a bright and witty girl and the daughter of a Braintree minister. She had never attended school but she had been tutored by her grandmother; she knew some languages and verse and could quote Pope and other English poets. Evidently, she did a good deal to restore him to the path of rectitude and to narrow down his prepossession with the other sex. They were married in October, 1764. A son, representing the sixth generation of Adamses in America, was born a year later, and in the next decade there were four more children—still more causes for worry.

There is evidence throughout his life that Adams was something of a professional hypochondriac. A few years after his marriage, he complained of some pains in his chest, which were diagnosed as trivial but were an agreeable and lifelong cause for anxiety.

When Adams was thirty, in 1765, he was elected a selectman of Braintree (soon to be renamed Quincy). This was his first upward step on the political ladder. But the real turning point of his career came five years later after the Boston Massacre. Popular hatred of British troops led to a brawl between the citizens and a British detachment commanded by Captain Thomas Prescott. The officer was indicted for murder and he could find no lawyer to defend him: Boston attorneys were well aware, of course, of the mounting detestation of the British authorities, and they side-stepped his pleas for defense counsel. In the end, Prescott went to Adams, with tears in his eyes, pleading that he defend him.

There is room for irony in the fact that Adams, subsequently the second President, consented to defend a British officer on a charge of murder. It is only just to point out, however, that Adams showed unquestionable courage in defending Prescott for whom he won an acquittal, as well as for six of his command of eight. Adams succeeded also in winning light sentences for the other two British troopers.

That act, however, did him no harm. It won him the approval, obviously, of the Loyalists, and even the insurgents throughout the colonies paid grudging tribute to his pluck and recognized that every man (even a British officer) is entitled to a defense. Adams had thought he had jeopardized his future; instead, soon after the trial he was elected to the colonial assembly where he promptly began to worry over the increasing likelihood of revolution. His diary at this juncture overflows with expressions of his fear and distaste of violence.

Now his practice in Boston began to increase and at least he was relieved of any anxieties on the score of personal finances. Samuel Adams, his cousin and later governor of Massachusetts, persuaded him to join the Sons of Liberty. He was not liked by patriots in that organization but at least one member conceded that this "vain, vaunting and bigoted" lawyer-politician had exceptional talents. In any event, and whatever the degree of dislike of Adams, those talents were such as to bring him into close association with the eventual leaders of the imminent American Revolution. Evidently, they quickly won him over to the conviction that an uprising was justifiable and inevitable, for he gloated over the Boston Tea Party (1773) and the audacity of its participants.

He was elected a delegate to the First Continental Congress, through the influence of Samuel Adams, and with him, Hancock and Robert Treat Paine rode to Philadelphia on horseback. This was his first prolonged absence from Abigail and the four children. While away, he wrote her letters that were given over chiefly to criticism of his colleagues at Philadelphia, and to complaints that they did not admit that Washington had been nominated commander in chief of the Continental Armies at his suggestion. He protested also at flippant references to him as "His Royal Rotundity"; Adams was not overendowed with humor.

Not much was achieved at Philadelphia, and the Massachusetts delegates, regarded as rabble-rousers by the Virginia delegates, went home to somewhat aroused constituencies. Nevertheless, Adams was sent to the Massachusetts provincial congress. Lexington and Concord came and went: he was unexcited, convinced now that revolution would burst on the scene in a matter of hours. The following year he was sent to the Second Continental Congress and while there Bunker Hill was fought, the action in which much of the youth of Massachusetts died. Abigail wrote that smallpox and dysentery were at every hand, and that at Braintree alone there were as many as four funerals a day. She wanted him home but Adams, working day and night, could not be spared. In December, 1775, Massachusetts appointed him Chief Justice of the Commonwealth, a post he accepted when he could leave Philadelphia. In the following June, he was named to the committee, with Jefferson, Samuel Adams, Benjamin Franklin, Roger Sherman, and Robert R. Livingston to draft the Declaration of Independence, and in that month he wrote to his wife that "British rule has come to an end in the Colonies." On July 4, 1776, the final form of the Declaration was approved, and a new nation was at war.

A few days later Adams was appointed chairman of the Board of War and Ordinance, the equivalent of a secretary of war. He remained in that post, criticizing every one from Washington down, until November, 1777, when he was appointed American minister to France by the Continental Congress. He took the young John Quincy with him on the voyage of forty-five days. Evidently the lad was far better liked in the French capital than his father. He had to play second fiddle to Franklin, who was seeking financial assistance of France and her intervention, and who treated this "fat, paunchy, vain New England prig" with undisguised contempt; for his part, Adams charged that Franklin surrounded himself in Paris with atheists, libertines and "with the ladies."

Two years later he sailed for home where he was elected to the Massachusetts Constitutional Convention. Two years later he was ordered back to France to attempt treaty negotiations with the British ambassador at Paris. Again, Franklin forestalled him—

"Franklin, with his eighteen mistresses." Soon thereafter he went to The Hague, as American minister, where he was rid of the disdainful Franklin.

Adams found the Dutch "pleasant people to deal with and, again, Old Ben Franklin is not here," he added with unabashed relief. He insisted that he was the only person in Europe empowered to discuss peace terms, and the Dutch believed him.

In 1780, Adams fell ill; he had worn himself out with worry. He wrote to Abigail in October: "I am sick, I have had too much trouble, I cannot take a pen in hand to write to anybody."

He learned that he had been appointed to a peace committee with Franklin, John Jay, Henry Laurens, and Jefferson. He was grievously disappointed for he had hoped to be the sole member. And Cornwallis' surrender did not cure him of his melancholia. During the five years he was to spend in Europe, he broadened in outlook, acquired some of the social graces so necessary to European diplomacy and after his own fashion he became a diplomat—that is, if a paunchy and vain New England lawyer might be called a diplomat.

He still detested Franklin, now seventy-six, old and infirm: "he has the gout and gravel and a stranguary, and cannot sleep." (Adams' tone here is frankly exultant.) Yet the old man was governor of Pennsylvania at eighty, and was active until eighty-four.

Adams returned to Paris for a third time, on this occasion with confidence. He returned to the same quarrels and bickerings. When the news came of his appointment to Great Britain as the first ambassador from the United States of America to the Court of St. James, he was inflated with pleasure. He sent for Abigail and the family; he had been away from most of them almost constantly for five years. They settled in London, and began preparations to meet George III. New clothes were purchased including expensive gowns which Abigail could never use again; that pained the frugal New England housewife who had become an ambassador's lady.

John and Abigail were coached in every move they were to

make. They must be letter perfect for every eye would see the least mistake made at the presentation. The Massachusetts lawyer and the parson's daughter met His Majesty, and John wrote it "was not such an ordeal" as he had expected. Abigail noted that "the women at Court are plain, ill-shaped and ugly."

John knew that he was unpopular. He settled down to live at an expensive hotel until he could find a suitable house in Grosvenor Square—"a large dwelling, well situated and comfortable, but terribly expensive withal."

Jefferson went to France as minister, and he and Adams worked well together. Each had respect for the other.

In appointing Adams as minister to Great Britain, there was less desire to promote harmony than to protect American interests from encroachment by a nation which still considered us incorrigible children. Great Britain had hopes of once again taking those children under her wing. Indeed, there were many within the new republic itself who believed that a mistake had been made, and that Americans should return to the mother country. (While the war had come to an end, Great Britain still held many forts throughout the West. There were interminable arguments as to reparations, boundaries, the citizenship status of the Tories, and always the demand when would the forts be evacuated? There was the issue of reciprocal trade agreements, dear to Adams' mind. He tried vainly to get definite answers from the British government. The minister fretted and worried. Little Abbie married the secretary of the American legation. He was "a poor secretary but a fine gentleman socially," the father-in-law observed.

There arose the problem of the Barbary pirates. The United States was paying $30,000 yearly for "protection." Adams met the Tripolitan envoy in London. He smoked a long pipe with him, one "with a stem more than two yards long." He came away from the conference to recommend that the bribes continue. Jefferson stubbornly refused to be a party to any such agreement, and the rest is history. The war with the Barbary states followed, and the older nations of the world were made to realize that the United States would not pay one cent for tribute: a good policy for a young nation to establish. For that, no award is due Adams.

He spent three years in London, stalemated on almost every side. He came to know that a complete reconciliation was impossible. So he went home, a defeated man. In the spring of 1787, he wrote of his "unutterable decision to come home at all events," but he did not wish to return without permission. Would his friends undertake to provoke his recall? He did not receive his instructions until December, when he received a letter from John Jay saying that his resignation had been accepted. His leave-taking was frigid. Nothing had been gained by his three years' stay in London. The prospects of a treaty were as remote as they were in 1785.

The Constitution had been ratified by a majority of the states and the new republic was preparing for its first general election. There was no doubt in the minds of Americans who the President would be. The only discussion was over the Vice-President, "the Heir Apparent." Many men were receptive to filling the post. Hancock felt that if the President were to come from Virginia, why should not the second highest office go to New England, and why not to the leading citizen of Massachusetts? Alexander Hamilton was not to be considered because of his foreign birth. In the end, Hamilton decided Adams might be the man, but he advised his friends not to cast too many votes for Adams and to scatter their votes.

Chinard in his *Honest John Adams* believes that Hamilton's advice was due to the fact that Adams had been known to disagree with Washington during the Revolution. Thus, if the Vice-President, constitutionally with little power, obtained the endorsement of a large majority, he might try to rally his partisans and become a burden to the first President.

When the elections were held, Washington was named President by unanimous choice, and Adams was made Vice-President. He had no definite knowledge what his duties were to be when he left Boston for New York. He left in elaborate style and he was careful to note that "a procession of forty carriages" escorted him on his way.

For eight years he presided over the small body of men who made up the United States Senate. They numbered twenty-four at first, later increased to thirty-two. As today, the Vice-President voted only in the event of a tie. In the small Senate of that time its members were more evenly divided than in later years, and the records of the Senate show that Adams was called on to vote many times. He invariably explained his vote at prodigious length. He delivered tedious lectures to the Senate on its conduct, morals, and on parliamentary law. He wore a "wig and a small sword" and was fond of discussing titles to be used in addressing the President. He discussed abstruse points in the Constitution.

He would visit the House of Representatives where the members spent much of their time lampooning him to his face.

With the President, he was on good terms. He liked the cabinet. Hamilton, brilliant and shrewd, was Secretary of the Treasury. Edmund Randolph, the Attorney General, was a Virginian and another man of accomplishments. Henry Knox, the Secretary of War, was from Adams' own state; Jefferson was Secretary of State.

Adams was asked occasionally to consult with the President, but he soon realized that no man could influence Washington. Adams wrote of him at this time, "he seeks information from all quarters, and judges more independently than any man I ever knew."

He entertained the President and the first lady. He was the President's host when Washington toured the New England states, and he basked in reflected glory.

Adams did some writing during this period. For *Fenners Gazette of the United States* he wrote a series of thirty-one essays forming the *Discourses on Davila,* a "dull heavy volume," to quote its author when he was old and infirm.

Adams was dissatisfied with the Constitution. He would have given the President the right to a veto without review on all bills. He would have made him a sort of monarchial President, elective but all powerful. Adams felt that the republic might not endure. It was interesting that Hamilton held the same view as did many leaders of what was later the Federalist party. Their apprehensions are perhaps understandable in that they were only a few years removed from kings and monarchial powers. But there were men who had opposite convictions. Washington, Lee, Henry, Randolph, Jefferson, and Madison, these men were certain the republic would continue; they felt that with a few changes the Constitution would work.

In 1791, Adams broke with Jefferson. That belongs to the stream of American history and cannot be treated in a chapter on the life of John Adams. It suffices here to say that in the publication of Tom Paine's *Rights of Man,* dedicated to Washington, Jefferson wrote the foreword in which by implication he attacked Adams, and for twenty years the two men, who had once been companionable, were implacable enemies. So they remained until they were old men when, through the efforts of a mutual friend the breach was healed and their friendship restored.

The second election was held in 1792, and again there could be no doubt as to who would be President. As Vice-President the newspapers of the country named as available candidates Samuel Adams, John Jay, George Clinton, James Madison, and at the bottom of most lists, John Adams. One New York paper asked its readers to "examine those who have endeavored to prepare the people of America for a King."

The contest was soon one between Clinton and Adams. When in November the ballots were counted, Washington was again President by unanimous vote of the nation. For Vice-President, John Adams received seventy-four votes; Clinton fifty; Jefferson (who was not a candidate) four; and Aaron Burr one. The sun of Burr rose over the horizon with that single vote.

In Washington's second administration there occurred the French Revolution, the Genêt affair, and internal dissensions. Jefferson said "it will require all the address, all the temper, all the firm men of Congress and the state to keep this people out of the European war." The nation did keep out of a shooting war. Adams continued to preside over the Senate. He read much, he wrote some.

Abigail had gone back to Braintree from Philadelphia. John was a lonely man of fifty-eight, growing fatter and his breath shorter. The Vice-President's salary was $5,000 a year, and he wrote that "it is difficult to maintain a ménage in Philadelphia."

Washington's cabinet had undergone some changes. Hamilton was no longer in the treasury; Oliver Wolcott had succeeded him. Tim Pickering, a Puritan, had displaced Randolph as Secretary of State, and Jefferson was another cabinet casualty. The second Washington cabinet was not of the caliber of the first. None save Randolph, the Attorney General, had more than mediocre ability.

Inevitably, intrigue was developing. Hamilton, on the outside, could now play politics. The treaties with France and England had been signed and were under debate by the Senate. They were imperfect but they were treaties. The senators discussed them behind closed doors and Adams listened. He did not vote.

Washington, tired, was determined to retire. For twenty-five years he had been in the thick of battle. He was surfeited with honors. Adams knew that here was his opportunity.

There were two self-admitted candidates, Adams and General Charles Pinckney. Jefferson was put forward by his friends in the South, but he was little interested. He made no campaign although he would serve if elected. General Pinckney was a man of undoubted qualities; he had been an outstanding patriot but he could arouse no enthusiasm among the electorate.

Adams campaigned energetically. He craved the Presidency. Hamilton came to his aid and his hopes grew. Jefferson, his enemy, went so far as to write him a letter in which he expressed hopes that he would be elected.

In the end, the ballots gave Adams seventy-one votes, Jefferson sixty-eight, and Pinckney fifty-nine. Burr received thirty votes and Samuel Adams, John's cousin, polled eleven. Adams swore roundly at elections in general, especially those held in republics.

He was President by five votes only. That unpleasant fact was kept before him by his enemies; he was never permitted to forget that he was President by the narrowest margin.

At the Inauguration, Washington welcomed and honored his successor. There were resounding cheers for the outgoing President, few for the incoming.

As President, Adams made many mistakes; he made more enemies, and he lost most of his friends. Trouble with France became more acute. Congress called for the reorganization of the army with Washington as commander with the rank of lieutenant general. He was empowered to name the officers to be under his command, and Hamilton became inspector general with the rank of major general. But war was avoided.

The consensus of most biographers of Adams is that he was a failure as the Chief Executive of the nation. Whether or not that is a harsh verdict, the fact remains that that was apparently the view of the electorate in 1800 when he ran third. But in fairness, it should be noted that Adams had to bear comparison, in his time, with Washington, then the only presidential criterion. That was no enviable assignment, historically or politically.

It is beyond the province of this volume, however, to deal with the Presidents of the United States, whose lives have been exhaustively documented. Adams died July 4, 1826, at the age of ninety.

The biographer of John Adams must strain and lean backward to find in the first Vice-President qualities of warmth and color, or those of intellectual stamina and resiliency. The times were dramatic and compelling; they encouraged and begged stature of any man with more than rudimentary education, with almost any degree of imagination, thoughtfulness, and awareness of the historic present.

In Adams, however, Americans have an incontestably unlikable, if not repellent, figure. It is true that men of education, in his lifetime, were not readily available; it is true that in his day he had neither precedent nor history to serve as a primer for the office of Vice-President; and, finally, in that post he had to serve under Washington, and when he reached the White House, he served with Jefferson as Vice-President.

The latitude for comparison worked profoundly against Adams, perhaps more in perspective today than it did when he lived. To another man this proximity to Washington and Jefferson and, indeed, Franklin, might have been provocative of greatness. But however liquid the period, Adams made little impact on American history. The first Vice-President was hypercritical, sanctimonious, boorish. He was vain, self-centered, a hypochondriac, and he had the aplomb and finesse of a crossroad's lawyer. He was honest, but what of it? As a Vice-President, he was the late eighteenth-century equivalent of Coolidge.

Valid or not, the point must arise, in a review of Adams' tenure as Vice-President, whether unwittingly he did not establish the historic precedent for the nondescript character of that office. He was by no means taciturn, and by petty devices he made himself felt; but in an era which promised memorable rewards, he established the precedent of Vice-Presidential puerility.

CHAPTER II

Thomas Jefferson

THE CONTRIBUTIONS OF Thomas Jefferson, second Vice-President of the United States, to the present-day United States can scarcely be overemphasized, although he died more than a century ago. The vaulting social ideals for which he fought and to which he gave lasting impetus, and which in his day impressed many men as merely utopian and even absurd, ended any possibility of an arbitrary class government of the United States—in an era, it must be stressed, when the conception of a king ruling over this country was by no means as provocative of merriment as it is today.

The second of the Heirs Apparent came of good antecedents. His mother was one of the Randolphs of whom there were so many that it was necessary to designate the communities from which they came. His father was the "Mighty Peter Jefferson," a man of great physical strength as well as intellect, the surveyor of Albemarle County, Virginia, and a lieutenant colonel of militia. The mighty Peter was a man "without book education," yet he had read widely. He had married Jane Randolph, daughter of Isham Randolph, a well-to-do Virginian, when she was nineteen and he was twenty-nine. There were six children of this union; Thomas was the third, the two older children being girls. There was a brother twelve years younger than Thomas.

The brick-red-haired, "seventy-five-inch," square-jawed Thomas Jefferson was born on April 13, 1743 at Shadwell, Albemarle County. Washington then was eleven years old; John Adams was eight; Madison was not to be born for eight years, Hamilton not until 1757; and Franklin was thirty-seven.

So little is known of Jane Randolph that one can only conjecture that she was a devoted mother to her children and a good wife to the mighty Peter. Thomas rarely mentions her in his journal. He records in his notebook "this day my mother died at the age of fifty-seven years." As a youth, he was influenced chiefly by his father and his "faithful mentor and friend," George Wythe, a man many years his senior, with whom he studied law for five years.

The young Jefferson studied Latin and Greek under Reverend William Douglas. He wrote that he studied "English at five and Latin at nine." For his tuition the father paid the clergyman "sixteen pounds yearly." This included room and board. Peter Jefferson was a devout churchman.

In 1757, Peter Jefferson died, and young Thomas, then fourteen, was left as the head of the family. A mother, four sisters, and a two-year-old brother were "under his care." The family was a well-to-do and respected unit of the better class of Albemarle County. They had some one hundred thirty slaves, thousands of acres of land, horses, mules, and a "farm well planted."

The head of the family, the lad of fourteen, wanted an education. He discussed that desire with his guardian, John Hardy. Hardy agreed with his ward, and Jefferson matriculated at the William and Mary College in March of 1760. He was seventeen, tall for his age, hazel-eyed, and of "a pleasant manner." On his way to Williamsburg he stopped at the town of Hanover. There he met a "cheerful young man," seven years his senior, one who impressed him and whose name was Patrick Henry. Patrick was a former storekeeper and a bartender at Hanover. Jefferson wrote that "Mr. Henry was filled with pleasantry and was a good dancer." Tom Jefferson played the fiddle at that time and read Homer as another absurdity.

Jefferson spent two years at Williamsburg. He made note that he "studied fifteen hours a day and ran a mile and back for exercise." Williamsburg was a lively and colorful little community. It was a town of "some two hundred houses," the capital of the province of Virginia, the seat of the college of William and Mary, and it was the center of the social life of Virginia. There were "six Reverends on the faculty," headed by the Reverend Thomas Dawson, who drew the fabulous salary of two hundred pounds yearly as president of the college. The Reverend Dawson was frequently drunk and when upbraided for intemperance, Lieutenant Governor Fauquier would go to his defense on grounds that the "intrigues of his long-faced and black-robed faculty probably drove him to it."

It was at William and Mary that Jefferson came to know two men who were to exert considerable influence on his future. They were Wythe, an able lawyer, and Dr. William Small, of the college faculty. Jefferson regarded Wythe as the greatest lawyer in Virginia. Dr. Small was a scientist of considerable learning, and Jefferson gave him credit for interesting him seriously in scientific research.

The two became fond of the thoughtful seventeen-year-old boy. Jefferson always remembered what they taught him, and he spoke of them with warmth throughout his life. He studied law with Wythe; he accompanied him to the Second Continental Congress and he gave Wythe the opportunity to be the first Virginian to sign the Declaration of Independence. Wythe, incidentally, was one of the few members of the Continental Congress whom John Adams would not criticize—which may or may not be a tribute, depending on one's point of view.

In 1764, when Jefferson was studying law with Wythe, the young man whom he had met at Hanover made his famous "Treason Speech." Jefferson was impressed. He heard Patrick Henry many times and his reactions are interesting. He wrote that he "would shut my eyes and listen raptured and enthralled" but that, when the speech was over, "I knew not what Henry had said."

Jefferson was never to become an orator; his voice was poorly pitched and he "was always shy when on my feet." But he wrote fluently and seemingly with little effort.

After Jefferson had studied law for five years, he was admitted to the bar and for seven years practiced in the courts of Virginia. He never cared much for the law, however, and would say that he was not mentally equipped to practice. His income as an attorney nevertheless was substantial. He wrote that he made "more than three thousand dollars" yearly from his practice and established a custom of "charging ten pounds to go into court."

In 1772, Jefferson married Martha Wayles Skelton, a young widow. He was twenty-nine and she was twenty-three and "rich," he wrote. She brought him "many slaves and much land" —in point of fact, 135 slaves and 40,000 acres. He related in his notebook that he paid the two ministers officiating at the wedding five pounds each, but borrowed back twenty shillings from one of them the same day. He paid ten shillings to the fiddler at the wedding and he paid forty for the marriage license, expenditures all carefully recorded.

He took his bride home in the most severe snow storm in the history of Virginia. The carriage collapsed and the couple was lost for hours. But they reached Monticello safely, if exhausted.

Jefferson had built Monticello two years before his marriage. He had drawn the plans, burned the brick in his own kilns, forged the nails himself and directed the construction of the home in which he was to live and die. There fifty-six years of Jefferson's life were spent; and there his children were born, only three of whom lived beyond infancy. Always when away he longed for "the home on the Hill." At this time Jefferson was acquiring a library and he wrote that he made it a practice to purchase four hundred books a year.

Late in life he sold this library to the United States for $23,-950. The volumes formed the nucleus of the Library of Congress.

In 1769, three years before his marriage, when he was twenty-six, Jefferson was elected to the House of Burgesses and in 1771 he was re-elected. He relates that his election expenses were four pounds, nineteen shillings, four pence, all of which went for "cakes and rum." Jefferson did not drink and, while he and his neighbors raised tobacco, he never used it.

In his fifth year in the House of Burgesses, he was asked to draft a reply to the governor's address. He "made a bungle" of the reply, he confessed, and it had to be rewritten; he was chagrined and "sensible of my inability."

Three years later he wrote that prose epic, the Declaration of Independence.

The colonies were dissatisfied; revolution was in the air; and Virginia was in turmoil. The people of that colony were divided, and many were Loyalists, afterward to be called Tories. Some of the great families of Virginia removed to England. One of the Randolphs was president of the First Continental Congress but his brother, a Tory, took his family to the mother country.

It was about this time that some of the younger members of Virginia's first families formed the Committee of Correspondence. Their meeting place was at Monticello and the membership was made up of men some of whom were to become the chief leaders of the movement to free the colonies. Besides Jefferson, there were Richard Henry Lee, Patrick Henry, Francis Lee,

"Mr. Carr and various others," Jefferson noted in his diary. Creation of the committee was Jefferson's first political move of importance.

In 1774, the time for the break was propitious. The leadership in favor of that rupture were the members of Jefferson's committee, led by the older, more stable George Wythe and by George Mason. They were middle-aged, more cautious than the young men of the committee. They were a "good brake for the young men," Jefferson recorded.

Jefferson was appointed to the First Virginia Convention at Williamsburg and had, as fellow members, Washington and Henry. He did not attend many of its meetings, however, as he was "at the time sick with the dysentry."

Nor did Jefferson attend the First Continental Congress at Philadelphia. He remained in Virginia, "working and recuperating." His kinsman, Peyton Randolph, was president of that Congress. A fat and critical little man of thirty-nine, a delegate from Massachusetts, was there and complained that "little was accomplished." The critic was John Adams.

At the Second Congress, in 1775, Jefferson was an alternate delegate to Peyton Randolph, who was again expected to be president. The alternate did not arrive in Philadelphia until Congress had been in session for more than a month. He lived in a "handsome house on Chestnut Street, owned by a carpenter," and he dined at the City Tavern with many of his associates in the Congress.

Jefferson was an active member in that Congress. He served on several committees, worked long hours, and was a leader of the younger, more militant members. He wanted to achieve something concrete; he had no patience with the "old men." When time came for the Congress to take a firm stand, Jefferson was appointed a member of the committee to draft the resolution. His fellow members on that committee were Franklin, then a spry gentleman of sixty-nine; John Adams of Massachusetts; Robert R. Livingston of New York; and Roger Sherman of Connecticut.

Jefferson wrote the Declaration of Independence. Men have tried to steal the glory but the members of the committee attested later that Jefferson was the author of the document. It is true that Franklin and Adams made a few alterations but there were no other changes by the committee.

On June 28, 1776, the resolution, "A Declaration by the Representatives of the United States of America in General Congress Assembled," was presented to the Congress. The debate on the resolution was warm and at times acrimonious. The Congress expugned a few phrases and added the reference to a "Supreme Being." Jefferson took no part in the debate. It was his work; he felt it would stand or fall on its merits. When the debate was over and the Declaration was adopted, Richard Henry Lee told him that "the thing is so good that no cooking can spoil the dish."

Jefferson now was tired, although only thirty-three. He wanted to resign. He was re-elected by his constituents but he preferred to return to Monticello. The president of the Congress, Edmund Pendleton, took him to task and wrote, "I hoped that you would get cured of your wish to retire so early in life." Pendleton persuaded him to remain as a member until the Articles of Confederation were adopted, at which time he went back to Monticello "to retire to private life." He was then the next youngest member of Congress.

In October of the same year, however, Jefferson was back in Williamsburg as a member of the Virginia House of Delegates representing his old constituency, Albemarle County. Here he learned practical politics as played quietly and behind the scenes. He made few speeches; he knew his limitations as an orator. With the help of three men who had been and were always his friends, he was able to control the House of Delegates. They were Wythe, "my mentor," George Mason, and a little, dried-up man of vast ability, in his middle twenties, named James Madison—"Little Jeemy." Wythe was always Jefferson's friend and advisor; Mason was "strong in council"; but Madison, the faithful, devoted follower, was almost a worshiper.

For three years Jefferson sat in the Virginia House of Delegates. He introduced and pushed to passage the bill to establish religious freedom. He was broadening and now thirty-six, had a widening circle of friends.

The governorship of Virginia was soon to be vacant. Patrick Henry had served three years and under the Virginia constitution could not serve again. In 1779, at perhaps the gloomiest stage of the war, the House of Delegates elected Jefferson governor over two of his close friends, John Page and General Thomas Nelson.

Jefferson was not a spectacular success as governor. Many explanations have been advanced for that failure. There was the fact that materially so much was demanded of Virginia toward assisting the war effort and that supplies were not to be had; that there was little money available, that a state militia had to be maintained as well as conscriptees to the Continental Army; that the British invaded the state and that there were no soldiers to defend her; that Cornwallis burned Norfolk and captured Richmond—the reasons are endless. Jefferson was not an executive nor a military expert. He barely escaped Colonel Banastre Tarleton's forces and was driven to flight. He offered as a reason for fleeing that he was governor of Virginia and could do more in that capacity than as Cornwallis' prisoner or "perhaps hanging from a tree." That was a convincing argument. But his failure as governor of his state was held against Jefferson as long as he lived.

Charges of ineffectual resistance were brought against the governor by a Mr. Nichols, a neighbor and subsequently a warm friend. The charges were investigated by the Assembly and Jefferson was acquitted. His constituents sent him back to the House of Delegates, where he again became the leader. He was also re-elected to the Continental Congress but declined to serve. Again he said he was finished with politics. He was thirty-eight, in 1781, and was not yet conditioned to the importunate demands of politicians, even the early American variety.

Jefferson now spent a year back at Monticello with his family, his slaves, his studies. He concentrated upon botany, mechanics, and geology. He invented the swivel chair, used to this day. The tide of the war began to turn. The French came and, at last, Cornwallis surrendered.

Life was sweet for Jefferson. Music could be enjoyed, poetry read. "The even temper of life is after all the best," he wrote. He could again enjoy his friends and entertain those who came to visit him and, incidentally, to "eat him out of house and home" —so his daughter protested. Then his beloved Martha died. Always fragile, she had given birth to five children in ten years; she died with the birth of the sixth in May, 1782. She left him and his three daughters, one an infant who died two years later. He was heartbroken; he did not remarry.

Little Jeemy Madison had suggested Jefferson's name as a commissioner to negotiate the peace with England. The appointment was approved and Jefferson prepared to sail but, owing to the hard winter, the sailing was postponed. In the meantime, a provisional treaty was signed. There then being no reason to go, Jefferson asked for and received permission to resign his commissionership. Again, he went back to Monticello to "retire to homely pursuits." He was then forty.

Late in 1783, Jefferson was back in Congress. His friends had insisted on his returning as a member of that body and he was in Annapolis, where the Congress was then meeting, in mid-December. He was appointed to the more important committees. As usual he made no speeches; there were "too many talking lawyers," he wrote in his journal. He drafted more than thirty important papers in the first six months of his tenure, but could not be "bothered" with speechmaking.

In 1784, he was appointed minister plenipotentiary to France, with instructions to work with Franklin and Adams in "arranging and negotiating treaties with European nations." He sailed from Boston in July and nineteen days later was in Cowes, accompanied by his eldest daughter, Martha.

Jefferson set up an establishment in Paris. He studied the old capital, it social life, parks, the Seine, the museums. He met men and women of all levels of society, he studied French and in time spoke the language well. He worked closely with old Franklin, then seventy-eight; he liked him very much—as contrasted to Adams. Franklin, in turn, was fond of a minister young enough to be his son. Jefferson spent much of his time in "reading, studying and visiting." He saw almost all of Europe. He smuggled rice out of Piedmont and hired a muleteer to smuggle out two additional sacks, so that he might take it back to the United States in hope that it would prove superior to the Carolina variety. It so proved.

Jefferson paid a visit to Adams, at this time ambassador to Great Britain, and together they were received by King George. The monarch, it will be recalled, turned his back on the author of the Declaration of Independence and Jefferson knew, he wrote, "that peace was not yet."

In 1785, Franklin returned home to become governor of Pennsylvania, and Jefferson was the sole American representative on the Continent. While he was in Paris, in 1787, the Constitutional Convention met in Philadelphia. Fifty-five men sat during that hot summer, and from their deliberations came the Constitution of the United States. Washington was president of the convention, and William Jackson its secretary. Jefferson was sent a copy of the completed document and "in general liked it," but was disappointed at the absence of a Bill of Rights.

On April 30, 1789, Washington was inaugurated as President of the United States and Adams became the first Heir Apparent. Jefferson now wanted to come home. "Europe is a prison," he wrote. He received permission to return and on November 30 he arrived at Norfolk. The first newspaper he seized told him that Washington had offered him the post of Secretary of State. On his way to Monticello, a courier overtook him with Washington's offer in writing. He wrote that he regretted the offer had been made.

Washington again urged him to accept the secretaryship, implying that next to the Presidency, it would be the most important position in the nation. Madison, that shrewd little man, at last persuaded his friend to accept, and Jefferson, at forty-six, became the first Secretary of State. His salary was $3,500 a year. (The other members of the cabinet drew $3,000.) He borrowed $2,000 from a neighbor to defray expenses of his estate during his absence.

The atmosphere was electric in the new republic. The French Revolution was under way. Here there was an element which wanted a monarchy—Adams spoke of the Chief Executive as "His Majesty the President." The debonair Hamilton was riding the crest of popularity. He had married into the illustrious family of General Philip Schuyler. Intelligent, shrewd, and realistic, he was now Secretary of the Treasury and had hoped to act as a sort of prime minister. Because of his foreign birth he could not be President. "If he could not be a king," it was written of him, "he would be a kingmaker." General Knox was Secretary of War. There was as yet no Secretary of the Navy, and the Attorney General was looked upon as a "lower member"; he was permitted to retain his private practice. All of the cabinet members were young. Randolph, the Attorney General, was forty-three; Hamilton was thirty-three; Knox was forty; Jefferson, the oldest member of the cabinet, was forty-seven.

Washington was, in the view of Jefferson, "slow in operation, being little aided by imagination, but sure in conclusion."

Jefferson reorganized his department. He kept in close contact with the representatives abroad, and acted on many of their proposals. For three years he was the senior member of the cabinet. He was in incessant conflict with Hamilton and with Adams, who had visions of the President surrounded by "slanderers," by those who would jeopardize the nation for their own good—perhaps not the most appropriate observation from the ambitious Adams. The fight became so bitter that Washington was forced to intervene. In a letter to both Hamilton and Jefferson, he asked that they forget their differences.

After three years as Secretary of State, Jefferson asked the President to accept his resignation. Washington was reluctant and asked Jefferson to go to Mount Vernon, where they might discuss the matter. The President said that he feared he "could not find another" to take his place. The resignation was postponed and Jefferson returned to Philadelphia and "eternal bickering" with Hamilton.

The election of 1792 was held. Washington had not wanted to run for the Presidency again. But Jefferson, Madison, and the "antimonarchists" persuaded him to accept another term, and he was unanimously re-elected.

The French Revolution had divided the nation. Jefferson was a friend of the French: he knew them better than most Americans. He did not approve all their actions but "they are to be admired more than the English with their George." "Citizen" Genêt came to the United States as the French minister. Both Adams and Jefferson had known him abroad. They liked him personally but he soon became *persona non grata* because of his interference on this side of the Atlantic.

Jefferson remained in the cabinet during the first year of Washington's second administration, when he again asked the President to accept his resignation. This time Washington acceded, and in January of 1794 Jefferson was on his way to Monticello to "be a patriarch." He was fifty years of age and he said, "never again will I be enticed into politics"—an egregious prophecy. He said he was too old.

Jefferson was at Monticello once more, and content. He worked at the plantation devising improved methods; he again studied botany and architecture, and invented a new reaper. He drew plans for the improvement of Monticello. He built a foundry for nails and employed twelve people in that work alone. He constructed a flour mill and contracted to grind wheat for his neighbors. Martha had married her second cousin, young Tom Randolph, and he was of great help in the management of the plantation.

Jefferson now began to devote much study to the slavery question. He realized that "conditions were rotten." He often spoke of "our colored brethren." In 1784, while a member of the Virginia Assembly, he had introduced a bill which would have given the slaves their liberty by means of a graduated system. This measure failed of passage only by one vote. What might not have been the savings in lives and property two generations later had Jefferson been able to bring about adoption of that legislation!

At Monticello Jefferson was contented for two years. Then the issue of the Vice-Presidency arose. Washington had refused to be a candidate for a third term. He had hoped to be succeeded by Jefferson or Madison, for he did not trust Adams. Pinckney was an active candidate for the Presidency as well as Adams. Clinton, who had polled fifty votes for Vice-President in 1792, was another receptive candidate while Aaron Burr also wanted the post. Jefferson was not particularly interested when Madison came to see him. But Madison, always an eloquent persuader, left Monticello with the promise that Jefferson would serve, if elected.

He made no campaign and yet he came within three votes of being elected. He had, moreover, written Adams a letter wishing him success in his campaign. Adams polled seventy-one votes, Jefferson sixty-eight.

Jefferson did some thinking. "If one is to be a candidate," he wrote, "why not a successful one?" He had lacked only Pennsylvania's solid vote. He had received thirteen of her fourteen votes. Adams had received one vote from North Carolina and one from Virginia. Two votes would have changed the election. He wrote to Madison that "next time, let us cultivate Pennsylvania, and we need not fear the universe."

In February of 1797, Jefferson went to Philadelphia, which was still the capital of the United States. As runner-up in the elections, he was now Vice-President, the Heir Apparent.

Jefferson's reaction to the position of Vice-President was probably typical of that of most of his successors. Adams had said in a letter to his Abigail, very presciently, that that office "is the most insignificant office that ever the invention of man contrived." Neither could grow enthusiastic over the post. It paid $5,000 yearly—"hardly enough to live on," Jefferson protested. He had nothing to do; he was compelled to listen to endless speeches—the Jefferson who made no addresses and detested oratory.

In the office of Vice-President, Jefferson was an able man in an innocuous position. Adams wanted to appoint him a special plenipotentiary to France to clarify a situation daily becoming more muddled. Some historians believe that the President was eager to rid himself of a potential menace to his own office. Vice-President Jefferson declined the mission abroad and convinced the President of the unconstitutionality of that appointment.

Jefferson sat for four years as the presiding officer over the thirty-two members of the Senate. He saw the passage of the Alien and Sedition Act. But he was merely the presiding officer; he had no voice, no influence and no vote, except in the event of a tie. The measure smelled "more of monarchy than any act ever passed by Congress," he wrote. It was eventually to be recognized as the greatest mistake of the many made by the Adams administration. Jefferson saw the nation almost at war with France; he saw the British repeatedly insult the American flag on the high seas. He saw Jay's "perfidious treaty" with England approved by the Senate. He did not like it; he knew that Jay had been outtraded by the British; but he could not raise his voice in protest.

Even with all these shackles, he was to be the ablest man to preside over the Senate.

Jefferson had now decided he was not finished with politics—that at the next election he would not fail by three votes. He went about his preparations methodically. He consulted with Madison and his friend, George Nicholson, the neighbor who had brought the charges against him when he was governor of Virginia, but who now had become an ardent supporter.

When the Congressional caucus met in the spring of 1800, its members named Jefferson for President and Burr for Vice-President. Adams was again the candidate on the Federalist party ticket with General Pinckney as his running mate.

That campaign was one of the bitterest waged in American history. It was not less than miserable and vicious. Jefferson's morals were attacked. His church affiliations or, rather, the lack of them, were held up to the voters. His mistakes as governor of Virginia, more than twenty years before, were dragged into the limelight. Jefferson endured it; he had toughened.

Adams, for his part, squirmed under attacks that were almost as vicious. He was called a monarchist and his political record was held against him. He had called himself, perhaps only jocularly, the "Duke of Braintree." Some authorities hold that that label defeated him. Adams always asserted that the title had been assumed only in humor.

Jefferson received seventy-three votes, Burr also seventy-three votes, Adams sixty-four, and Pinckney sixty-three.

Here was a political situation the nation had not foreseen. Burr, who had had no hopes of election, had succeeded in tying the man desired by the majority of the nation. The election was thrown into the House of Representatives where each state voted as a unit. Nine votes were required for election.

Hamilton was no longer in the cabinet but he was a power in the Federalist party; in fact, he was the Federalist party. He had provoked the dislike of Jefferson but when it came time for a vote he said that he preferred a "hypocrite to one entirely unscrupulous." He came out for Jefferson against the "unscrupulous Burr."

The House of Representatives began voting to break the tie on February 11, 1801. Eight states voted consistently for Jefferson, six for Burr, with two states divided. Nineteen ballots were taken the first day. On February 12, the ballot was taken nine times. In the next three days, six ballots were taken. Feelings ran high. There was even talk of secession and a real fear of disunion if Burr were elected. Jefferson was asked to compromise. He refused and told James Monroe, his valiant young assistant, that "attempts have been made to obtain terms and promises from me."

On February 17, six days after the voting began, Hamilton, seeing that "Burr is an impossibility," persuaded some of the

Federalist congressmen to change their votes. Jefferson was elected President by the votes of ten states.

On March 4, 1801, Jefferson was inaugurated in the new city of Washington—"a small town with great possibilities," he noted. There were a few small houses, most of them wretched and nearly all of them boardinghouses. The President's mansion, "which would need thirty servants," was unfinished and the town, as yet, "hardly in the making."

Jefferson walked from his boardinghouse to the Capitol and was sworn in by John Marshall, a kinsman, although always an enemy. Marshall had been appointed Chief Justice as one of Adams' last acts as President. Jefferson had an indifferent opinion of Marshall's legal ability, and asserted that the Chief Justice had studied law only six months.

The outgoing President was not in Washington to witness his successor's inauguration. The apparent truth is that Adams ran away. He left Washington as the sun rose so that he would not see Jefferson inducted.

Jefferson's inaugural speech has been described as a masterpiece, clear and concise. In it he reaffirmed his principles that twenty-five years before he had written in the Declaration of Independence. He was then fifty-eight, a little gray, now at the height of his powers.

Adams' cabinet had been either weak or disloyal. In contrast, the cabinet appointed by Jefferson was strong and intensely loyal to the President. Madison became Secretary of State. Albert Gallatin, a Swiss, was Secretary of the Treasury. Henry Dearborn was Secretary of War, and the Attorney General was Levi Lincoln. The Postmaster General, not yet a full cabinet member, was Gideon Granger. A new cabinet position, the Secretary of the Navy, was held by Robert Smith. Three of the members were from New England; Smith was from Maryland, and Gallatin came from Pennsylvania; only Madison was from Virginia. Burr was Vice-President and, while there was a certain amount of cordiality between the two, Jefferson never trusted him.

Jefferson lowered the national debt. He sent out exploring groups and looked to the time when the United States would take its position as a "first-class power in the galaxy of nations." Despite the purchase of Lousiana and the Embargo Act, Jefferson and Gallatin, his Secretary of the Treasury, reduced the national debt by $27,000,000, a huge sum in those days.

In Jefferson's administration, practical politics began to have meaning. When he went to the White House, there were less than four hundred persons in the federal employ. Everyone was a Federalist. Jefferson replaced more than a hundred with Republicans. Adams had done a great deal of "midnight appointing," but Jefferson made changes where he considered he could place "good Republicans in the place of bad Federalists." Most of his appointments were well reasoned.

Jefferson had a long memory. He had been snubbed by King George when that monarch turned his back on him on the day he paid his official visit with Ambassador Adams. In reprisal, he embarrassed the British minister "almost to tears" by receiving him in an "old suit and carpet slippers." The President and Madison had a chuckle over this, and over another incident when Jefferson refused to give seating precedence to the same British ambassador, leaving him to find his place at the dinner table without assistance.

In 1804, Jefferson was not seriously opposed for re-election. Burr was passed over and Clinton of New York was the Vice-Presidential nominee. General Pinckney of South Carolina was put forward by the Federalists while their candidate for Vice-President was Rufus King, a former senator from Massachusetts.

The election was a landslide. Jefferson received the votes of fifteen states. Ohio had been admitted to the Union. Pinckney received the votes of two states. Of the 176 votes in the Electoral College, Jefferson received 162.

Even Adams voted for Jefferson, to the astonishment of the electorate.

It was during this second term that the Burr trial for treason was held. Chief Justice Marshall presided at the trial; and Jefferson "knew that Burr would be acquitted," but he had always felt, he wrote, that Burr had been "guilty of treasonable intent."

Jefferson was sixty-six in 1808, and he would not consider running for a third term. Madison, the devoted Jeemy, was entitled to the succession, in Jefferson's view. He was elected by an overwhelming vote, and, after seeing him inaugurated, Jefferson mounted his horse and rode back to Monticello—this time to stay. He was weary after a lifetime in politics. He had been a justice of the peace at twenty-one, a member of the Virginia House of Burgesses, a member of the Continental Congress and the Virginia state legislature; he had been governor of Virginia, he had written the Declaration of Independence, he had been ambassador to France, Vice-President and, for eight years, President of the United States.

For the next seventeen years Jefferson remained at Monticello, but he was not inactive. He continued to study and to write.

Virginia, he decided, should have a university worthy of her. At seventy-five years, when most men are content to live on memories, Jefferson launched his crusade. He stormed the Virginia legislature with the enthusiasm of one half his age. He first obtained an appropriation of $15,000. But he demanded far more. In the end, he persuaded the legislature to appropriate $300,000 for the university, and persuaded a Committee of Twenty, which the governor had appointed, to establish it at Charlottesville, in his Albemarle County.

He achieved that by some unconventional arguments. He stressed the "salubrious climate"; he cited his own longevity. He showed them that Charlottesville was the center of population as well as the geographical center of Virginia. The bombarded committee "threw up their hands." The university went to Charlottesville.

Jefferson himself drew the plans for the first beautiful structure of the University of Virginia. He superintended its contruction and, taking a chisel himself, helped with the marble work.

Jefferson and Adams again became friends. They wrote long

letters in which they discussed everything the two old enemies could recall. Jefferson had been thrown from his horse and had fractured his left wrist; the right he had broken many years before in the same way. Writing was difficult, but he persisted. Tom Randolph, his son-in-law, later found twenty-five thousand letters among Jefferson's effects, every one of which he had answered.

The Marquis de Lafayette visited him, and the two men, who had known and loved one another almost a half century before, renewed their acquaintance. The physical body was failing but the mentality of Jefferson remained strong. He survived the hard winter of 1825-1826. With the spring he knew his remaining days were not many. He was eighty-three. He died on July 4, 1826, the fiftieth anniversary of the signing of the Declaration of Independence.

Adams died the same day.

Jefferson's last days had been a period of financial hardship. It was at this time that he sold his library to the government. The nation heard of his difficulties and thousands of dollars came to him, unsolicited. New York raised $8,500 at one meeting, Philadelphia $5,000, Baltimore $3,000, and other cities in proportion until almost $40,000 was contributed by grateful Americans.

Jefferson wrote his own epitaph: "Here was buried Thomas Jefferson, author of the Declaration of American Independence, of the Statute of Virginia for Religious Freedom, and Father of the University of Virginia." There is no mention of the governorship, of his long political career, of his terms as Vice-President and President.

Toward the end, he had written down his religious philosophy. It reads:

"The doctrines of Jesus are simple: that there is only one God; that there is a state of future rewards and punishments; that to love God with all thy heart and thy neighbor as thyself is the sum of religion."

That Jefferson was by far the most eminent in the line of Vice-Presidents is incontestable. Yet the four years during which he presided over the Senate were of little moment in the rich career of the man; and it is, indeed, doing Jefferson a disservice to highlight four years which, in contrast to other periods in his life, might be said to have been almost somnolent ones. The student of Jefferson's life must often feel that the occurrence of the Vice-Presidency in his career came as a sort of fortuitous impertinence, and that it is similarly impertinent and injudicious of the historian to direct the spotlight to them.

But even in an office that must have been nondescript to Jefferson, he found the provocation to write his *Manual of Parliamentary Practice,* which still guides the Senate and popular assemblies throughout the world.

It is a safe assertion that no Vice-President since Jefferson has felt altogether comfortable in that office. It is not that his achievements, as presiding officer over the upper house, were momentous; the truth is that he devoted much of those four years to overseeing improvements to Monticello made possible by the salary of the Vice-Presidency. But the knowledge, for example, that one occupies the office of the author of the Declaration of Independence must inevitably make for restiveness, if not frustration. Doubtless it would amuse Jefferson to know that he made the office of the Heir Apparent an uneasy one for his successors.

CHAPTER III

Aaron Burr

IT IS ONE OF THOSE IRONIES and injustices of history that Aaron Burr, the third Vice-President and sometimes held to be the ablest, is remembered by posterity chiefly for events in his long life that were unrelated to the office he held (incidentally, he only narrowly failed of election to the Presidency). Those events were, of course, his duel with Alexander Hamilton, in which Hamilton lost his life; his abortive trials for treason; his countless affairs with women of all classes on both sides of the Atlantic; and his marriage late in life to that elegant and eminent strumpet, Madam Jumel of New York.

These somewhat irrelevant issues have almost invariably overshadowed his exceptional talents as presiding officer over the Senate, which is the primary function of the Vice-President; Burr's outstanding abilities as a lawyer—few of his contemporaries were more able; and the persuasive charm, wit, and generosity he exercised when so inclined.

Burr came of a line of eminent men. He was born February 6, 1756, at Newark, New Jersey. His father was the Reverend Aaron Burr, the president of Princeton University; his grandfather was Dr. Jonathan Edwards, who preached the doctrine of "eternal hell fire," and Aaron, along with his four-year-old sister, Sally, went to their uncle, Timothy Edwards, to be raised in a "strict manner and with many thrashings."

Aaron Burr was a precocious child. He was graduated from Princeton at sixteen. (There were four colleges of note in the colonies at that time: Harvard, William and Mary, Yale, and Princeton.)

Burr wrote that at sixteen he was thrown into the Kill van Kull channel, off the Staten Island shore, by a father and three brothers of a young lady with whom he was trying to elope. He does not mention the young lady's name but he wrote, in disillusionment, that "the water was dirty, and I will never have dealings with Cupid again!" He was never more mistaken in his life.

His friends and neighbors pleaded earnestly with Burr to become a Presbyterian minister. He studied theology and discussed the possibility of embracing the church with the Reverend Joseph Bellamy. But suddenly he made a momentous decision. That decision was to become a lawyer.

Burr consulted with his brother-in-law, Tapping Reeve, and was making preparations to begin studying for the bar when in 1775 the Revolutionary War began. Burr, immediately aroused, hastened to join the Continental Army. Then twenty, the "Bantam Burr," five feet, six inches tall, and weighing less "than ten stone," became a captain in the colonial army. He was with Colonel Richard Montgomery, Benedict Arnold, and Colonel William Campbell on that snowy night of December 31, 1775, when they stormed the Heights of Quebec. Burr charged up the bluff with the giant Montgomery and the audacious Arnold. He saw Montgomery killed, and the "little Burr" dragged the body of his leader back through the deep snow.

Arnold had a wounded leg; Montgomery was dead; and the gallant Campbell, "who wept as a child," would not allow Burr to lead another attack.

Burr went to see Washington. The commander in chief retained him as his aide along with another "diminutive young man," Alexander Hamilton, who was to be opposed to Burr for the next thirty years. Burr, moreover, did not get along with Washington. He chafed at the slow pace of the war and was critical of the general's cautiousness. He demanded action. He soon actively disliked Washington and that soldier, in turn, developed an antipathy for Burr. Burr, promoted to a colonelcy, was at Valley Forge during the unforgettable winter of 1777-1778. He was a strict disciplinarian and ruthless in his punishment of shirkers. A plot was hatched to murder him. Burr had wind of the conspiracy and cut off the arm of one of the plotters. There were no more such conspiracies at Valley Forge.

Burr participated in the Battle of Monmouth. There his horse was shot from under him.

He was assigned as aide to General Israel Putnam and was later a close friend of the big, bluff, and unlettered Rhode Island farmer turned soldier. For his part, Putnam had "much faith in the ability and bravery of Colonel Burr."

While with General Putnam, Colonel Burr met Margaret Moncrieff, the pretty daughter of a British major. It would appear that he promptly seduced the young lady who, on her part, was not adverse to an affair with the gallant American soldier. Many years later, when she had been married, had been the mistress of many men, and was an elderly woman in England, she boasted of her friendship with the colonel.

Burr did not immediately recover his health after a sunstroke at Monmouth. He asked Washington for leave without pay. The two men could not agree on anything and, as a result of their disagreements, Burr resigned from the Army. (Throughout his long life, Burr charged that Washington's military ability had been exaggerated and that while he was an able executive he was not an outstanding military leader.)

In 1777, Burr met the widow of a British army officer, Theodosia Prevost, a woman of thirty-two and the mother of five children. Burr at that time was only twenty-two. He was impressed with the intelligent widow. He "admired her greatly" and eventually proposed. They were married on July 12, 1782. Burr then was twenty-seven and the "widow Prevost" was thirty-seven, with two sons in the British army. Burr noted that he had only "half a Joe" with which to pay the preacher, which amount "appeared to satisfy the parson."

Burr, out of the Army, had studied law for six months and in 1781 was admitted to practice in New York. The statutes of the state demanded three years study before an examination could be had, but Burr argued with the Board of Examiners that his army experience should count in his favor. The board listened to that unique and unprecedented argument, and in the end permitted him to take the examination, fully expecting him to fail. He astonished them by passing with a high grade, and there was a new attorney at law in Albany, where he lived for a year "continually in want of funds."

He and Theodosia went back to New York City where he soon achieved success and where, by 1786, he was, along with Hamilton, one of the best-known members of the legal profession in that city. He had adopted the five children of his wife and, with "Little Theodosia," who had been born to his patient Theodosia, he was happy at Richmond Hill. Burr at this time was planning to purchase the great Morris mansion, but Madam Jumel was the victorious purchaser.

Burr was becoming interested in politics and, in 1791, he was elected to the United States Senate by the New York legislature. His opponent was General Philip Schuyler, the father-in-law of Hamilton.

Burr's record in the Senate was average. He attended the sessions regularly and he was noted as a party man. He boarded with the "Widow Todd," along with Madison, who was to marry her pretty daughter, Dolly. Burr asserted that he introduced the two and was responsible for the match. Theodosia, his wife, died in 1794.

In 1792, Burr had polled one vote for the Vice-Presidency. In 1796, he was active in the Presidential campaign and polled thirty votes. This was the year Adams was elected President by only three votes and it was on this occasion that he cried "Damn, damn all elective governments!"

In 1797, Burr was out of the Senate but again a member of the New York Assembly. He had been Attorney General by appointment of Governor George Clinton and was a candidate for governor of New York, only to be beaten by 7,000 votes. The voter at the time was allowed to cast a ballot only if he could show that he possessed property to the amount of $500.

In the campaign of 1800, the forty-five-year-old Burr was an active candidate for the Vice-Presidency. He was able to steal the New York delegation from Governor Clinton and then almost stole the election from Jefferson. The electors clearly intended that Jefferson should be President and Burr the Vice-President, but by some shrewd maneuvering, some "pulling of the wool" (said Clinton), and some chicanery, when the tallies were read off Jefferson had seventy-four votes for President and Burr an equal number. The election was accordingly thrown into the House of Representatives where, after thirty-six ballots, Jefferson received the votes of ten states and Burr those of four; two states cast blank ballots.

Jefferson was declared President.

Again Burr, now Vice-President, had made an enemy, and from that day Jefferson did not trust him.

As the presiding officer of the Senate, Burr was a success, one of the ablest ever to preside over that body. He was fair; he was an excellent parliamentarian; he followed the rules as laid down by his predecessor, Jefferson; and he was well liked by the members of the Senate.

His daughter Theodosia had married Joseph Alston, an able young attorney of South Carolina, who was later governor of that state and an "ever good husband." She had given birth to a son, Aaron Burr Alston, "Gampy" to his adoring grandfather, who loved him and played with him and who grieved inconsolably when the little boy died of a fever during Burr's exile in France. Burr wrote in his journal, "All is sorrow, for Gampy is gone."

In New York there were three divisions of the Republican (Democratic) party, one headed by Burr, one by the Livingstons, and the strongest by the elderly Clinton, the perennial governor. As had Jefferson, the Clintons and the Livingstons concluded at last that Burr could not be trusted and together they had made short work of the "little Bantam." He could not be elected governor of New York, but he came close to becoming President of the United States.

Burr's enmity for Hamilton grew with the years. While Burr

was Vice-President, Hamilton circulated bitter criticism of him and he wrote that he "knew more libelous ones which I could tell." Burr demanded that he produce evidence to sustain his accusations. Hamilton refused and informed Burr's friend, Van Ness, that he would stand by his accusations and that Burr could do as he saw fit.

Burr considered this to be an invitation to a duel. He challenged Hamilton and on July 11, 1804, the Vice-President of the United States fought a duel with the former Secretary of the Treasury at ten paces, with pistols.

There have been many versions of this affair. Hamilton wrote his letters of farewell on the night of the tenth. From these letters one would infer that he expected to be killed. Burr wrote a letter to his beloved Theodosia the same night but did not mention the duel. At 7 A.M. in two parties, they rowed across the river to Weehawken, New Jersey, with their respective seconds. With Burr went young Samuel Swartwout, Van Ness, and Davis, who was to be one of Burr's biographers. Dr. David Hosack was the "physician in attendance."

The seconds met and a coin was passed between Van Ness and Pendleton, representing Hamilton, for position. Hamilton won. The coin was passed a second time for the word of fire and Hamilton won again. The duelists took their stand ten paces apart and the word was given to fire.

Burr's seconds said that Hamilton fired first and cut a limb off the tree under which Burr was standing. Burr then fired deliberately and Hamilton fell, mortally wounded in the chest. He was taken to his home where, thirty-two hours later, he died, surrounded by his wife and seven children.

Burr ate a hearty breakfast at home and went to his law office. There are details of this affair which have never been explained. Dueling was looked upon with no disfavor. During the same year, in New York, there had been three duels with the principals all prominent men of the city. DeWitt Clinton, a future mayor of the city, and a United States senator, had wounded his adversary, who was one of Burr's seconds; the captain of the Port of

New York had been mortally wounded, and one of Hamilton's own sons was killed in a duel. Old and pompous General Wilkinson had lost caste by refusing a challenge. Andrew Jackson fought more than one duel, and men prominent both socially and politically met their opponents on the field of honor with no criminal charges resulting against the participants.

But with the death of Hamilton, willful murder was charged and Burr was indicted for that crime in Bergen County, New Jersey. He was charged with a misdemeanor in New York for issuing a challenge. The situation looked ominous, and Burr skipped town. The apparent reasons were that Hamilton's friends were numerous, that Burr had made many enemies, and that there were too many people in the city and state whom he had offended. In 1804, he went to South Carolina to be with Theodosia and his little Gampy. He was happy with them that winter and indifferent to what the rest of the world thought of him.

There was much excitement in New York. Friends of Hamilton reiterated their demands and there were public threats to lynch the "murderer Burr." He stayed in the South with Theodosia during the winter. Burr's sun had set and in the national elections of 1804; George Clinton was elected Vice-President.

There was much speculation now whether Burr would be in Washington at the meeting of the Senate in February of 1805. But when that body was to be called to order, the dapper little Vice-President walked into the chamber and brought the Senate to order. He presided over the impeachment trial of Supreme Court Justice Samuel Chase. In the end, there was a simple majority vote for impeachment but not the necessary two-thirds majority. President Jefferson was chagrined. But Burr had presided with dignity, showed no bias, and Justice Chase made no complaint at the treatment he received.

The morning came when Burr was to vacate the chair to Clinton, old George who had no use for the "unscrupulous Burr." The Vice-President called the Senate to order and spoke for twenty minutes. It was has farewell address. Senator Mitchell noted that "this day I have witnessed one of the saddest days of my life; he (Burr) spoke with so much tenderness and concern that it wrought up the Senate in a most uncommon manner. . . . There was a silent and solemn weeping for perhaps five minutes. Burr is one of the best presiding officers who ever presided over a deliberative assembly."

Burr ended his speech, walked down the aisle of the Senate, and slammed the door as he left, carrying off a situation in the grand manner.

He was fifty, and he was through.

Burr knew that he could not return to New York. He discussed his future with his friends, senators from the South and West, who advised him to go West, practice law, and run again for Congress. The advice seemed sound. From Pittsburgh, in the spring, he drifted down the Ohio river in a craft with bedrooms, kitchen, and an elaborate dining room. He stopped at Marietta, Cincinnati, Louisville, and Nashville. In Nashville, he met General Andrew Jackson, then forty-four and an ardent soul "whom I love to meet." He consulted with General James Wilkinson, who was later to appear as a witness against him in the trial for treason. He held many conferences with the traitorous general, who was governor of Upper Louisiana, and at the time was in the pay of the king of Spain.

At this period, there was talk of secession of the Western territories. Other men had talked of secession but with Burr on the scene the project was more serious. In New Orleans, a "goodly town of nine thousand souls," he was popular; he had an opportunity to exercise his charm with the women and he met the beautiful Madelaine Price. He was serious in his desire to marry that charming daughter of a hotelkeeper, but she could not make up her mind and there passed out of his life a woman who might have influenced him greatly.

He returned to the East and, after a visit to Theodosia and Gampy, he was again in the West in July of 1806. He drilled a regiment at Marietta. His enemies charged his activities there

43

were suspect but Burr's answer was that this was merely an honor the officers of the regiment accorded him because of his role in the Revolutionary War.

Burr wrote several letters in cipher to General Wilkinson, who promptly altered them to suit his purposes. Burr said that these letters had to do solely with a projected colony in Louisiana in the Bastrop grant. General Wilkinson charged later that they were treasonable.

In the summer of 1806, Burr was arrested by the United States district attorney for Kentucky, Joseph Davis. Henry Clay, then a rising young lawyer, acted as Burr's counsel and the charges were dismissed, but he was again arrested and Judge Rodney held him for trial for treasonable conduct. Burr feared that he would not receive a fair trial and hid from the arresting officers. He wrote to the governor of Kentucky but was given no aid. Finally he was arrested because an attorney named Lewis recognized him in his homespun outfit. Lewis said that he also recognized Burr by his eyes and, knowing that there was a reward of $2,000 for his arrest, he took the smaller man by force to the army authorities. With Lewis and a squad of soldiers, Burr started for Richmond, Virginia, where the treason trial was to be held. On the trip to Richmond, Burr again made an attempt to escape, calling upon the populace to assist him. Lewis threw the little Burr across his shoulders and carried him back to his guards, Burr kicking and squirming.

At Richmond, Burr was indicted for treason and for misdemeanors. He was lodged in the Virginia penitentiary—in a suite of three rooms. He was entertained by the ladies of Richmond and indeed Burr was lionized by some although the majority of the nation believed him guilty of treason.

The trial dragged on through the hot summer of 1807. The United States District Attorney, Hay, was assisted by Alexander McRae, lieutenant governor of Virginia, and by young William Wirt, afterward to be Attorney General of the United States. Burr had as counsel the staid and elderly Edmund Randolph, who had once been Attorney General, senator, and the Secretary of

State. He had as associates four other well-known attorneys, one of whom was the great pleader Luther Martin, a man of much ability and a "prodigious drinker of brandy."

Chief Justice John Marshall presided at the trial and when Jefferson heard this he knew that "Burr would not be convicted." Unquestionably, Justice Marshall did show some favoritism and was known to have dined with Burr while he was on trial. General William Eaton testified and the pompous and traitorous General Wilkinson was a prosecution witness. Scores of witnesses took the stand; speeches endured for days and the charge to the jury was prolonged. Some men asserted that Marshall was guilty of favoritism in the charge and wagers were laid that the jury would acquit.

After long deliberation, the jury brought in the odd verdict that "Aaron Burr is not proved to be guilty by any evidence submitted to us. We therefore find him not guilty."

Burr was cleared of the charge of treason, but he had no place to turn. The people of the nation believed him guilty. He went to Baltimore and into hiding there for fear of lynching parties. Later at Philadelphia he again had to flee for fear of violence.

Burr could not enter New York or New Jersey because of the charges standing against him in the Hamilton duel. Reluctantly, he decided to leave the country and on July 16, 1808, he arrived in London. He had sailed on a British ship under an assumed name which he used until he was safe in England in the home of relatives of his wife, the Prevosts. Now Burr, former Vice-President of the United States, proceeded to charm the people of London. For some time he was entertained by royalty.

Burr had schemes: he revived the plan to invade Mexico. He had a countess for a friend; he charmed a duchess; and he made love to country maidens, charwomen, scullery girls, and barmaids. The beautiful Duchess of Gordon entertained him with "much drinking, Maderia, champagne, claret, port and sherry." He was arrested for debt and was a prisoner for three days.

Burr was then asked to leave the country. He was looked upon as dangerous. The Americans in England would have none of him. He wandered over the Continent for four years. He had been in Scotland; he went to Sweden; he was in Germany for a time where, at Weimar, he had an affair with a Madame de Reisenstein. He thought seriously of marrying her but he soon tired of her and wrote in his journal that she was a "sorceress." Again he was on the move, forever changing his place of abode.

Burr went to Paris. The French did not want him. He was a political embarrassment and the French authorities had threatened to arrest him if he landed in France. They could offer no reason, however, for the threatened arrest when he called their bluff. So to Paris went the wandering expatriate, and there he lived for three years.

In the French capital, Burr lived precariously. He kept his journal and once noted, "This day I have only two sous, but thank God they clink together." He met women of every strata, and mentions as his mistresses more than a dozen. He slept in their houses; he ate their food; he borrowed money from them; and he lived off the women he hypotized. He made few men friends and he continually was borrowing money from those he did make. He made loans from the gullible who were impressed with his ostensible prestige as a former Vice-President.

Burr had get-rich-quick schemes. He was interested in a new process to make vinegar. He had purchased a new set of teeth from a French dentist and planned to sell false teeth in England. He had a plan to speed up the transatlantic crossing to six days.

Always Burr lived on the ragged edge of poverty and in his journal he tells, for example, of his hunger—"this day I had one potato." "Today I was able to eat having been invited to dine with F." He even repaired chimneys. There were times when this fifty-five-year-old "best Presiding Officer the Senate ever had" was acutely hungry.

Burr made efforts to ingratiate himself with the American Minister and members of the consular corps. They would have no dealings with him. He came to be desperately lonely for Theodosia and Gampy. It was then he decided to return home and face the music. But there were difficulties. The American consul refused him a passport and for months he waited and starved. He borrowed money from the French girl with whom he lived. He was cold as well as hungry; sometimes he had "no fire with which to heat the vermicelli."

Burr met a French count who, because Monsieur Burr was a "celebrated" citizen of the United States, loaned him ten thousand francs. Again Burr was happy; again he could buy flowers for Fleurette and the countess, and presents for Theodosia and Gampy—presents he afterward pawned or sold before he was to see his native land.

Finally, after nearly four years of exile, Burr was given his passport. He sailed for America but his ship was seized on the high seas and he was brought to England as a captive. Ashore, Burr again faced poverty and winter. He pawned everything, even his clothes, and he lived in the kitchen of a public house; seduced the scullery maids and a pretty barmaid who gave him food and drink.

Burr haunted the Alien Department of the British Foreign Office. He met a Mr. Reeves, who gave him the money for his passage and made arrangements for his return to the United States. This benefactor would not accept his last book, a *Boyles Dictionary*, which Burr offered in return for his help in obtaining his passage back to America. Burr wrote that he afterward sold the book for $30 and used the money to live while he was waiting—ever waiting—in Boston.

Burr came home in May of 1812. He had been an exile for four years, he was fifty-seven, and admitted that he was weary and tired. This time he was traveling under the name of Arnot.

For several weeks "Mr. Arnot" remained in Boston. He had written his friend, John Swartwout to see if it were expedient to return to New York. "Have the people forgotten?" "Will I get the limit?" He was eager to see Theodosia; wanted to play with Gampy—he had not yet heard of his grandson's death.

Swartwout wrote him that it was safe to return to New York. Burr went back at last to the only town for which he ever cared.

He opened a law office in New York. He was an able lawyer.

Men who did not approve of him knew that, however, and some were willing to meet him in a business way, if not socially. Burr wrote that 500 people came to his office the first day. Five hundred of a population of 25,000 was a good percentage, and meant business. He would no longer be hungry and he could again see Theodosia.

He noted that he made $2,000 the first week he opened his office.

Burr never saw Theodosia. Gampy was gone and Theodosia had lost her life at sea while going to join her father abroad. She had sailed on the *Patriot*, with a guarantee of safety from a British admiral. The ship was never sighted after it sailed from Charleston. Burr waited and worried; he haunted the docks; he questioned sailors and hoped against hope. One old seadog told him that he had seen Theodosia walk the plank from a pirate ship.

Finally, Burr gave up all hope.

Burr practiced law for the next twenty-four years. He made money and he spent it. He gave much of it away.

Burr adopted two young girls and a boy; it is possible they were his natural children, for there were many of them, more than records show, more possibly than Burr knew himself. He sent to France and brought over a son, born to one of the women with whom he lived while there, and apprenticed him to a watchmaker.

In the heyday of his political eminence Burr had known Madam Jumel, the most notorious woman in New York and the mistress of the richest man in the city, Stephen Jumel. She had been Betty Bowen, the illegitimate daughter of a sailor and his girl. Betty had been a woman of the streets in Providence, Rhode Island. She had inveigled Stephen Jumel into marrying her by pretending to be dying and then "miraculously" recovering. Later Jumel was killed by falling off a load of hay, and Betty Bowen Jumel was left the richest woman in New York.

When she was fifty-seven and Burr was seventy-seven, their paths again crossed. She was now frowsy and he was a stooped and bewigged little man who walked "well bent over." Burr proposed marriage to her. She was at first hesitant but in the end she said "yes" and July 1, 1833, when Burr was seventy-eight, he married Madam Jumel. The wedding was held in the Jumel mansion. Fifty-one years before a young man of twenty-seven had married the pretty Prevost widow and he had given the parson "half a Joe." This time he paid him handsomely.

They honeymooned in Connecticut and returned to New York and to continual bickering. After little more than a year, Mrs. Burr sued for divorce. She charged infidelity and named as corespondent one Jane McManus. Aaron contested the divorce and a merry fight began. New York laughed long and loud at the two old souls each accusing the other of infidelity. Betty simply ceased calling herself Mrs. Burr and again became Madam Jumel. The old lady lived to ninety and saw the Civil War fought; she died in 1865.

Burr suffered a stroke. He made a will in which he designated two illegitimate daughters as heirs. One was only two years of age, the other six. When Burr was questioned about these daughters and told that he could not possibly be the father of two such young children, he said, "When a lady sees fit to name me as the father of her children, why should I deny that honor?"

The old man became weaker. His friends moved him to Staten Island where he sat and watched the ships come and go. His good friend, the Reverend Van Pelt, went to see him and prayed for Colonel Burr. The old man listened, and then died. He was eighty-one, and the date was September 14, 1836.

Burr's was a kaleidoscopic life. He rose to the heights and he was dashed as quickly to mean circumstances where he subsisted on the dregs of life. He knew nothing of constancy in his friendships. Washington, generous, slow to anger, even phlegmatic, hated him. Jefferson, who was fair to all men, regarded him as entirely untrustworthy. George Clinton, Philip Schuyler, Robert Livingston, men who knew him in New York, lost faith in him and were his personal and political enemies. Hamilton's hatred may perhaps be discounted, for in some ways he had much of the same temperament as Burr. The two were both small men

49

physically, pugnacious and unreliable in their relations with other men.

As against the dislike he provoked among his contemporaries, there is the unquestionable fact that he was a brave soldier. At Quebec he won honor; at Monmouth he was in the thickest of the battle. General Putnam was his friend as had been Montgomery and the brave Colonel Campbell. He was a prodigious worker and a remarkable disciplinarian. Certainly he was one of the best presiding officers the Senate has ever seen.

Burr asserted to the day of his death that he had no traitorous ideas in his plans for a Western empire. He was never on the defensive in respect to his duel with Hamilton. He said that he had challenged Hamilton with justification, that the challenge had been accepted, that Hamilton fired first, missed him and was then killed—as scores of other men had been under that code. He was a mixture of charm and unscrupulousness, a man with countless enemies, with only a few friends. He lived long and hard, and in that life he loved only three people. They were Theodosia, his lovely, loyal daughter, Gampy, his grandson and his namesake, and above and beyond them was Aaron Burr. In color and verve, the office of the Vice-Presidency of the United States, almost invariably a haven for mediocrities, has never had his equal.

CHAPTER IV

George Clinton

THE FOURTH VICE-PRESIDENT of the United States reached that office embittered that he had failed of election to the Presidency. He had been governor of New York for seven terms, a record never since attained, and he had built a political dynasty in New York so strong and all-powerful for so long that he felt his party owed him the top office in the country—as perhaps it did. In any event, he went to Washington with the conviction that he was to serve a party (if not a nation) of rank ingrates, and his disgruntlement obviously contributed nothing to heightening his efficiency as the presiding officer over the upper house.

George Clinton was born in New Britain, Ulster County, New York, on July 26, 1739. He was the youngest son of Charles and Betty Denison Clinton.

There was an elder brother, James Clinton, a Revolutionary general of note, an "unsociable man but a great soldier." James Clinton fathered thirteen children, one of whom, DeWitt, enjoyed much political prominence in the early years of the nineteenth century, became mayor of New York, and was a United States senator at thirty-three. DeWitt Clinton hoped that he would be the President to come from the "Clinton Clan." He was a shrewd man and, with the experience gained as secretary to his uncle, George Clinton, it looked as though he might succeed. But George was always to be the leader—George, the giant of a man who never went to elementary school, a natural leader of men who, had he been able to talk at least as well as Adams, would most assuredly have been a President of the nation he loved so much.

While Clinton never went to school, he studied for a time under a Dr. Thaine, a graduate of Aberdeen University, who found George a "likely student." But there was never a day of formal schooling.

Clinton was seven years younger than Washington who was his closest friend. Clinton once lent Washington $25,000 to buy land, and they were to be partners in various undertakings. Clinton was four years younger than Adams whom he disliked cordially.

Early in life Clinton evidenced a bent for adventure and during the French and Indian Wars, when he was eighteen, he was a privateer on the *Defiance*. He became a steward's mate but he wrote that the expedition was "not very successful." He returned home in 1758, a strong, pugnacious young man. He had learned that which was to stand him in good stead throughout his long life—how to take orders and adapt himself to discipline. Later he was for some time a lieutenant in his brother's company which served in the latter part of the French and Indian Wars, and he gave a good account of himself.

He was frequently in the field, even when governor of New York, but he never prided himself as a military man. Clinton soldiered as a duty; he went with the troops when circumstances demanded. He was content to serve in whatever capacity was necessary. But he was at all times a disciplinarian. The condition and the fighting spirit of the New York militia was evidence of his ability, and Baron von Steuben, as inspector general of the colonial forces, once commended Brigadier General Clinton on the "appearance of your line."

George Clinton's father, Charles, had been a surveyor, a post of considerable standing in the colonies. George followed in his footsteps. He studied law under William Smith the Younger, an author of note, a leading lawyer and afterward one of the leading Tories of the state. George Clinton was "sorrowful" over the lapse of his tutor and friend when he cast his lot with the Loyalists, along with hundreds of the leading families of New York. New York produced more Tories than any colony in the federation and Clinton became an effective Tory baiter. He hated them and, while governor of New York, he confiscated more than £260,000 of their "personal goods and chattels" and lands worth considerably more.

Clinton was a member of the colonial legislature, and was admitted to "practice the profession of law in the Mayor's court." In 1763, he had sufficient practice to employ a clerk. In 1759, he had been appointed by his distant cousin, the colonial Governor Clinton, to be clerk of the court of Ulster County and for fifty-nine years he either served or delegated his authority in that port. He never relinquished that minor position even during the Revolution and his terms as governor and Vice-President.

The "big Clinton boy" became quite a leader around the little center of Kingston, New York. He spent several years as a member of the Assembly and met the eminent Philip Schuyler, the Livingstons, the Yateses, and the Lewises, men who were later to be close friends or enemies, socially and politically.

The Revolution was approaching. Men of foresight in the colonies knew it in their bones. George Clinton became a leading Whig, indeed a "wild-eyed Whig." "He could see no justice in any cause but the Revolutionary cause"—that was accurately written of him.

In 1770, Clinton married Cornelia Tappan, then twenty-six, a "plain girl from a good family," who was to bear him six children.

Clinton was again in the New York Assembly from 1769 to 1775. In 1775, he was sent as a delegate to the Second Continental Congress. At this time he met the commander in chief of the newly formed Army. Washington appointed him as a brigadier general in the Continental Army.

Along with Clinton, to this meeting of the Continental Congress went John Jay; the "squint-eyed Duane"; Philip Schuyler, the "Aristocrat"; two of the Livingstons, Philip and Robert Jr.; and six others—twelve in all. They had decided among themselves that any five might constitute a quorum and act for the body. They received thirty shillings a day for their services, which was substantial payment for the times.

Clinton, the "rabid Whig," was "violent and quarrelsome." A consistent Anglophobe, he would not consider reconciliation with Great Britain: he "could never see eye to eye with an Englishman."

In the Continental Congress, Clinton was an industrious worker. But he had not yet become a fluent speaker and was seldom heard in debate. He missed few meetings and yet he did not sign the Declaration of Independence. He had been in the Congress during the hearings; he had attended the debates and naturally would vote affirmatively on all matters touching the independence of the colonies. He was not only a member of the

Congress but an army officer as well, and he was away on troop duty when the Declaration was signed.

As a soldier Clinton excelled as a procurer of supplies for the Army. He fed much of Washington's Army during the terrible winter at Valley Forge (1777-1778). The general was then governor of New York but he never forgot that he was an army officer as well. He sent Washington "one hundred cattle and one hundred and fifty hogs heads of salt pork" and on another occasion three hundred barrels of pork.

At White Plains, where Clinton's task was to defend the Hudson River, he had no patience with "shirkers and deserters" and wanted to shoot them all. General Clinton claimed that the Army was "too democratic"—a curious observation from this staunch patriot. Officers up to and including captains were elected by members of their companies; higher officers were usually political appointees and unquestionably there was inefficiency.

The first New York Constitutional Convention met in 1776 and extended well into the next year. Clinton approved of the constitution the delegates drafted.

General Philip Schuyler was eager to be governor. He was well-to-do and well placed socially. John Jay, later to be minister to England, Chief Justice of the United States, and finally governor, after many years of trying, was also an active candidate. John M. Scott, an able lawyer and a "good Presbyterian," was another in the race. Clinton did not particularly want the governorship. He was elected to that post seven times and yet only once did he ever show a lively desire to campaign.

This first election was scarcely a contest. The soldier vote was almost unanimous for Clinton. When the votes were counted, Clinton, then thirty-eight, had not only been elected governor by a large plurality, but he had also been "elected" lieutenant governor—that is to say, he had the two highest totals.

In the eyes of the "aristocracy," headed by Schuyler and Jay, Clinton had "no right to be governor." But Schuyler was a good loser and he congratulated Clinton. They maintained a degree of friendship. Jay, on the other hand, was not a good loser and refused to offer his felicitations. Jay could never beat Clinton and in the end he was governor only because the "mighty George was tired and refused again to be a candidate."

One clause in the New York Constitution was the source of much dissatisfaction to Clinton in his many campaigns for the governorship. This was the property clause which stipulated that only those electors who possessed property to the value of $500 were permitted to vote for governor; the clause remained in the constitution for many years and often cut into Clinton's majority.

Clinton was an able governor. He was a firm executive. Under the constitution he did not have full veto power but he showed much patience in his negotiations with the legislature, particularly when the majority was against him. He watched carefully over state finances; he was shrewd in his own affairs, and he carried that canniness into the affairs of the state. He personally lent thousands of dollars to the federal government and he transacted a good deal of business for Congress. He never accepted any commission for his services. Congress afterward repaid him the loan he made to the United States in its time of need.

Cornwallis surrendered and, to most people of the new nation, the war was over. To the farsighted Clinton, it was not over for at least thirteen years. There was the vexatious problem of the Tories, of the boundaries and the frontier forts. Britain refused to abandon the forts and would not discuss boundaries as long as Tories were "persecuted."

Clinton detested the Tories with all the hatred of a "strong and violent man." He had seen the terrible results of the Tory-agitated Indians in the Mohawk Valley and in "the Wyomings," and he had seen some of his best friends turn their backs on the cause when the going was at its hardest. They claimed to be "Loyalists"—he flatly called them traitors. As governor, he confiscated their property, sold their estates; he drove thousands of them out of New York. Many of the "best families" emigrated to Canada (the Chief Justice of Canada, incidentally, was a former citizen of New York).

In 1787, the Constitutional Convention again met in Philadelphia. Hamilton, a former officer in the Army, a small man physically but a giant mentally, the son-in-law of Philip Schuyler and a leader of "The Aristocracy," as opposed to George Clinton and his "rabble," was the only New Yorker to sign the constitution. Clinton disapproved of that document and became its most caustic critic. He charged that the lower house had too many members and that the terms of the President and the senators were too long. He feared that the President "might become a Monarch"—a king in his own ten square miles. He also asserted, plausibly enough, that there was no valid reason for a Vice-President.

Clinton encouraged Burr to run for the United States Senate against Hamilton's father-in-law, General Schuyler, and the "Bantam Burr" beat the old gentleman. For that act, Hamilton hated both Clinton and Burr, a mutual abomination.

In some election years, the Federalists did not trouble to make a contest. Clinton seemed to be a fixture. He saw Washington inaugurated as President and he and his "good wife" came to be "very friendly with His Excellency and his Lady." George Clinton named his only son George Washington Clinton and a daughter, Martha Washington Clinton.

In 1789, Clinton appointed Burr as attorney general of the state of New York. Burr was forty-four years of age and considered a "comer" in politics; he was a great trial lawyer and Clinton at the time had no reason to regret the appointment.

The governor's daughter, a "smart and sensible girl," met and married "Citizen" Edmond Charles Genêt, the French ambassador to the United States. He was friendly with her father and, in turn, Clinton was friendly with France. He was still trying to get Great Britain to relinquish the forts in the western part of the state and, while not fond of "French Popery," he would side with anyone against "Great Britain and Her George."

There had been a good deal of commotion over the desire of

Vermont for statehood. New York rightly claimed the territory as part of her domain. Ethan Allen and his "Green Mountain Boys" fought earnestly to be admitted. Clinton claimed that he postponed the admittance of Vermont into the Union for ten years. But in the end Ethan Allen, "a profane man" to Clinton, obtained what he wanted, and Vermont was admitted in 1791. While Clinton had fought the admission of Vermont, he had ceded to the Union that territory in the Western part of the state which was later admitted as Ohio.

In 1792, Clinton refused to be a candidate to succeed himself as governor, but nevertheless he listened to the persuasive voice of his nephew, DeWitt, and to "many friends." He was elected for his sixth term, but he wrote that he was "not happy." Now he wished to devote his energies and trust his future to the national field.

In 1792, almost without any campaigning, Clinton had polled fifty votes for Vice-President as against seventy-seven for John Adams. Some historians believe that had Clinton actively entered the field at that time, success might have been his. He was fifty-four, vigorous and healthy, and it would have been a propitious time for him to have entered the contest for the Presidency. But because he listened to the counsel of DeWitt and friends, he was forced to wait until he was sixty-six before he won the consolation prize.

It has been said that Adams was much chagrined that Washington was unanimously re-elected while he, Adams, was the victor by such a close margin. Fourteen additional votes would have elected Clinton the Vice-President.

In 1795, Clinton "would no more have the governorship." This time he stuck to his refusal. Burr, an active candidate, was beaten by Jay, largely through the efforts of Hamilton, who had retired from the Treasury and actively entered New York politics.

Clinton retired to his estate and bided his time until the next national election.

In 1800, Burr had to carry New York state to be President. He persuaded the former governor "to serve in the Assembly if elected." The elderly Clinton was not interested—he had been governor for six terms—but again DeWitt persuaded him to accept, and with his name on the ticket, New York was once more safe in the Republican fold. No one could beat "The Leader," as he was called, but he was bored and rarely attended the Assembly meetings. Why should he, who had been governor and had never been defeated for office, trouble himself about the Assembly? In addition, his wife was failing in health.

Clinton had no particular desire to see Jefferson become President: he feared he might be dominated by those partial to monarchism. He did not know the Sage of Monticello and he did not then realize what a champion of democracy Jefferson was to be.

Clinton was prominently mentioned as Jefferson's running mate in the campaign of 1800. He even went so far as to consult with Jefferson's friends, Albert Gallatin and Nicholson, and he made the odd stipulation that he might become a candidate if promised that he could resign, once elected. But Burr engaged in some of his political manipulations, and won over the New York delegation.

Burr became Vice-President and the weary Clinton was governor of New York for a seventh term.

The governor was growing old; his wife was dead; his daughter was in the West Indies with her husband, Genêt, and his son George was of no help to him, a black sheep and "an unappreciative son."

The Republican (Democrat) party was in the saddle nationally and was to remain so for more than twenty years. Burr had muffed his chance by his inability to play square with his friends. He had attempted to steal the Presidency from Jefferson but, although an able presiding officer of the Senate, he was not to be trusted and he was finished as a national figure. Clinton, no longer the giant but a stooped old man of sixty-five, was to be Vice-President.

The Twelfth Amendment had been ratified early in 1804 by

all the states except three, and the manner of electing the President and Vice-President was changed. The position was no longer so desirable, but an old man of almost sixty-six craved it nonetheless. He wanted to be the Heir Apparent since he might succeed to the one real inducement to that office. Again DeWitt, his nephew, came to his assistance. He obtained the endorsement of the New York delegation and, when the caucus met, the venerable Clinton was nominated for Vice-President. The vote in the caucus was sixty-seven for Clinton and twenty-two for John Breckinridge of Kentucky. There were twenty-one scattered votes.

Nomination along with Jefferson was tantamount to election. The electoral vote for Jefferson and Clinton totaled 160. The Federalist candidate, General Pinckney, polled fourteen.

When Clinton went to preside over the Senate, there were thirty-four members, but only a few of them were more than mediocre. The Vice-President himself, moreover, was no longer the man he had been. The honor to which he had looked forward came as an anticlimax. Vice-President Clinton was not a success as the presiding officer of the Senate. He was loved and respected, but he was too old. "He would forget to put the vote"; he was "incapable of presiding over the Senate." He voted eleven times while president of the Senate, two of his votes on major issues. He voted against the First United States Bank Bill, and that vote killed the act temporarily. He also voted to postpone action on "an Act to prohibit the importation of Slaves," and by that action delayed enactment of the measure until 1808.

Clinton did not like the little and provincial city of Washington. He spent as much of his time as he could at his beautiful estate in Kingston, New York. He ate at a Mrs. O'Neal's boardinghouse and he grew fond of "Little Peg," who was to cause consternation in capital society, a quarter of a century later, as Peggy Eaton.

Clinton vainly opposed Jefferson's Embargo Act and showed some of his old spirit in opposition. The act proved a failure and was subsequently repealed.

In 1807, the Republicans of New York asked the old man to return to his native state and run again for governor. They "knew he could be elected." This time he refused their pleas and not even his favorite, DeWitt, could change his mind. Seven times was enough and he was now the Vice-President. His salary was only $5,000, incidentally, but the astute Clinton, unlike Adams and Jefferson, was untroubled with financial worries.

In 1808, Madison was named by Jefferson as his successor. Some of the party members, among them John Randolph and some of the Virginia, Maryland, and New York representatives, who did not approve of Little Jeemy Madison, proposed Clinton as a successor to Jefferson. But little strength developed for Clinton, and Madison, at the party caucus, received the nomination with eighty-three votes. Clinton and James Monroe each received three votes. On the balloting for Vice-President, Clinton received seventy-nine votes. This caucus was called a rump caucus because its leaders had designedly neglected to notify those whom they knew were opposed to Madison. Clinton claimed he had known nothing of the meeting and declared in writing he would not abide by its decision. In addition, he proclaimed himself a candidate "for the First Office."

As much as his friends—enemies of the "Virginia Oligarchy of Country Gentlemen"—would have preferred Clinton, they knew that he could not hope to be elected. He was too feeble; he was almost senile; and he was no diplomat.

The Federalists nevertheless almost nominated the old gentleman. They were desperate for a candidate. Their fortunes were at a low ebb and they were ready to clutch at straws. Two of the leading Federalists of Massachusetts, George Cabot and Harrison Gray Otis, were willing to lead the fight for Clinton's nomination, and felt they might elect him over Madison. When the votes were cast, however, Clinton had received six ballots, all from New York: Madison 122, and the Federalist candidate, C. C. Pinckney, forty-seven.

History rarely mentions Pinckney, but he was a perennial candidate for President for twenty years. For Vice-President,

Clinton received 113 votes as against forty-seven for Rufus King, a former United States senator from New York.

The aged Vice-President did not see Madison inaugurated. He did not come back to Washington until May of 1809, when he again climbed painfully into the presiding officer's chair in the dusty little Senate chamber located in the basement of the Capitol. Clinton was ill; he "had no enjoyment out of it all." His daughter had died, and he was more lonely than ever. His eyes bothered him; he could no longer read; altogether he was not a very happy old man.

It was during the Madison administration that Clinton was able to kill the United States Bank Bill. It was one of the few important votes a Vice-President has ever cast. Many years later a senator from Kentucky, Henry Clay, claimed that he wrote the speech which the aged Clinton delivered in extenuation of his negative vote. There was none then to deny his claim, since Clinton was dead.

The hour struck when Clinton could no longer preside over the Senate. He was seventy-three and he wrote that he was "tired of confinement and fatigue." He died on the morning of April 22, 1812. He did not live to see his native land again go to war with the "hated British," to use his phrase. The old patriot, the friend of George Washington, who had been governor of New York for seven terms and who had refused the governorship on two other occasions, received all the honors a grateful nation could bestow. The senators wore mourning for a month, and the Vice-President's chair was draped with crepe. Gouverneur Morris, whom Clinton disliked, delivered the funeral oration. He was buried in the old Congressional Cemetery in Washington but almost a hundred years later, in 1908, his remains, in a lead casket, were taken to Kingston.

George Clinton was unquestionably a remarkable man. He was strong in his likes and dislikes; he was honest and faithful to his friends. He was an able executive and financier, a rich man for his time; he left an estate of $250,000. He was by no means an indifferent soldier, although he wrote he had "no bent for military life." He did much to finance the Revolutionary War and no hint of profiteering or dishonesty ever touched him.

But as Vice-President, the defect in Clinton was that of advanced age. He was sixty-five when he first reached that office, and his eighteen consecutive years as governor of New York had extinguished the fire and bounce in a man who, with all charity, cannot be said to have possessed much mental vigor. In 1808, he was embittered over the election of Madison and, although he received the Vice-Presidency, his defeat for the White House post rankled and did nothing to make him a more than indifferent presiding officer over the Senate.

CHAPTER V

Elbridge Gerry

THE FIFTH VICE-PRESIDENT and the "last of the boys of '76" to sit in the high chair in the basement Senate chamber was that "Massachusetts Boy, little Elbridge Gerry." He was "just an ordinary boy," was written of him in his time, and for most of his life he was infrequently capable of rising above the mediocre.

His father was James Gerry, a sea captain who had arrived at the Massachusetts Bay Colony in 1730 and settled in Marblehead. James Gerry became a leading citizen of Marblehead; he was captain of the Fort, a shipowner and a businessman. He shipped dried codfish to the Barbados and Spain. His bottoms returned with Spanish goods for the colonies.

Elbridge Gerry went to Harvard College with the sons of the "well-to-do families of the Colony." He was fourteen when he entered and was an "ordinary student." In 1762, he was graduated twenty-ninth in a class of fifty-two. He was scarcely known there. But John Adams and John Hancock, also graduates of Harvard, were two men with whom Gerry was to associate during his long life.

In 1764, when he was twenty, and an associate of his father and brother—the younger James was in the dried codfish business—Elbridge made a trip to New York where he met a tall, red-haired young man, Thomas Jefferson. Gerry mentioned that he "liked Mr. Jefferson." Indeed, he was always to like Mr. Jefferson.

For ten years he was a business associate of his father and brother. He was the third of twelve children born to James and Elizabeth Gerry. James Jr. became, as did Elbridge, "a great patriot," but history does not mention the other ten children.

In 1772, when Gerry was twenty-eight, he grew interested in the political situation. He met "old rabble-rousing" Sam Adams, who was a brewer, always without funds, always a disturber, always an ardent patriot and "completely devoid of diplomacy." Adams was older than most of the men with whom he was associated in the Revolutionary movement. He was twenty-two years senior to Gerry whom he considered a "young man of cause" and who became his "ever-faithful disciple."

Gerry was elected to the General Court in 1772 and re-elected in 1774. That year there was a political battle which provoked Gerry and the members of the Committee of Correspondence to resign in a body. A hospital had been constructed for smallpox patients, financed and built by the General Court. The apprehensive people of the community, described as "incensed and indignant," promptly burned the hospital to the ground. The committee registered a protest and asked that the perpetrators, whom they said they knew, be punished. They could obtain no redress, however, and so the resignation resulted.

In 1774, Gerry was sent as a member to the First Provisional Congress of Massachusetts, and he was again a member in 1775. He had as fellow members Sam Adams and John Hancock. Gerry was appointed to the Committee of Safety and was a "good and faithful member." He was always a tireless worker, meticulous as to detail, the bookkeeper type; a thin, little, dapper and "square" man with small hands and feet and with a forehead "ever furrowed."

It was during Gerry's membership on the Committee of Safety that there is recorded perhaps the only amusing event in his life. This was a seriocomic affair and could have been historic had events taken a different turn. On April 18, 1775, the committee was meeting at Menotomy (now Arlington). To Gerry, then thirty-one, information came that the British under a Lieutenant Colonel Smith were to raid the meeting. He spoke to Adams and Hancock. They moved discretely to Lexington, but Gerry went to bed in the local tavern. In the middle of the night, cries were raised that "the Redcoats have come!" Gerry hurriedly arose from his bed and, clad only in his nightshirt, ran down the back stairs and out to a cornfield where he spent the night "cold and near frozen to death."

In January of 1776, Gerry was in Philadelphia as a member of the Second Continental Congress. His colleagues were the two Adamses, "Old Sam," a man of fifty-four, and portly John Adams, as well as Hancock.

Gerry was a disciple of Sam Adams and he came to like John Adams "after a fashion," but he was never a follower of the "Duke of Braintree." He did not like Hancock. Gerry indeed was always to be leader of the anti-Hancock faction in Massachusetts politics.

As a delegate to the Second Continental Congress, Gerry was appointed a member of the Treasury Board and served until 1779, when he refused that committee assignment. This committee work came to him because he was an accountant. During this period and, in fact, during his entire service in Congress, Gerry supplied the Continental armies with munitions, food, ships, and dried codfish. He and his brother James equipped privateers and were "diligent and patriotic." Gerry was never a profiteer and, while he was a shrewd merchant, he kept his dealings with the government on a high plane of honesty.

In 1780, Gerry broke with fellow members of Congress and

for three years he did not attend its meetings although he was still a member of that body. The breach came about through his loyalty to his native state. He thought that Congress expected too much from Massachusetts in the way of munitions, food, and equipment for the armies as compared to the amounts furnished by the other colonies. During these three years, Gerry was always busy and he never forgot his duty as a good patriot. He spent his time in Boston sending supplies to the army and running his privateers with his brother. He was a friend of Washington.

Gerry was an active participant in the pre-Declaration discussions and made addresses in one of which he spoke of the "prostituted Government of Great Britain." He voted in the affirmative on Jefferson's Declaration of Independence but did not sign the document until September 3, 1776. Gerry also signed the Articles of Confederation and was a "diligent member of Congress."

Gerry was also something of a moralist. He pleaded with Congress, as did Arthur Lee, to recall "Old Man Franklin" from his ministerial duties in Paris. He called Franklin a "corrupt man and libertine." Adams, it will be recalled, had been of the same opinion when he was serving with Franklin. While a member of the Massachusetts legislature, moreover, Gerry voted with Samuel Adams to "prohibit stage plays in the Commonwealth of Massachusetts."

In 1786, Gerry refused to be a member of the pre-Constitutional Convention which met in Annapolis, but the year following saw him an active member of the Constitutional Convention in Philadelphia. John Adams wrote that Gerry "opposed everything he did not propose." Gerry was prone to speak on the spur of the moment on any subject whether or not conversant with it. He would be for a given clause one day and the next would oppose it. His temperament in general was to oppose everything. Gerry proposed a clause in the Constitution which would limit the standing army to 300,000 men. He wanted the President to be elected by the state governments, not by a vote of the people through the Electoral College. He believed that the

Treasury Department should be in charge of a commission because a "department which might come to handle three or four millions of dollars should not be entrusted to one man."

Gerry later fought the adoption of the Constitution and, with George Clinton of New York, was its most consistent opponent; yet he realized that "there must be one" and his objections were centered on the "details of the instrument."

The Constitution was adopted, and the legislatures of the various states met to ratify it.

Gerry was not a member of the Massachusetts Ratification Convention. He was invited to "sit on the floor," however, so that he might answer "such questions as may be propounded to him." He became such an active disputant that this privilege was rescinded and he was bluntly requested to leave.

In 1786, the dapper little "Columbia Patriot" was married to Ann Thompson, of New York. He was forty-two, small, bewigged, immaculate, and a social leader. He and Ann began immediately to raise a family and by 1793 Gerry would not run for Congress because he wanted to "raise his young and numerous family." He had United States bonds sufficient to "render him an income of three hundred dollars per month," he wrote, and was willing to live at his estate at Elmwood, an imposing residence which had belonged to a Tory and which was long the home of James Russell Lowell.

In the election of 1796, Gerry had voted for Adams. The President, wishing to repay a political debt and desiring a "non-Party man," appointed Gerry a member of the three-man commission to deal with France. The other members were John Marshall and Pinckney. These two able men soon found themselves stalemated at every turn by the third member. Gerry was violently Jacobin in his feelings. His hatred for England was so intense and his lack of diplomacy so evident that he came to be a millstone around the necks of Marshall and Pinckney.

The shrewd Talleyrand saw his opportunity and proposed to Gerry that he deal with him alone, leaving the other two out of all future negotiations. Gerry was agreeable and attempted to usurp all the power of the commission.

When Marshall and Pinckney heard of this move on the part of their colleague and Talleyrand, history records there was a "painful scene."

Marshall, a Virginian of the frontier type, a man who had "studied law six months," an "able and profane" man, cursed long and loud. Pinckney, who was less vituperative but equally displeased, told Gerry that he was through and that Gerry could carry on alone as he and Marshall would no longer serve with him. They left and Gerry found himself without authority and, at the same time, at the mercy of the cleverest politican in Europe. He too came home without accomplishing anything. Gerry always claimed, however, that he had kept the United States out of war with France. But history attests that of all the various American commissions to go to Europe, only "Old Man Franklin" and Jefferson made progress.

In 1800, the Republicans (Democrats) nominated Gerry as governor of Massachusetts. He was defeated by a large majority although he carried Boston, a feat no other Republican had done. The governor of Massachusetts served a one-year term. In 1801, 1802, and 1803 Gerry was a candidate again but was each time defeated. In 1804, he was "tired of carrying the vain hope."

But in 1810 Gerry was once more a candidate for governor— the fifth time his name had gone before the people of Massachusetts. The 1810 campaign was peculiar in that while Gerry was not a popular man the Federalists had nominated Christopher Gore, the "most unpopular man in the state." Gerry was elected by a small majority, again carrying Boston.

In this, his first term, Gerry was a moderate governor and in 1811 he was re-elected. He was "wild and pugnacious" during his second term. He discharged all Federalist officers; he replaced them with "worthy party members." There was a loud outcry. Gerry received many letters of protest, some of them threatening "tar and feathers." He was "much maligned," he wrote, sensitive to the criticism. In retaliation, Gerry proposed to the legislature that it pass a bill making criticism of the governor tantamount to contempt of court.

It was during this term of office that Gerry framed and succeeded in passing a measure which has left his name on the pages of American history. Gerry is at least remembered as the author of the "Gerrymander Bill," by which the votes of a few could dominate a district and elect one who would normally poll a minority vote. He divided the Congressional districts in such a way that there were "shoestring" strips and boundaries, excluding areas which would have polled a majority vote for his opponent. While the bill was under discussion, a Federalist member called it a "Salamander bill." Someone said, "No—a Gerrymander Bill," and such it has been since.

Gerry was defeated for re-election by ex-governor Strong and again he was out of office. He had been a candidate for governor seven times; he had been elected twice.

Clinton had died and the country was without a Vice-President at the time of the election of 1812. The "Virginia Oligarchy" wanted a running mate for little Jeemy and for the first time came the geographical selection method. Madison and Monroe and their political allies were looking for a Republican vote getter from New England to be second man on the ticket, which they felt sure would be victorious. They selected the old patriot from Massachusetts and the election went as they had predicted. Gerry could not carry Massachusetts, but he and Madison were elected by a large majority.

The country was at war with England and Gerry was "glad of it." He said: "We have been at peace too long, a good war will help us." He was much provoked with the people of Boston who were apathetic in their attitude toward the war. Gerry called them rebels and secessionists. Indeed, the conduct of New England in general was subject to criticism throughout the War of 1812. Elbridge Gerry, approaching sixty-nine, had no patience with its people. He was still the "Columbia Patriot," he was still the consistent hater of England, as he had been more than a generation before.

Gerry went to Washington to preside over the Senate and on May 24, 1813, he delivered a long and fire-eating oration. He was frail and old; he had lost "all his competence," as was said of him; but he was still the little dandy and fighting cock he had always been. Vice-President Gerry became the social leader of expanding Washington. His "young and numberous" family were grown young men and women. There were three sons and four daughters and they required more money than his $300 monthly, which he had thought would be sufficient for his and their needs.

Gerry saw the British capture and burn the town of Washington. They did not annoy the seventy-year-old Vice-President, who sat in his home a sick man. He announced he would not vacate the chair of the Senate. Madison was grievously ill and Gerry would not give the "partisan Giles" the privilege of becoming President. Senator Giles was President pro tem of the Senate.

Madison recovered, however, but the old man from Marblehead, driving in his carriage to a meeting of the Senate, was stricken "with a lung hemorrhage," and he died on November 23, 1814.

Gerry had been a rich man in 1800. He was nearly penniless when he died. His family had been too numerous for his pocketbook. Congress paid the expenses of his funeral but the House of Representatives refused to pay Gerry's salary to his widow for the remainder of his term.

Elbridge Gerry was an honest man. No tinge of scandal touched his official or private life. He was suspicious by nature, but he was unquestionably a devoted patriot. But fundamentally he was an ordinary man, in not the best sense of the word. He was a cipher as a diplomat, and his conception of the science of politics was scarcely more sublime than that of the ward heeler of today. To be recalled primarily as the author of the appallingly transparent Gerrymander Bill is of meager interest to posterity.

But like Adams, he unconsciously furthered and fostered the odd American tradition that the Vice-President must be a spectacular nonentity.

CHAPTER VI

Daniel D. Tompkins

A SUBSTANTIAL NUMBER of American historians have been capricious in their treatment of the handful of leaders who, if immobilized during their terms as Vice-President, at least demonstrated at other times in their careers that they were not only men of good will but also possessed marked administrative ability. Particularly may that be written of Daniel D. Tompkins, the sixth Vice-President who, among other achievements that required courage, almost singlehanded fought the apathy (if not outright treason) of pro-British New England in the two years of the War of 1812.

With the election of Madison as President, the days of the "Boys of '76" were coming to an end. Forty years had passed since the signing of the Declaration of Independence. The men who had played outstanding rolls during those memorable days were now old or dead. Their places were being taken by men who had grown up politically during those forty years.

Monroe had played only a minor part in the Revolution. He had been a twenty-year-old aide to General Washington, as had Hamilton and Burr. Now he was sixty, the last of the Virginia Oligarchy to be President.

The nation had been in existence twenty-eight years, and for twenty-four of them Virginians had been President. Add to these twenty-four years the eight in which Monroe served, and it may be noted that during the first thirty-six years of the nation's history, thirty-two years were given over to Presidents from the Old Dominion. During this period, the Northern states had furnished an equal number of Vice-Presidents.

The running mate chosen for Monroe was Tompkins, then governor of New York. He was forty-two, astute politically, a suave gentleman who got along with people and yet was an able and aggressive governor.

Tompkins—he had added the middle initial "D" to distinguish himself from another Daniel Tompkins, who had been a schoolmate—was born at Fox Meadows, now Scarsdale, in Westchester County, New York, on June 21, 1774. He was the seventh son of Jonathan Tompkins, who had been one of the three leaders of the Revolutionary movement in Westchester County. It was once said that there were only three patriots in Tory-dominated Westchester County, and that Jonathan Tompkins was their leader.

The son was graduated from Columbia University in 1795, and studied law for two years. He was admitted then to law practice and went to live in New York where he joined the Republican party in the fifth ward. There were then seven wards of which the Federalists usually carried six in the local elections. The Republicans could regularly elect Clinton as governor, but they generally lost the city elections. They could not beat Jay, Hamilton, and the other "aristocrats" in their stronghold.

But 1800 was a crucial year. The Republicans collected a fund of $2,000 and formed the Tontine Club, a political organization which later became a part of the Sons of Tammany. Some of the founders of the earlier political group were men whose careers were spectacular. There was Tompkins, to become governor and later Vice-President; Robert Livingston, who had been at Philadelphia during the Second Continental Congress; and William Van Ness and John Swartwout, those two friends and loyal followers of Burr. Swartwout was to be wounded in a duel with DeWitt Clinton. Van Ness carried the Burr challenge to Hamilton, and both he and Swartwout were seconds to Burr on that fateful morning in July, 1804, when Burr mortally wounded Hamilton.

These men, working with their supporters in the Tontine Club, carried the fifth ward in the city elections, but their votes were thrown out by the Federalist incumbent on grounds that the Tontine Club had been formed contrary to the city charter. This wholesale disfranchisement irked "Big George" Clinton, and he spent hours planning revenge on Hamilton and Jay. Hamilton tried to steal the senatorship and there are letters on record in which he sought the aid of Jay. Judge Jay would not be a party to the larceny and wrote Hamilton to that effect.

Tompkins was active in this campaign and was rapidly becoming a leader in Republican circles. His law practice was growing. He had the knack of ingratiating himself, and he "never forgot the name or the face of anyone with whom he had conversed." The politicians recognized the value of that facility. He was elected to the State Assembly in 1803, and in 1804 was sent to Congress. The thirty-year-old attorney was offered an appointment to the New York Supreme Court, and resigned his Congressional seat to accept it. He had not attended any meeting of Congress. He served on the court for three years. His youth belied his ability: he "had a mature mind, a judicial manner, and was a credit to the bench of New York."

In 1807, the race for governor was narrowed to a contest between DeWitt Clinton and Judge Ambrose Spencer. There was a deadlock in the caucus and neither man would yield. The members from the fifth ward offered a compromise candidate—Tompkins. The deadlock was broken, and at last there was a governor of New York who did not stem from the Clinton dynasty.

Tompkins took his seat as governor in January, 1808. He ran into opposition at once from the Council of Appointments. The council was composed of four senators and the governor. The governor had no vote except in case of a tie. They had become an "arbitrary and brutal machine." It was the custom of the council, on organizing each term, to rescind every act of the presiding council and make wholesale changes in officeholders. Tompkins wrote that their maxim was to "strip the Governor of as much power as possible." His direct manner of circumventing the council was to ignore its members, which he did for seven years. He made his appointments as he saw fit, regardless of the council's wishes.

Tompkins had an abundance of courage. He had no influential friends or family; he had no political debts to pay and he was a resolute governor. President Jefferson was a friend of Tompkins —and against Clinton—and the same could be said of Madison, who was to become President on March 4 of that year. The political patronage for New York went to Tompkins and his recommendations have been described as sound.

During Madison's administration there occurred the second conflict with Britain, the War of 1812. Tompkins was re-elected governor after he received the unanimous nomination of the Republicans (Democrats); his opponent was General Kiliaen Van Rensselaer.

Governor Tompkins was "heart and soul for the war." He said "we must devote all our energies to fighting England," and was earnest in his support of President Madison. Indeed, Tompkins is chiefly remembered because of his civilian contributions in support of that struggle.

There were few outstanding individuals and still fewer heroes in the War of 1812, but even so an authoritative history of the struggle has never been written; as to many individuals who were leaders, it is not the most inspiring story. There was Commodore Oliver H. Perry and a few naval commanders who served ably and sometimes spectacularly. And there was, of course, "Old Hickory" Jackson of New Orleans. But there was a pitifully small number of military leaders. In that struggle Tompkins, the governor of New York, was the outstanding political figure. More, he was a constant source of men, money, and munitions. A loan of $32,000,000 was floated by the federal government and through Tompkins' efforts New York absorbed half of it. At one time he raised $1,000,000 on his own pledge. He belabored the Federalist leaders whom he charged were "traitors and friends of the British."

Governor Tompkins held more positions of trust than have ever been held by one individual in the history of the United States. He was governor; he was military commander of the Third District and vested with the authority of a major general; he was quartermaster, disbursing officer for both New York and the United States; and he was offered the position of Secretary of State by Madison. Tompkins, who had refused to serve in the Congress, similarly refused the secretaryship. He had a job to do as governor of New York, he felt, and the thirty-eight-year-old Tompkins did it. His enemies contended that he drank a lot of whiskey in doing his work, but no one ever said that he failed as a war governor. (Perhaps what the United States acutely needed in the War of 1812, as Lincoln reportedly said of Grant, was more whiskey-drinking leaders.)

His was an unpopular post. The North was opposed to the war. The New England states refused to contribute to loans to underwrite the struggle. The people met in Hartford and discussed secession. The leaders of these "rebels and traitors," as they were called by Tompkins, were Governor Strong of Massachusetts, Governor Gitman of New Hampshire, Governor James of Rhode Island, Governor John C. Smith of Connecticut, Senator Harrison Gray Otis of Massachusetts, Cyrus King, a half-brother of Senator Rufus King, and Governor Chittenden of Vermont. These were the men who made every effort to stultify the war efforts of President Madison and of Governor Tompkins. Tompkins wrote that Chittenden was "more seditious and treasonable" than the others. That governor actually ordered all Vermont officers in the Vermont Brigade to leave their commands and return home. To their credit, many of them "absolutely and positively refused." The officers of the regular Army arrested General Jacob Davis of the Vermont militia. Governor Chittenden took the case to the Supreme Court, which upheld the arrest. But with the exception of New York, there was little or no aid from the

Northern states—or indeed from Maryland—given the nation in its conduct of the War of 1812.

New York, Pennsylvania, Ohio, and Kentucky, with the Southern states, carried on the struggle.

When peace came, Governor Tompkins again took up the lesser struggle on behalf of the people of New York and went back to his duties at Albany.

"The City," as New York was then referred to, had become the most populous in the country. It had a population of 100,-000; steamships plied up and down the Hudson; the port was the largest in the nation; and some of the streets were paved. Governor Tompkins was encountering trouble with the legislature, which was Federalist. The first United States Bank had gone out of existence and those who had been its backers undertook to form the Bank of America in New York. The governor was opposed to its formation. He contended that "it was conceived in sin and its purpose is corrupt." Nevertheless, the bill creating "The Bank of America of the State of New York" was introduced. A bribe of $600,000 was offered to the state by way of $400,000 to the Board of Education, $100,000 to the Literature Board, and $100,000 to the treasury, "provided the Legislature of the State of New York would issue no other bank charters." As an additional bribe, the promoters offered to lend to the farmers of New York $1,000,000 at 6 per cent interest. They sent a large lobby to Albany "with gold to bribe the members of the Legislature." The measure came to a vote in the assembly, and passed by fifty-eight to thirty-eight.

Tompkins felt that the bill would pass the senate. But under the constitution of the state he could temporarily dismiss the legislature. He did so in a message which "bristled with charges of bribery." The opposition cried "Despot and Dictator!" They called Tompkins a tyrant, but the man who had fought all of New England during the War of 1812 was unafraid of the legislature of his own state. He defeated the bill; to him the methods were irrelevant to the larger issue.

Tompkins was an opponent of slavery and one of his last acts as governor was to obtain passage of a bill to prohibit slavery in New York after 1827.

In 1816, Madison came to the close of his administration. He had been "overly cautious"; his administration had not been the success for which his followers had hoped. Little Jeemy was a great scholar and, in many ways, a great man, but he was not much of an executive.

Monroe was to be his successor. He had been Secretary of State and acting Secretary of War. Governor Tompkins had hopes that he might be chosen. The Southern delegates, who controlled the caucus, contended that he was not well enough known. There was also the fact that slavery was becoming a national issue and that the governor of New York was an implacable opponent of Negro bondage. In the caucus not a single vote from south of the Potomac was cast for Tompkins. They handed him the Vice-Presidency, however, and in 1816 he was elected with Monroe, as most of the country had expected.

Monroe and Tompkins received 183 votes in the Electoral College. Rufus King had thirty-four, while John E. Howard received twenty-two for Vice-President. Chief Justice Marshall received four.

In January of 1817, Tompkins resigned the office of governor and went to Washington, now grown to be a "sightly city."

Tompkins was called a "dignified presiding officer of the Senate." His duties were even less pressing than those of his predecessors. The country was at peace and there was little controversial activity in the upper house until the Missouri Compromise Bill came up for passage; and then Tompkins handled an obstreperous Senate in a "cool and calm manner." He had been a supreme court judge of the state of New York; he had been governor for seven years; he had handled difficult situations before.

Tompkins was a strict parliamentarian and followed Jefferson's rules, as had Burr sixteen years before.

But there was a period of trial which beset the Vice-President shortly after he arrived at Washington. He had disbursed millions of dollars for the state of New York and the United States during the war. Tompkins was not an accountant; he was a lawyer, a judge, a fair executive, and a strong and able governor during a critical period. Unquestionably Tompkins was honest and even his worst enemies would not bring a charge of dishonesty against him. But he was not a bookkeeper and after an audit of his accounts, an audit for which he asked, it was claimed he was short $120,000.

Tompkins then asked for a judicial inquiry which was granted. It was determined that not only was he not a defaulter, but that the government was in his debt. Henry Clay, the Speaker of the House, was his friend and counsel, and the President commended his efforts in a letter to Congress.

Tompkins brought suit against the government for the money owed him. This was a friendly action and Tompkins was awarded judgment for some $111,000. The money was not paid in full until 1847 when the last installment, overdue almost two years, was paid to his heirs.

In the cabinet during Monroe's administration were John Quincy Adams as Secretary of State; John C. Calhoun, later to be Vice-President, as Secretary of War; William H. Crawford, Secretary of the Treasury; Richard Rush, Attorney General; Smith Tompson and Samuel Southard were successively Secretary of the Navy.

Henry Clay was Speaker of the House. In the Senate were Rufus King, William R. King, and Robert Y. Hayne. In the House was James Buchanan of Pennsylvania and, in 1823, Daniel Webster of Massachusetts. The great triumvirate of Clay, Calhoun, and Webster would soon be in the Senate to control that body for thirty years.

In the election of 1820, Monroe came within one vote of unanimous re-election for President. The one adverse vote went to John Quincy Adams, who was friendly to Monroe, but felt that no man should ever receive the unanimous vote for the Presidency. He said "that honor should ever be George Washington's."

Tompkins received 218 votes for the Vice-Presidency and Monroe 232 for the Presidency.

By 1822, the Vice-President was a sick man. He could go to the Senate chamber only occasionally. He was only forty-eight but he had overworked himself. Tompkins had gone to New York in 1821 to preside at the State Constitutional Convention. While there he had brought about the elimination of many obstructive clauses in the old constitution. It was said of him that he performed an "exemplary job." He had performed one more duty for his native state. He was tired; he had given too much during the hard pull as war governor; but he lived out his second term at Washington.

With the elections of 1824 he was indifferent to the Presidency. He had once wanted it "above all things in my life," but now he was weary and no longer interested. He was sick and "sometimes given to melancholy."

On June 11, 1825, shortly before his fifty-first birthday, Tompkins died. The truth was that he had worked himself to death.

The state historian of New York wrote of Tompkins that "he had a remarkably well-balanced, self-controlled, and judicial mind. His great work was in the War of 1812." He was the outstanding statesman of that critical period. He stood like a rock and never faltered. The efforts he expended ruined his health, threatened his finances and nearly wrecked his reputation. "He might have been careless, he was inexperienced, but no man can ever impugn his honesty," the state historian remarked of him.

In his two terms as Vice-President, Tompkins was absent from the Senate for such prolonged periods that he left little impression on that office. But he stands out, nonetheless, in contrast to many others who occupied this nondescript post, for his broad human sympathies and, particularly during his service as governor of New York, for his liberal reform measures—he contributed, for example, more than lip service to the abolition of slavery and to more humane treatment of Indians.

78

Probably because these are not qualities of mind indispensable to the Vice-Presidency, history has pigeonholed and forgotten him.

CHAPTER VII

John Caldwell Calhoun

IT WAS ONCE APTLY SAID of John Caldwell Calhoun that he was pre-eminently a man who should have been President.

In the Jacksonian era, he was one of that great triumvirate of Webster, Calhoun, and Clay. He had none of the oratorical sparkle and magnetism of the other two, but he far surpassed either in political prescience, in political daring and in tenacity of will. He was an ardent supporter of States' rights, in the fateful years preceding the Civil War, and while it is incorrect to utter the conventional indictment that he was an enemy of the Union, the truth is that that great American dedicated his life to the protection of the interests of the South—first among which, of course, was slavery.

In 1730, three brothers went to the colonies from Ireland and settled in Pennsylvania. They called themselves Colquhon, Colhoun, and Calhoun. In that day, the spelling of surnames was a matter of choice and frequently various members of a family spelled their names in as many ways as there were individuals.

In time the three brothers made their way to Virginia and finally to South Carolina where at Abbeville a son of the original Patrick Calhoun had a son, born on March 18, 1782, who was named John Caldwell Calhoun. The child was named after an uncle killed by a Tory in the Revolutionary years.

The Calhouns were prosperous slaveholders in a land where

wealth was counted by land and slaves whom, it may be noted, they treated well. Patrick Calhoun sat in the state legislature for thiry years and died in 1796, when John Calhoun was fourteen years old. Up to that time, John had little schooling. He had studied with one Reverend Moses Waddel, and because he was not strong, his mother set him to hunting and fishing. He grew stronger and returned to study with the Reverend Waddel. He spent two years at Yale and was graduated at the head of his class. He studied law with Tapping Reeve, a brother-in-law of Aaron Burr.

After young Calhoun, tall and gangling, had spent two years as a student with Reeve, he returned to Abbeville and after a short apprenticeship he was admitted to the bar.

Calhoun never liked the law. With Jefferson he believed that he was not temperamentally suited to that profession. The tactics of delay, the postponements, the details of trial work did not appeal to the tall, spare young man of twenty-five and, in 1807, he decided he would not practice.

His political activity began about this time. He was invited to make a patriotic address which so impressed his neighbors that they sent him to the South Carolina legislature.

His father had represented the Abbeville district for many years and it seemed logical to elect the son of Patrick Calhoun to the same seat.

In 1810, his friends in Abbeville sent him to Congress. He had served ably in the state legislature and the promotion was well-deserved. Governor Ashton, the husband of the beautiful Theodosia Burr, thought well of Calhoun and called him "a forthright and independent young man," but feared that he might "become too independent."

John married his second cousin, one of the Calhouns, a well-to-do young woman ten years his junior, who for many years was one of the social leaders of Washington.

At Washington, Calhoun began a career which was to continue forty years. Madison was President; Henry Clay a member of Congress; but Webster was not to gain prominence until 1813.

The War of 1812 was imminent, and the national atmosphere was tense.

In the War of 1812, Calhoun was a consistent supporter of the struggle against England. He voted for every appropriation for men, money, and munitions. He defended Madison's administration, and he asserted rightly that our military unpreparedness was due, in large measure, to the shortsightedness of previous administrations. Adams and Jefferson had allowed the Army to deteriorate until there were no effective fighting units left.

As has been noted earlier, the New England states, as well as Maryland, were opposed to the war. For example, Webster said "we will do what we have to do, and no more." Governor Tompkins of New York and the Southern governors, aided by Calhoun and the other members of Congress from the Southern states, saw to it that money was provided and that the war was prosecuted with vigor.

There was indifferent leadership. There was inefficiency and there was some actual treachery but there was also a navy and there was General Harrison and "Big Dick" Johnson and, finally, "Old Hickory" Jackson to save the nation's honor. When Clay, who was in France on a mission, heard of Jackson's victory at New Orleans, he said, "Now I can go to London without hanging my head."

Before the election of 1816, the electorate knew that Monroe would succeed Madison. The "Virginia Oligarchy" was still in the saddle. It was not a matter of who would be elected; it was merely how large the majority would be. Calhoun had been a strong member of the House and Clay, who had been Speaker during a part of Calhoun's term, admired him. Calhoun had been chairman of the Currency Commission, which had drafted the tariff bill, and he had consistently supported the war effort and been an advocate of a well-disciplined army.

In November 1817, Monroe offered Calhoun the War portfolio. Earlier, Monroe had considered three men for the post. First was Clay, who refused the offer, as he had hoped to be Secretary of State. Isaac Shelby, of Kentucky, the first governor of that state, was then given consideration, but Monroe's advisers considered him too old, while General Jackson wrote he "did not want the damn job." The President had had Representative Calhoun in mind from the first, but he was afraid that Calhoun would refuse the position, and he held back the offer for that reason. William H. Crawford of Georgia, the Secretary of the Treasury, prevailed upon Monroe to take up the matter with Calhoun. But before offering the position to Calhoun, the cautious Monroe consulted with the army leaders and found sentiment strongly in favor of the gentleman from South Carolina. Monroe then tendered the secretaryship to Calhoun, and he accepted.

With Calhoun in the cabinet, Monroe's official family was well-balanced. John Quincy Adams was Secretary of State; William H. Crawford was in the Treasury; and Calhoun was Secretary of War—three strong men. Old John Quincy Adams was not a success as President, but he was an able man; and Crawford was a strong administrator who, had he not had a stroke of paralysis, might have been President.

Secretary Calhoun brought his wife, Floride, and their two children to Washington and established a home on E Street where Mrs. Calhoun entertained the socially elite of the growing town of Washington as only a well-born Carolina woman knew how. She was a great help to the thirty-five-year-old Calhoun.

Some American historians argue that there have been only two genuinely great Secretaries of War in the United States, and that next to Jefferson Davis, Calhoun was the most able Secretary of War the country has had. He strengthened the Army, put it on an efficient basis, made promotions on a merit basis, and improved the United States Military Academy at West Point and made it an institution of standing throughout the world. When General Jackson refused to obey orders and encouraged his officers to refuse to obey those already given, Calhoun promptly threatened to court-martial him. Secretary Calhoun drew around him technical experts and he established various branches of the Army in Washington where he could superintend their activities. He brought to Washington the Commissary Department, the Quartermaster Corps and the Surgeon General. Calhoun also put the War Department on a sound financial basis. When he became Secretary, there were outstanding obligations of $45,000,000; he reduced these to $5,000,000.

Although Secretary of War at this time, Calhoun was vitally interested in the Missouri Compromise Bill. There was a bitter fight in the Senate over this attempt to delimit slavery by geographical lines. Webster, Hayne, Clay, and Benton were "hot and wrathy in debate." The Compromise Bill was passed and both Adams, the Secretary of State, and Calhoun were much interested in its enactment, but from conflicting viewpoints. Adams, a New Englander, was naturally opposed to slavery. Calhoun had the viewpoint of the South and, while "realizing that slavery was not an ideal condition, we have it with us." He argued that Missouri had been obtained as a part of the Louisiana Purchase, which came to the United States as slave territory, and that its status should be unchanged. As the bill was finally passed, Missouri was admitted as a slave state, but slavery was to be prohibited in any future state north of her boundary.

In the campaign before the 1824 election, there were four active candidates for the Presidency. Calhoun was receptive but the men openly campaigning were General Jackson, John Quincy Adams, Clay, and Crawford of Georgia. Calhoun even was willing to accept the nomination as Vice-President. Clay was the perpetual candidate, always eager to step into the race as a compromise candidate. That year he was particularly eager and had his ear to the ground as early as 1822, two years before the nominating caucuses. The Vice-President, Tompkins, was an ill man, and not interested in another term.

The race was soon one between Adams and Jackson and when the votes were counted Jackson received a majority of the popular vote. He had made his plans and actually started to Washington for the inauguration when there developed a "combination of Bargain and Corruption"—what John Randolph called a "combination of Puritan and Blackleg." Clay frankly traded his support to Adams for the appointment as Secretary of State, and again Randolph charged "Billfold and Blackleg." Clay challenged Randolph to a duel and a farcical one was fought in Virginia, in which neither was injured.

The "Virginia Oligarchy" was gone, never to return, and fat and senile John Adams, the "Duke of Braintree," saw his son inaugurated. He was inordinately happy that "my son is President as I once was." His son was as unpopular as had been the father. These two men, able though they were, could be depended upon to do the wrong thing always. John Quincy Adams, like his father, was a poor loser and did not stay in Washington to see Jackson inaugurated. Calhoun had been elected Vice-President, as he had hoped, and an alliance was made with General Jackson, who was bitter over the deal made to defeat him.

For seven years Calhoun served as Vice-President. He was an able and fair-minded presiding officer of the Senate and followed Jefferson's rules of procedure. He had virtually no opportunities to cast a deciding vote except once in the matter of confirming Martin Van Buren as ambassador to Great Britain. He voted no, and Van Buren did not get the post.

Vice-President Calhoun became a strong States' rights supporter. He realized that on a mathematical basis the North could always outvote the South and that it was only suitable that he become associated with men who would protect the South by working as States' rights advocates.

As Vice-President, Calhoun had few duties to perform. He was conciliatory to the men with whom he had disagreed while in Congress and as Secretary of War: he was planning for the future and it was no secret that he wanted to be President.

In 1828, there was introduced to the House, and later to the Senate, a bill dubbed the "Tariff of Abominations." It was passed through the efforts of the New England states and Pennsylvania, along with a scattering of other votes. This was the original of all protective tariff measures and its passage and subsequent signing by President Adams brought consternation to the South. The only hope offered them was by Randolph, the maker of epigrams, who said, "It is a pirate under a Black Flag—its only manufacture being the manufacture of a President."

Calhoun was opposed to this act, but was unable to fight against its enactment since, as the presiding officer of the Senate, he had no rights to the floor.

In 1828, Adams was a candidate to succeed himself, with Clay and Webster as his chief supporters. But Calhoun, along with the South and the West, was a staunch supporter of Old Hickory. So strong proved the feeling against Adams that he did not receive a single electoral vote outside the North, with the exception of the split Maryland vote. In the South and the West feeling ran so high that men who had voted for Adams were hunted down in the woods and tarred and feathered.

Jackson was the seventh President of the United States and again the "cast-iron man" from South Carolina was Vice-President. The President was sixty; he had fought in the Revolutionary War as a boy of fourteen and carried a scar from that conflict. He was the idol of the Army.

Calhoun was now forty-six, in the prime of life. He was a well-liked and respected member of his party. The future looked bright and he felt that eventually he would sit in the newly renovated house at 1600 Pennsylvania Avenue.

There are few anecdotes told of Calhoun which have any tinge of humor. He was a serious man and was seldom seen to smile. It is said that when Clay was defeated for the Presidency he was heard to say, "I had rather be right than President." Calhoun, who had just been elected Vice-President, retorted, "Well, I guess it's all right to be half right—and Vice-President."

The cabinet appointed by Jackson showed early signs of partisanship. Van Buren was Secretary of State. He was the real Heir Apparent since he had been the leader of Jackson's campaign. General John Eaton of Kentucky, who had been implicated with and who was afterward a witness against Burr in his trial for treason, was Secretary of War. William Barry, also from Kentucky, was Postmaster General.

These men were staunch followers of Jackson. The other members of the Cabinet were Samuel Ingham, of Pennsylvania, the Secretary of the Treasury; John Branch, of North Carolina, the Secretary of the Navy; and John M. Berrien, the Attorney General. The three were friends of Calhoun and looked to him as leader. There was discord within the cabinet ranks and Congress was wrangling over the tariff.

The social life of Washington, meanwhile, was at boiling point because Peggy Eaton, wife of the Secretary of War, was *persona non grata* to Washington. Peggy was the daughter of a Washington innkeeper. She had married a pay clerk in the Navy who committed suicide under unexplained circumstances. General Eaton, while boarding at the hotel run by her mother, fell in love, married her, and tried to present her to Washington society. The social leaders, foremost of whom was Mrs. Calhoun, refused to receive "Pot House Peg," and derided the lady with such names as the "Harpy of Degradation" and others even more abusive.

The battle came to a climax when President Jackson ordered the cabinet to receive the wife of his Secretary of War. Mutiny broke out and only Secretary Van Buren—a widower with no wife to offend and thus nothing to lose—would attend the levees when Mrs. Eaton was present. Mrs. Calhoun, whose husband was Vice-President, an elective office, and who thus was not "subject to Mr. Jackson," stood her ground and eventually won out. During this Peggy Eaton "scandal," at one time, more than a hundred Congressmen threatened to resign and "Eaton Malaria" was a regular and convenient epidemic.

General Eaton resigned the war portfolio and was appointed governor of Louisiana while Jackson became an avowed enemy of Calhoun. The breech was never healed; it has been said that that social contretemps was the chief factor in preventing Calhoun from reaching the White House.

"Little Matty" Van Buren had engineered the Eatons' transfer to Louisiana and later persuaded President Jackson to appoint the general minister to Spain. It was a clever move, and endeared Van Buren to Old Hickory.

The States' rights fight grew more bitter. Vice-President Calhoun chafed at his enforced inactivity. He had definitely broken with the President, and he was eager again to enter the lists as a defender of the cause in which he was so vitally interested. He had been on the sidelines too long.

Senator Hayne had been elected governor of South Carolina and accordingly there was a vacancy in the Senate. One day Calhoun paid a visit to the President. When he left the White House, there was no Vice-President of the United States; instead there was a new senator from South Carolina. Calhoun's resignation is the only withdrawal in the history of the Vice-Presidency.

In the Senate, Calhoun for eighteen years led the fight of the States' rights men.

Before the election of 1832 was held, President Jackson brought in Van Buren as the Heir Apparent. Van Buren was to be President in 1836—Old Hickory would see to that. But Calhoun would not be subservient to Jackson. He had no fear of the old general, who scared most men out of their wits. Calhoun told the President to his face, in a meeting of the cabinet, that he had once recommended his court-martial, when he was Secretary of War, and when Jackson had disobeyed orders. The old man ranted and raved while Calhoun, who never raised his voice, told him "I would do it again under the same circumstances."

But Van Buren became President.

Calhoun remained in the Senate until his death, in 1850, excepting the short time he was Secretary of State during Tyler's administration. Had John Calhoun seen fit to defer to Jackson, the history of the era might have been different. Calhoun would undoubtedly have served two terms as President; Van Buren would have been a minor character, and William Henry Harrison would have been merely the general who defeated Tippicanoe.

The National Bank Bill, always a thorn in the flesh of Congress, the President and the nation, again came up for consideration. It was passed by both houses of Congress and Van Buren promptly vetoed it. He said that he "would put the damn rascals out of the bank," and did it. Calhoun, the Vice-President, took no part in the debate. He was opposed to the bill, however, and John Tyler consulted with him on the fight which the Southern senators made against its passage, and especially on sustaining the President's veto.

The issue of the tariff came before Congress again as aging John Randolph had predicted it would, and once more it was Calhoun against Clay and Webster. Clay, always the compromiser, saw that he could not pass his original bill so he approached Calhoun on an alternative measure, and out of the meeting of the minds of the two came a bill which Calhoun could support. When Calhoun announced the compromise—for as a part of the trade he had forced Clay to allow him to make the amendments —there was tumultuous applause. The two warriors had at last come together and for once Webster had to fight both Clay and Calhoun. The debate raged long and earnestly. Randolph left the Senate chamber and told a colleague, "Webster is dead, I saw him dying an hour ago." Calhoun, of all the members of the Senate, could handle old "blustery, boisterous and blowsy Webster."

Slavery was becoming more of an issue each day; Texas was knocking at the door of the Union for admission, the Oregon boundary was a matter of dispute between the United States and Great Britain; and the old men were passing from the picture. Jefferson and Adams were dead ten years; Madison, Marshall, Monroe, Crawford, and the long-forgotten Burr were gone. Clay, Calhoun, and Webster were the leaders. Old Hickory was through and would go back to the Hermitage. Van Buren was President. A young man named Abraham Lincoln was coming to the front and was serving his only term in Congress, and an aristocrat from New York, who would just miss becoming President, William H. Seward, was in Washington.

The country was at peace. Van Buren ran for re-election. Old General Harrison was a popular choice for the Whig nomination for President, and with him was nominated an amiable but not particularly able former governor of Virginia and senator, John Tyler. They were elected by a large majority over Van Buren and Colonel Richard Johnson, and one month after the inauguration the first Vice-President to come to the high office by reason of death moved to the White House.

Unquestionably the most able man in the Senate at the time was Calhoun. He was the Rock of Gibraltar to the States' rights men. General Upshur was Secretary of State. When on a sea trip the U.S.S. *Princeton* blew up and General Upshur was killed, President Tyler went to Calhoun to offer him the secretaryship. They talked at length over the offer. Tyler needed a strong man in the Department of State: he had the question of the Texas annexation and the Oregon boundary matter to settle. Would Calhoun accept?

Once more Calhoun, no longer young, moved his personal belongings from the Senate chamber and became a cabinet member. He had made an agreement with Tyler that he would be permitted to resign when the Texas annexation and the Oregon boundary issues were settled. These two vexatious problems were literally tossed in his lap. Secretary Calhoun handled them both as he had always handled problems—"in a direct and fearless manner." He realized he could not hope to persuade Great Britain to yield to the fifty-four forty frontier. He knew this was not feasible and that the logical solution was to place the boundary at the mouth of the Columbia River. He settled the dispute by means of the Ashburton Treaty, which was an equitable settlement of an explosive controversy. Calhoun said frankly that he had no "desire to go to war over the matter of a boundary."

Texas, now a republic, had fought for her independence and was recognized among the galaxy of nations. She had asked to be admitted into the Union. Only the most rabid antislavery elements were opposed to her admission. Secretary Calhoun prepared the bill for her entry and one of the last acts of Tyler as President was to sign the bill admitting Texas into the Union as a state where slavery was permitted.

In 1846, Calhoun was sixty-four, and his hopes of becoming President had faded. James K. Polk, of Tennessee, a little-known man even though he had been Speaker of the House of Representatives, was elected President. He had defeated Clay and Van Buren; Clay had campaigned for the last time. Polk was fifty, colorless, but of determined character. He could not be swerved when he made a decision and he was to prove a strong President who did not want a second term.

One of the senators was willing to resign and again Calhoun was a member of the upper house from South Carolina. He took his seat in December of 1845, and for the last five years of his life he again represented his state.

The Mexican War was provoked as a result of the annexation of Texas. Boundaries were in dispute and General Zachary Taylor and General Winfield Scott made short work of the pathetic Mexican Army. Calhoun did not approve of the Mexican War, but he supported it as he had the War of 1812. Mexico soon sued for peace. There was agitation to dismember Mexico and take her into the Union as a number of slave states. There was the much-discussed Wilmot Proviso which provided that no state acquired by war or through purchase should be admitted into the Union as a slave state. The debate on that proviso was acrimonious.

The leaders in it were no longer young and vigorous. Clay was seventy; Calhoun and Webster were sixty-six. The younger men listened to them but they would not be swayed by the orations of old men; they would make the decisions themselves.

In the elections of 1848, "Rough and Ready" Zachary Taylor, a Virginian transplanted to Louisiana, who had been a regular army officer, who "knew not whether he was a Whig or a Democrat," and who had never voted, was the candidate chosen by the Whigs at their convention in Philadelphia. Millard Fillmore of New York was his running mate. The convention was ruled by young Thurlow Weed who snubbed both Clay and Webster and brought about the nomination of Taylor, a slaveholder, whom he believed could carry some of the Southern states. It is interesting to note that the Whig ticket, headed by a slaveholder, received the hearty support of Lincoln and of Seward, both strong antislavery men.

90

Taylor was elected. California was admitted to the Union as a free state, although the South was strongly opposed to her admission, and once more secession and nullification talk was in the air.

Senator Calhoun again led the fight for the South but, as he had long known, the North could outvote those states.

The United States now was a nation extending from the Atlantic to the Pacific and from Maine to Texas, but a nation divided on two great issues, slavery and States' rights. There was no union within the Union. When Congress met in December of 1849, sixty-three ballots were required to elect the Speaker. The Civil War was only a decade away and the men who were to be the leaders in that struggle were coming to the fore. Jefferson Davis, the tall Mississippian who was soon to be Secretary of War, was fast emerging as the leader of the Southern element in the Senate; Senator Stephen Douglas of Illinois and his chief political opponent, Lincoln, were the new leaders among the antislavery men of the Middle West. The afore-mentioned Weed, Seward, and Salmon P. Chase were to be contenders for power for the next twenty years. Robert E. Lee, U. S. Grant, Albert Sidney Johnston, men who were to be future enemies, were friends and associates. The Union was breaking up but only the farsighted saw the handwriting on the wall.

Three old men were prophets of the debacle to come. They knew that the patched-up compromises could not be made to endure much longer.

Senator Calhoun was in fact decrepit, and on March 4, 1850, he was supported to his seat in the Senate chamber by John Hamilton of South Carolina; that day the elderly man from South Carolina was to sing his swan song. He was sixty-eight, and since boyhood he had been afflicted with weak lungs. As for Clay, he was ready to die; and old "blustering" Dan Webster was "unclean," his vest, once so ornate, was now covered with the "remnants of many dinners." Webster was speaking when Calhoun entered the Senate, and talking of the gentleman from South Carolina. His address was laudatory and when he had finished the Senate applauded the old orator. The President of the Senate then recognized the Senator from South Carolina. That gentleman was wrapped in flannels and bundled in warm clothing to protect his frail body from the raw March weather. He could not talk and he motioned to Senator Mason, of Virginia, who was to read his last speech.

A part of this last address is worthy of a rereading:

Disunion will come, not suddenly but gradually. It has already begun. Disunion must be the work of time. It is only through a long process that the cords can be snapped until the whole fabric falls asunder. Already the agitation of slavery has snapped the most important. How then can the Union be saved? In no way but by removing the cause of the trouble, by satisfying the Southern states that they can remain in safety.

Senator Mason read on while the Senate sat spellbound. They were listening to the last words of a dying man.

The impression created by Calhoun's speech was mixed. His colleagues loved him, they respected him, they crowded around and shook his hand. The Senate knew that his words were prophetic, that what he said would certainly come to pass. But they also knew that this disunion might be postponed. Clay, Calhoun, and Webster would not live to see that tragic day, but those who had listened to Calhoun's last speech, who would listen to Clay and Webster a few times more before they too would make their farewell addresses, would see the breakup of the Union which these three men had valiantly tried to save.

Calhoun was finished; he had run his course. On March 11, he was on the floor of the Senate for a short while. He listened to Webster once more and now he heard younger members speak disparagingly of the "three old men." He went home. He wrote a few letters to his family telling them not to be alarmed, that he had "pulled through before, (he) would do so again." But this time he could not. He died on the early morning of March 31, 1850.

Calhoun was a statesman, much more than a politician. For forty-three years he was active in the life of the young nation.

He saw it grow from the thirteen colonies along the Atlantic coast until it lapped the shores of the Pacific. He saw Louisiana, Florida, Texas, and the Pacific slope come into the Union. He saw slavery become the major issue and the provocation of disunion. He consistently fought for States' rights, and he resigned the second highest office in the gift of the nation to make that fight. He saw the South lose its power and its prestige, and the West become the balance in the balloting strength of the Electoral College. He was a good legislator, a hard-working congressman, a singularly able Secretary of War, a brilliant senator—the one man who could "whip Clay and Webster the same afternoon, and have time for Benton during recess."

Calhoun's forthrightness, there would seem little doubt, deprived him of the Presidency. He was not a man of Jefferson's stature, but the Vice-Presidency was not an incidental office in his life, as it was in that of Jefferson's, and it is a fair statement that he was, up to his time, the most proficient presiding officer of the Senate.

President Adams, by no means an articulate or precise man in his judgment of his contemporaries, appears to have had an interlude of singular clarity when in his *Memoirs* he wrote this summation of Calhoun:

"Calhoun is a man of fair and candid mind, of honorable principles, of clear and quick understanding, of cool self-possession, of enlarged philosophical views, and of ardent patriotism. He is above all sectional and factious prejudices, more (so) than any other statesman of this Union with whom I have acted."

CHAPTER VIII

Martin Van Buren

THE LONG AND NOISOME history of machine politics in the United States begins early in the last century with the rise of Martin Van Buren. The eighth Vice-President started life as a tavern dishwasher, and his education was the sketchiest; although he succeeded in winning admission to the New York state bar, in adult life his speech was often grossly ungrammatical, his writing frequently indecipherable, and his spelling a matter of phonetics. But he was a highly accomplished gentleman at constructing an efficient political machine, and at developing the spoils system to a level resembling closely its present mode of operation in the nation.

Some of the early Van Burens came to the New Netherlands as far back as 1631. They came as indentured servants and for more than a century and a half that was their position. From the time they landed at what was later New York until the birth of Martin Van Buren in 1782, they were always servants—indeed serfs. They waited on the patroons, and none ever became a patroon. History fails to disclose a soldier among the more than three hundred descendants of those first Van Burens.

It is doubtful if Van Buren was precisely their name. There were no scholars among the early Van Burens; few of them ever learned to read or write; and fewer still learned to speak English with ease.

The father of Martin was Abraham Van Buren, the keeper of a tavern which catered to the comforts of man and horse. His long, low clapboard tavern was at Kinderhook in Columbia

County, New York. It was a place of small repute with a back room in which the "gentry could be accomodated" when they stopped on their way to and from Albany, and where they need not come in contact with the neighborhood farmer talk.

Abraham Van Buren was a man in his late thirties when he married Mary, a widow with children and a woman given to prayer, who bore him two daughters, and who on a wintry night in December of 1782 "came to bed of a son," Martin. He was a small child with piercing blue eyes who in a few years would resemble the young Aaron Burr. Burr, incidentally, spent much time at the Van Buren tavern during the last years of the Revolution. The later mental resemblance to Burr was even more marked than the physical, and portraits of the two obviously show a similarity of features that might be found in father and son.

H. M. Alexander in his biography of Van Buren scoffs at this "scandalous implication" but John Quincy Adams, in his *Diary*, also was struck by the resemblance. He recorded that rumors of Van Buren's illegitimacy were heard throughout his acquaintance with Little Matty. To the foregoing it may be added that the two men were friends of long standing and that late in life Burr lived for a while with Van Buren.

Young Matty attended the local academy and could read and write English. He became a potboy in his father's tavern and once he began serving patrons he had time for no more schooling. He had attended the academy with William Peter Van Ness and little Hannah Hoe. Van Ness was to be a friend for many years but later a hated enemy; Van Buren was to marry the daughter.

Martin was fourteen when he was apprenticed to Francis Silvester as a law student. He cleaned the office; he carried documents; he ran errands, studied law, and by the time he was sixteen he was attending court with members of the firm.

At this period it was customary for the older apprentices to appear in court in minor cases and soon Matty was summing up in petty trials. He was even then a good trial lawyer and could wring tears from a jury.

At eighteen, Van Buren made his first political deal, a profession at which he was soon to become a master, and ultimately perhaps the greatest political trader the American people have ever known.

John Van Ness wanted to become a member of Congress. Martin offered to manage his campaign and "elect him" if, in turn, he would keep Matty in funds for two years while he finished his law studies in New York. The offer was agreeable to Van Ness and young Van Buren proceeded to do as he had promised. Van Ness became the Representative from the Columbia District and Van Buren, at eighteen, was in New York as an advanced law student. Van Buren had difficulty keeping Van Ness to his promise and that gentleman frequently complained that "money was not to be had."

Van Buren had been a delegate to the convention that nominated Van Ness to Congress, he had managed his campaign and he had elected his candidate, and all this before he was of voting age. Martin studied law in New York for two years and passed the examinations in the supreme court of the state of New York. In his autobiography he wrote of the hard times he had, and how he often was hungry. At this time he borrowed money from his half-brother, who loaned him "thirty or forty dollars," and he visited Burr at his palatial home on Richmond Hill. He wrote that he was treated "with attention." He was five feet six inches tall—he was never to be any taller—and until past sixty he was to be slender as a reed.

Politics were seething in New York. The Clintons and the Livingstons aligned themselves against the "upstart" Burr, who had exploited them to become Vice-President. They combined against the Little Bantam and thought they had relegated him to obscurity by beating him for governor. They took over the state administration and kept a tight hold until driven from power by the diminutive but astute Matty.

Nepotism during this period was rampant. At one time the Clinton family held eight state offices and the Livingstons sat in thirteen official posts. There was scarcely a state post that one of the members of these families did not control.

When Burr ceased to be a political factor in the state of New York, by reason of killing Hamilton, there stepped into his place a man who was just possibly his natural son.

Matty had joined the Tammany Society and eventually came to be its honorary Grand Sachem. He did not live in the city but kept his voting address in Kinderhook, but for thirty years he carried Tammany and its braves in his pocket. He showed them how to win elections. He was never an open party to their skullduggery but he would formulate the strategy and the braves would do the dirty work. He believed in the political "payoff" for the braves. Friendships were made for political advantages and were to be cast aside when no longer profitable.

Young Van Buren was soon a political power in New York City and in the state. This youth of just voting age played both ends against the middle. He was ambitious to the point of unscrupulousness. He bearded powerful DeWitt Clinton and blandly demanded favors. He did not come as a novitiate but as one of proved political ability. Because he helped to elect Daniel Tompkins as governor he was appointed surrogate of the court. This little red fox of Kinderhook was making progress. He improved his finances, his law practice grew and he saw a state senatorship in the offing. Van Buren made a bold stab for that office, and the staid dignified senators soon saw a youngster sitting among them. He was the youngest member of that body and the youngest man to ever sit in the state senate.

In 1812, Van Buren's friends went off to war; his neighbors took up arms; and the charge of slacker was leveled at him. But little Van was no fighting man and he remained in the state senate.

During his decade as a state senator he was primarily a political leader and a dispenser of patronage. He fostered few bills of importance. But Van Buren sponsored one piece of legislation of particular interest. If he never wore a uniform, he nevertheless introduced into the legislature a bill providing for universal conscription. It is altogether possible that had the War of 1812 lasted longer, the measure would have passed. Tompkins, the war governor, would undoubtedly have signed it and New York would have been in a position to furnish more men for the armed forces than all the rest of the nation combined. Senator Van Buren supported the war effort although he refused the commission which President Madison offered him. He preferred to play politics with DeWitt Clinton and the older men. He stayed home and eventually became President by means of political horse trading.

Van Buren decided in the elections of 1816 to enter the stage of national politics. He was now thirty-four, and he had become a well-to-do if not an actually rich man. He had been in state politics for sixteen years and the alluring idea occurred that perhaps he might become a kingmaker. He determined to elect Tompkins to the Presidency—affable, good-looking Dan who had been the leading patriot of the War of 1812—with Senator Crawford of Georgia as Vice-President. He was only partly successful in this first venture in national politics for the Virginia Oligarchy were to remain in the saddle for another eight years. Monroe was elected, but Tompkins became Vice-President in a trade in which even Van Buren learned a little about political deals from the smart boys from the South.

With Tammany Hall, he created a machine the like of which New York or the new nation had never seen. That machine endured until another political boss in the person of Thurlow Weed destroyed the "Little Magician's" regency and raised in its stead the modern machine system.

Van Buren had indeed become a kingmaker in a small way; he was on the way to becoming a power in the nation. To achieve that, however, he had to go to Washington and he persuaded Governor Tompkins to appoint him attorney general of New York. The post was a lucrative one. The salary was small but the opportunities in the way of fees were many and Little Matty could use the money since he had a growing family. But his $5.50

per day plus traveling expenses, added to the sums to be obtained as fees, would give him a fair income. He regarded the attorney generalship as a steppingstone, and the realistic little Van exploited it to every advantage.

In 1821, Van Buren was elected to the United States Senate. He had come far from the glorified hovel which old Abe Van Buren had called a tavern. He was not yet forty. He had learned the game of politics in the big league. He had climbed over the bodies of his friends; he had been unscrupulous, and he had kept his word only when it was to his advantage. He had never been proved guilty of the crimes for which his henchmen were known to be responsible but he certainly had a guilty consciousness of much fraud. He owned the controlling interest in the Albany *Argus,* and he unquestionably knew that its editor was a counterfeiter. He was associate of the Tammany Society, some members of whom flouted the law—to put it mildly.

They could not convict Little Matty, although at forty-five he retired from the practice of law with $200,000, then a very substantial fortune. Where and how he accumulated that sum of money, no one knew. He offered no information as to its source. Outwardly, there was little change: he dressed a little better; drew his corset laces a little tighter and thought of becoming a social leader.

His little Hannah was dead. She had died in childbirth. Martin was a widower with four growing sons whom he farmed out among his relatives. When he went to Washington in December of 1821, Monroe was President and in the Senate were some of the most able men that body has ever had. There were the redoubtable Clay and Webster, along with Benton of Missouri, the nearly insane Randolph—the great coiner of epigrams and the most vituperative man the country has ever known; and Hayne of South Carolina. These men, who were to be the leaders of the nation for thirty years, discussed abolition, the tariff, and States' rights.

Little Matty could not compete with these men as statesmen but he could and did outsmart them. He became a social climber.

He ingratiated himself with Mrs. Calhoun and the granddaughter of Jefferson, the beautiful Ellen Randolph. He said he fell in love with Ellen and proposed to her. She was impressed with the restive and dynamic Van Buren and possibly would have married him had he not had four growing sons.

Senator Van Buren played his hand very well. He carefully noted the way the wind blew and deliberated a long time over whom he would support for President when the time came to choose Monroe's successor. Big Bill Crawford, the able Secretary of the Treasury in Monroe's cabinet, looked as though he might be a winner. Jackson was the idol of the people—and the people were at last becoming a power. The property clauses were being set aside in the voting qualifications and the well-to-do were no longer the only enfranchised citizens, as had been made possible by the early state constitutions.

Little Matty was fully aware that the common man must be weighed in the coming election.

Adams was Secretary of State. That post was now recognized as the springboard to the Presidency. Who would be a winner? The junior senator from New York must not be a loser. He had too much at stake.

Van Buren made few speeches in the Senate. He was diplomatic—that is to say, it was difficult to learn which side of the tariff issue he supported. He must build his political fences so that he might eventually become President himself. He injected himself into the patronage fight and insisted that he be given the privilege of dictating federal appointments in New York. Where Tammany Hall or its friends were a party to a political claim, he insisted that they receive the appointment they sought.

Van Buren made trouble for President Monroe and his Postmaster General, but Monroe was about to retire and Van Buren felt that he must not lose his prestige in New York. He would want to come back to the Senate and the way back was by way of the patronage he could deliver over to Tammany. But because Tammany men could not be depended upon to remain honest, Matty was always in hot water. They would persist in absconding with any money they found loose. One enterprising New Yorker absconded with more than $1,000,000 while the postmaster of Albany was short in his accounts at the same time. Such men were an unremitting headache but Senator Van Buren helped them when they met trouble. In return, he demanded implicit obedience. It was a profitable arrangement for both Van Buren and for Tammany's braves.

Washington was provocative to Van Buren. He was an adventurer and there was adventuring to be had in the capital, now a city of 25,000 inhabitants. For example, there was the Supreme Court; he cast an acquisitive eye on that body and asked Senator King to recommend him for a seat. The senator made the recommendation but for once a political deal fell through, and Smith Thompson was moved up from the cabinet to the Supreme Court. This loss was a blow to Van Buren and it severed a friendship of long standing. Van Buren had named one of his sons after Thompson; Matty never was a good loser.

But Van Buren was resourceful. He had an agreement with Crawford to support him for the Presidency in return for which Van Buren was to get the Vice-Presidency. But fate played the cards differently. Crawford was stricken with apoplexy and the little political magician realized this was not the propitious time for the junior senator from New York to offer himself as a candidate for the Vice-Presidency. He looked around for a strong man as running mate for Crawford, as he still felt that the ill man from Georgia might still be elected. He then made a grievous mistake. He choose as Crawford's running mate the aged Gallatin, who had been Secretary of the Treasury during Jefferson's administration. This knowledgeable man, who had aspired to the Supreme Court, would have placed in nomination for the Vice-Presidency a man who was not a native-born American— Gallatin was Swiss-born. The Constitution stipulates that both the President and the Vice-President must be native born. The members of the Senate, his fellow party members, and particularly his political enemies were prompt to poke fun at Van Buren for his ignorance of the Constitution.

The Presidential campaign soon developed into a race among Jackson, Clay, and Adams, with little thought of Crawford as a serious contender. The results seemed to show that Jackson had received a majority of the popular votes, with Adams and Crawford running in second and third place. There followed the infamous compact between Clay and Adams. Contrary to the pre-election predictions, Crawford had beaten Clay and he had no hope of election. No candidate had received a majority of the electoral vote and, when the election was thrown into the House of Representatives, Clay threw his thirty-seven votes to Adams and old John's fat son became the sixth President of the United States. Clay was immediately appointed Secretary of State, and Old Hickory Jackson was accordingly furious. This was the second time the national elections had been decided by the House of Representatives.

Jackson immediately began to plan for the campaign four years later. He made friends with Van Buren and found a flattering supporter. Van Buren knew that the old man had been jockeyed out of the Presidency, and he knew also that his own plan to become Vice-President had failed because he had backed the wrong horse and that it would have been the part of discretion to have trailed with the old general from the start.

Jackson was the idol of the Army and of the common people of the nation. He was the last of the Revolutionary heroes; he had been a soldier in the South Carolina campaign more than fifty years before. The scheming, adroit Van Buren now felt that by associating himself with the general he would not be picking a loser.

Adams was a hard-working President. He kept his thoughts to himself and went his own way, and he was to last for only one term. He was beaten the day Clay was named Secretary of State. Calhoun was Vice-President. Clay and Webster were in the Senate. But the country was waiting for 1828 when it knew that the hero of the Battle of New Orleans would sit in the Presidential chair.

Van Buren returned to the Senate, this time as the senior

senator from New York. He cultivated Jackson assiduously and, when John Quincy Adams' days came to be numbered as he had felt that they would be, he nominated himself Jackson's manager—in fact, if not officially.

Little Van had weighed the matter more carefully this time and he was not to be beaten again. He knew that Jackson was temperamental and opinionated, but he had seen the popular vote the old man had received and he felt that the aging general, who had saved the military reputation of America that cold foggy morning at New Orleans, who had killed men and who carried bullets in his body—one so close to his heart that the surgeons would not remove it—who had many faults but greater virtues; he felt that this man could not be beaten. Why not then make it a partnership between Old Hickory and Little Van?

He decried Adams in the Senate. He lauded Jackson at every opportunity. Van Buren gained a small reputation as an orator. He could not, of course, match the great quartet of Clay, Calhoun, Randolph, and Webster, but he talked forever in favor of General Jackson and he brought into play his gift for political intrigue. If he could never hope to compete with such men as the increasingly senile Randolph, he could still pull the strings behind the scenes.

With the campaign of 1828, Matty found new reserves of energy. He stumped the country; he wrote pamphlets; he even eschewed the social activities of Washington. He knew he must carry New York for Old Hickory. Were he to lose his home state he would not only lose prestige but, in all probability, lose the election for Jackson. New York had thirty-six electoral votes and they could easily decide the election.

Senator Van Buren decided to run for governor of New York. With the assistance of Tammany, he felt that he could win himself as well as elect his chief. And he could always resign the governorship to enter the cabinet.

Jackson and Calhoun were elected. Adams might just as well not have run. Little Matty not only carried New York for Jackson but was elected governor. For six weeks there was a new governor of New York and there was as well a new Secretary of State in Jackson's cabinet. Van Buren had been a senator, a governor, and Secretary of State all within the space of two months. The Little Magician was forty-six; he had almost arrived at journey's end. Old Hickory could make him his successor.

The inauguration of Jackson and the day and night which followed was a riot and saturnalia. The people's choice was President. No longer was the aristocracy in power. That Virginia clique would never again come to power. Its sun had set and for the next century elections were to be run and won by political bosses.

Van Buren was Secretary of State and was the confidant of the sixty-two-year-old Jackson. He planned the campaigns; he prepared the papers which the President signed. Van Buren cleansed the administration of every holdover. He said, with candor, "We do not explain our removals."

The tariff question was again the main issue. Feelings ran high. Calhoun resigned the Vice-Presidency and returned to the Senate to become the hope of the States' rights men. The Eaton scandal broke and Van Buren was in the midst of the fight. He had no wife to offend so he came out boldly for "Tap Room Peggy." He reasoned that every man he could alienate from the President was one more man out of his way. As Secretary of State he gave a magnificent reception and invited the official family. He persuaded two ambassadors to attend, and he noted with relish that Mrs. Calhoun and the other social leaders were absent. He was drawing closer to the President each day; his prospects were bright.

As a way of ending the fight with Washington society, which he and the President were fast losing, Van Buren persuaded Jackson to allow Secretary of War Eaton to resign. The old man wanted Eaton near him and, above all, he hated to lose a fight, but Van Buren talked him into it by offering to resign along with the entire cabinet. The tempest in the teapot ended. General Eaton was made governor of Louisiana and was later to go to Spain as ambassador. Van Buren was "reluctantly persuaded" to become ambassador to Great Britain.

But not for long. Clay, Calhoun, and Webster played a Van Burenesque trick on little Matty. They refused to confirm his appointment. He had settled in London and looked forward to a pleasant winter in England with the chargé d'affaires of the embassy, Washington Irving, another upstate New Yorker. The dapper "almost Ambassador" hid his disappointment and came back leisurely to the United States.

On his return trip Van Buren passed through Holland whence his ancestors had come two hundred years before. The descendant of the humblest forefathers, he was embraced by the king of the Netherlands merely because his name was Van Buren and because the king, in addition to his other titles, was Baron of Van Buren.

He returned to Washington to become Vice-President. No one could hope to beat Old Hickory, and Jackson had decided to continue in the Presidency another four years. Van Buren was somewhat disappointed: had he not been told by the general that he was to be his successor? He felt he had only to wait, however, and as Vice-President he could mend his fences, make friends in strategic places, and keep an eye on New York.

Van Buren was nominated for the Vice-Presidency at the convention in 1832 with Jackson again the Presidential candidate. In the face of strong opposition from the Whigs, predictions of financial depression, and a general breakdown of the governmental setup, the two were elected. One could not beat Jackson, which was the equivalent of saying one could not beat his running mate.

As Vice-President, Van Buren sat on a powder keg which was likely to explode any moment. Nullification was in the air; slavery was an increasingly acute issue; the Texas question was coming to the fore; the Oregon boundary was another controversy; and the Bank was always a thorn in the flesh of the President. In the Senate, Van Buren sat in the Vice-President's chair with pistols by his side.

Although Little Matty sat with his brace of pistols ready, he was in a conciliatory mood. He did not want to make more enemies since he was determined to be President. He would avoid any stand on controversial subjects. Clay attacked him from the floor of the Senate but he would not answer the angry Kentuckian. He schemed and planned and carefully watched New York. He made a trip to his state and, with the help of the party, he won the elections of 1834. (He also won considerable money betting on the elections.)

Van Buren had two major addictions. He drank enormous quantities of whiskey and he bet huge sums on elections. The whiskey did not seem to affect him and he usually won his bets.

Back in Washington, Van Buren was challenged to a duel by Senator Poindexter over an article which called the senator a "bloated mass of corruption" but, as David Crockett said, he "wriggled out of it." Poindexter threatened that he would "beat him on sight." Van Buren wrote a letter disclaiming any knowledge of the article, but he continued to keep his weapons beside him.

In the campaign for the election of 1836, there were four avowed candidates for the Presidency. They were Senator Webster of Massachusetts, Senator Mangum of North Carolina, Senator Hugh White, and old General William Henry Harrison, who had been unearthed by the Whigs. The Whigs felt that they needed an outstanding candidate of the Jackson type, and believed that they had found him in the hero of Tippecanoe. He had been a congressman, a territorial governor, minister to Colombia and clerk of the court of his home county in Ohio. In any event, General Harrison was the most surprised man in the country when he was approached to be a candidate for the Presidency. He was willing—indeed, he felt the nation owed him a living and would have accepted virtually any federal office offered him. For one thing, he had eight children.

For his part, Van Buren felt that now was his opportunity. He was fifty-four. He had been state senator, attorney general of New York, United States senator, governor of New York, Vice-

President, and ambassador to Great Britain. The ambassadorship had been brief and unconfirmed by the Senate, but he put it down on his list of achievements.

Van Buren played the field. He egged on the candidates one against another; he set the North against the South, the East against the West; and he circulated tales which hurt his opponents. Old Senator White, who was past seventy, had a young wife and that was used against him. Senator Mangum was accused of being a Nullifier, Webster of being a drunkard, and General Harrison of "imbibing hard cider," the most innocuous drink in an era when men drank whiskey for breakfast instead of coffee. Matty, in turn, was attacked.

The incomparable David Crockett, who was to die a glorious death at the Alamo a few months later, wrote a biography of "Blue Whiskey Van." It is an amusing lampoon on Van Buren. With a vengeance, Crockett told stories out of school. Crockett wrote of Van Buren that "at one year of age he could cry out of one side of his face and laugh out of the other. . . . He wears corsets and, if possible, he wears them tighter than the women. He struts and swaggers like a crow in the gutter. But for his large red and gray whiskers it would be difficult to tell whether he was man or woman."

This was typical of the campaign methods of 1836.

The election was close but Van Buren pulled through and was the eighth President of the United States. Little Matty had come a long way since his days as a tavern potboy. He was on the heights; there was no higher hill to climb. He had trampled down all the opposition; he was in early middle age; and he was President. Richard M. Johnson of Kentucky was the Vice-President, elected by the Senate as he had not polled a majority vote.

In 1837, the country suffered a great depression, provoked by land speculations, paper money, and wild-eyed legislation passed during the last days of Jackson's administration. Factories closed, clearinghouses shut their doors and more than 90 per cent of the banks failed. Conditions were desperate throughout the nation and Little Matty was blamed, whether at fault or not. There was actual fear of civil war.

Had Van Buren possessed the courage during his senatorial days to take a definite stand on Nullification, the Bank issue, and the Distribution Act, he might have withstood the storm. But he had no following in Congress or the nation. No one knew where he would stand on a given issue. He was now reaping the whirlwind. He made an energetic effort to right conditions. The House and the Senate, however, would not believe in his sincerity. But when Congress met in September of 1837, President Van Buren sent a message to that body which heard it with astonishment. The nation was surprised. Little Van had written one of the great messages of all times. In that message to Congress, Van Buren showed a style that was almost comparable to Jefferson at his best. Whether it was written by Van Buren or "ghostwritten," it is great political literature. Historians of the times are inclined to believe that it was written by one of the Cabinet members or possibly by the Cabinet collectively in collaboration with the President.

Little Matty had troubles from all sides. Texas had gained her independence from Mexico; there was trouble with Great Britain over the Maine boundary and at one time war was threatened. He sent General Scott to Maine to protect American interests and took a firm stand with regard to Texas. The nation was surprised. Here was a man who had never shown any semblance of genuine statesmanship who was striving to be a strong President almost overnight. He could not gather his forces together, however, for there were few who had faith in him and fewer still who had reason to be loyal to a man who had never been loyal to anyone. He had only New York behind him but even in the Empire State ultimately he was beaten by a tall young man of swarthy appearance who became the second of the great political bosses, Thurlow Weed. Weed elected young William Seward as governor over old Marcy, the war horse. Van Buren had lost his own state.

He was on his way out.

The President tried desperately to gain prestige by paying court to the great men of the nation. He offered the position as Secretary of State to Washington Irving; he invited to the White House men who he hoped would be of aid. There came Clay, the great compromiser, the austere and learned Calhoun, John Quincy Adams—men whom he had long known, had schemed against, and double-crossed times without number. They came; they drank his wines; they ate his rich foods; and they met his new daughter-in-law, Dolly Madison's niece. They enjoyed themselves at his expense, but to them he would always be Little Matty, the intriguer.

Stranger than this perhaps was his inability to maintain his influence in New York. Van Buren could not beat Weed. He had been the regent but Weed was an obvious boss; Van Buren had schemed, whispered, conspired while Weed gave orders openly, and he was obeyed. Van Buren's efforts had always been to advance Van Buren but Thurlow Weed wanted no political office. . . . It was beyond comprehension. But the tall, saturnine Weed would be the leader for the next thirty years.

The next campaign began in 1839. General Harrison was the Whig candidate as he had been in 1836. Weed now dictated the strategy, and he could not be hoodwinked by Van Buren as had the others in 1836. He summoned Webster out of the Senate chamber and offered him the Vice-Presidency. "Blustering" Dan refused—he wanted the "big job or none." The Vice-Presidential nomination ultimately went to Tyler of Virginia, a man who had once been a Democrat. Then began a real campaign, run by a master campaigner. "Tippecanoe-and-Tyler-too" was the Whig campaign song and victory seemed to be in the offing for the Whigs, who had been so long on the short end.

In the half century of the nation's history, the party had elected only two Presidents, John Adams and his son, John Quincy, each of whom served only one term. Washington had been nonpartisan while Jefferson, Madison, Monroe, Jackson, and Van Buren were all Democrats. A change was due and Little Matty was to be the victim.

Van Buren was again the unanimous choice of the Democrats and Colonel Richard Johnson, the hero of the War of 1812 along with General Jackson, was the choice as running mate, as he had been four years before.

President Van Buren made a trip through the North, ostensibly to visit his relatives at Kinderhook, New York, but he made speeches both on the way there and back to Washington. Colonel Johnson spoke throughout the South and Senator Tazewell, who had polled eleven convention votes for the Vice-Presidency, worked throughout Virginia. Calhoun, who could not tolerate a Whig, did yeoman service in South Carolina.

The fight was to no avail, however. When the votes were counted, Harrison had 234 electoral votes to sixty for Van Buren. It was a landslide. Van Buren's day was done and the Whigs were in power. (The sixty-eight-year-old hero of Tippecanoe was President for one month when he died of a cold, and Tyler became President.)

The Little Magician was fifty-eight years old when he went back to Kinderhook to build himself a home which he hoped would rival Monticello and Mount Vernon as shrines for posterity. He built Linderwald, but people did not come to visit him. He was a candidate again in 1844, and at one time had more than a majority of votes in the convention, but could not muster the two-thirds majority. Van Buren made another effort to come back in 1848 as the head of the Free Soil party. As the candidate of that party he did not poll a single electoral vote.

The former President lived at Linderwald as he hoped a sage might have lived. He rode horseback and jumped fences. He made every effort to establish himself as a social leader. He paid court to Mrs. DeWitt Clinton, the widow of the long dead governor, and that lady promptly snubbed him. He proposed marriage to the spinster daughter of Francis Silvester, with whom he had studied law long ago, and she also refused him. He grew restive and decided to do a grand tour of Europe. He was now seventy-three. For two years he traveled over England and the

Continent. In Italy he met Pope Pius IX and wrote that he was "almost converted."

In Holland, the one time potboy had a coat of arms made for himself. With that vanity accomplished, he returned home. On July 24, 1862, when he was eighty, "Little Matty," "Blue Whiskey Van," the "American Tallyrand," and the "Red Fox of Kinderhook"—to cite a few of his sobriquets—died at Kinderhook.

Van Buren must be regarded as the most colorful and dynamic among the Vice-Presidents, even with due regard for Aaron Burr's histrionics. For all his shortcomings, his blatant opportunism, and his abiding and exclusive interest in Van Buren, it is difficult to regard him without a sort of amiable tolerance, if not outright admiration. The tavern potboy who fought his way, "upward and onward," to the Presidency deserves a Horatio Alger for an official biographer.

He was the prototype of the expert in realistic, organized politics in America, necessarily not the most immaculate vocation. For all his gregariousness and affability, he was a model of consistency in laboring twenty-four hours a day on behalf of Martin Van Buren. The perennial officeholder, his only concrete achievements were the Conscription Act of 1814 and the enabling legislation creating the Sub-Treasury. For the rest, he devoted very nearly all of eighty years to an unswerving crusade to advertise the indispensable political virtues of Van Buren.

CHAPTER IX

Richard Mentor Johnson

THERE ARE THREE SALIENT points of interest in the career of the ninth Vice-President of the United States, an American now almost forgotten. One is that he was the man who in combat killed Tecumseh (at least, most of the available evidence supports that assertion), who was probably the ablest Indian chief about whom there are any reliable accounts. Another is that he missed election as the Chief Executive by the narrowest margin. And the third is that he was the first Vice-President from the West.

In the spring of 1779, Robert Johnson, the father of Richard Mentor Johnson, along with his brother Cave and two neighbors, went from Orange County, Virginia, to Fincastle County in the same state. Times were hard in the Piedmont country; the Revolution was bogging and money was tight. It looked to Robert Johnson as though a move westward might be the best thing he could do for himself and his growing family.

They looked the country over, returned home, and began preparations to move to Daniel Boone's country. That fall saw Johnson with his wife, Jemima, and their four children on their way to Bear Grass, a settlement which in time became Louisville, Kentucky. Fincastle County was the most westerly of Virginia's counties and it was from that county that Kentucky was carved.

In 1780, there was born to Jemima and Robert a son whom they called Richard. He was a large baby and later a big boy with a charm of manner and a stout spirit. His father was a well-thought-of citizen of the new country, a pillar of the Baptist church and the man chosen by the congregation to be moderator of their assemblies and arbitrator of their disputes. He was a member of the Constitutional Convention of Kentucky of 1792, a friend of Isaac Shelby, the first governor of the state, and he was frequently in the company of Boone.

He was also a member of the state legislature, a candidate for Congress and, on two occasions, he ran for lieutenant governor of Kentucky. He married for a second time, when seventy years of age, a girl of seventeen, the daughter of a Baptist preacher. He died within six months and was buried beside his first wife.

The son Richard received an education superior to that of most boys in the new state of Kentucky. He had as instructors two professors from Transylvania University and from them obtained a knowledge of Latin and Greek as well as general schooling. He became interested in politics and in 1804, when he was twenty-four, was elected as one of two members of the state legislature from his home county of Scott. He was the youngest member of the Kentucky Assembly and the first native son to be elected to that body. Despite his youth, he soon became an active member and effective debater. In 1807, he was elected a member of Congress and served in that capacity for ten years from the Third Kentucky District. He was elected during Jefferson's second term and the young Kentucky representative, who soon met Jefferson, was a faithful supporter of the President. He voted for Jefferson's Embargo Act and felt that that act would have been workable had it been enforced.

In 1810, Johnson was re-elected to Congress by a large majority. His influence was growing among his colleagues. Before the War of 1812, he was a strong advocate of hostilities against England. In a speech made on the eve of that struggle he stated, "I feel rejoiced that the hour of resistance is at hand." He was on the House Military Affairs Committee and urged Congress to prepare for the "conflict which is sure to come."

Soon after the declaration of war, Johnson left his seat in Congress and went into active duty with the Army. He had offered his services to his country and volunteered to raise a regiment of mounted volunteers to fight in the West in any capacity needed. The offer was accepted and, assisted by his brother James, he formed a regiment of mounted infantry.

Colonel Johnson was an effective leader of men and, for those days, something of a military genius. He was a sound planner and drew up the strategy for the battle of the Thames, in which he was the outstanding hero. He told General Harrison, "You take care of the English—I will take care of the Indians." When he advised the general to change his plan of attack, the old man said, "Dammit, then do it your way." Johnson's regiment charged through the lines of the British, turned, and attacked them from the rear. The battle was won.

There has been much debate by historians over who killed Tecumseh, the great Indian chieftain, who had joined with the British. Men who were in the battle and near Johnson say that the colonel killed the Indian leader and that they saw Johnson rise up on his elbow and shoot Tecumseh just as the chief was about to tomahawk the colonel. This moot question has never been settled to the satisfaction of everyone, but it would seem from the evidence that Colonel Johnson did kill the Indian leader.

Eventually he was elected Vice-President on that assumption.

Colonel Johnson was wounded five times in the battle of the Thames and invalided home. He spent several months in hospitals and went back to Congress on crutches; for he had not resigned that office while at the front. Congress presented him with a sword for heroism in action.

Johnson was made chairman of the Military Affairs Committee and, as such, was a strong supporter of the administration. He was incensed at the carelessness displayed by officers of high rank and by the general inefficiency shown in the top command. His feelings were especially wrought up over the surrender of General William Hull, who lost Detroit to the British, and the burning of Washington. He felt there was traitorous conduct in the fall of the capital, and it is said that he tore out his hair when he heard of the conduct of the New England governors at the Hartford Convention.

While in Congress the colonel introduced and pushed to passage the Congressional Compensation Bill. The Senate passed the bill and it became law. This measure gave to the House and Senate a salary instead of the per-diem pay they had been receiving. Since 1789 the members of Congress had received six dollars a day while Congress was in session. Under the Johnson bill, members of both bodies were to receive a salary of $1,500 yearly, with the Speaker of the House and the President pro tem of the Senate getting $3,000 yearly. Strange as it may seem, the people of the nation rose in anger over passage of the measure. So much pressure was brought to bear on Johnson that he made an effort to repeal the bill. A committee was appointed to determine the merits of the repeal bill. Its members decided that the cost of living justified an increase in pay for representatives and senators and recommended that the boost be approved.

This legislation nearly caused Johnson's defeat and he had a difficult time when he came up for re-election.

In 1819, Johnson notified the House of Representatives that he planned to retire from public life. Johnson had a motive in leaving the House. He planned to return to Kentucky and run for the Senate. In his first effort he was defeated by a small majority. Soon another opportunity arose when Senator John J. Crittenden refused to stand for re-election. Johnson was elected the junior senator from Kentucky. He was a better than average member of the upper house.

It was at this time that Johnson and his brother James suffered a major financial setback. The government had sponsored an expedition to the Yellowstone country and the Missouri River. The Johnson brothers undertook to furnish the necessary steamboats and the provisions for the expedition. They soon learned, however, that they were to be left holding the bag. They lost their inheritance and spent many years paying off the obligations they had undertaken.

During Johnson's tenure as senator, the upper house numbered a good many of the most able men in its history. Buchanan, Clay, Calhoun, Webster, William R. King, who was then Vice-President, Grundy of Tennessee, and Franklin Pierce, were all in the Senate. It was a training ground for men who have since left their names on the pages of American history. In the House there was still John Quincy Adams, who had been President, James K. Polk, who was Speaker, and Millard Fillmore.

In 1824, during the hot Presidential campaign, Johnson was at first inclined toward Clay for President but he finally concluded that General Jackson was the better man. He worked earnestly for Jackson's election and was shocked at the deal Clay made with Adams to defeat the old general. Johnson was never, after this, a friend of Clay, but was always to be a follower of Jackson. He had been a member of the committee to investigate the general's conduct in the Florida matter—the time Jackson went over the boundary of Florida and hanged two Englishmen—and he signed the report exonerating Jackson. That was another favor the irascible general owed to Johnson. Johnson was also opposed to the Bank Bill and was one of the President's most faithful workers in preventing its passage.

In 1829, due in a great measure to his falling out with Clay and his support of President Jackson, Johnson was defeated for re-election to the Senate. Johnson had been in the House for ten years and he had served the same period of time in the Senate. He had sponsored much legislation and he had sat on many major committees. The last piece of legislation he sponsored had been the bill to prohibit imprisonment for debt. The House failed to pass the bill and this most vital measure waited several years before reaching the statute books.

From 1829 to 1836, Johnson was back in Kentucky attempting to mend his depleted fortune. He went back and forth to Washington and in 1835 he visited General Jackson, feeble physically but still, as ever, a driving force in the nation and the dictator of the Democratic party. Would the colonel like to be Vice-President? Of course, the colonel would appreciate the honor. The old general had kept faith with the man who had fought the losing fight for him against Mrs. Calhoun and the social leaders of Washington. Thus, the decision was made. The ticket would be Van Buren and Johnson—New York and Kentucky.

The Democratic convention met in Baltimore on May 20, 1836. The sessions were held in a Presbyterian church, but the six hundred delegates and alternates who assembled proved too large a crowd and the convention adjourned to a near-by theater.

Two days later Van Buren was unanimously nominated for President. In conformance with the decision of the caucus held the evening before and, after much argument, the convention named Colonel Johnson for Vice-President. The vote was 178 for Johnson, eighty-seven for Senator William C. Rives of Virginia. There was a virtual riot in the theater, the Virginia delegates howling at length. Kentucky applauded. Senator Mason declared that Virginia would not vote for Johnson for fear he would not support the political principles the state held important.

The Democratic party was to remain in power another four years. When the electoral votes were counted Van Buren had 174, General Harrison had seventy-three, and Daniel Webster had the fourteen votes of Massachusetts.

In the Vice-Presidential contest, however, the situation was different. Johnson had polled 147 votes, a large plurality but not a majority. Granger, the Whig candidate, polled seventy-seven votes, three more than Harrison had received for President. John Tyler of Virginia had polled forty-seven, including Kentucky's eleven, and Virginia gave her twenty-three votes to Smith. Since there was no majority, the election was thrown into the Senate, the only time in the history of the nation that the upper house had to elect a Vice-President.

The Senate met and the President pro tem called for the ballot on the two highest candidates, Johnson and Granger. The vote was viva voce and Johnson was declared the winner. It is interesting to note that the Virginia senators voted for Johnson while the Kentucky senators cast their ballots for Granger. Johnson received thirty-three votes and Granger sixteen votes. William R. King, then President of the Senate, voted for Johnson. There were at that time twenty-six states in the Union, and the full number of senators who could have voted was fifty-two.

For the next four years Johnson served as Vice-President. That is, in the majority of cases, about all one can say of most Vice-Presidents. He voted often in tie votes, a frequent situation in the Van Buren administration. The records show that on one day alone there were three tie votes and the Vice-President cast the deciding ballots. Johnson was an average parliamentarian and a just presiding officer. The colonel had been a member of the Senate for ten years and the Senators looked upon him as one of them.

The campaign of 1840 was bitter, both as to the feeling between the opposing political parties and bitter within the Democratic party itself. Pressure was brought to bear on Johnson to restrain him from running for re-election. It was foreseen that Van Buren would have a difficult enough time and the party knew it would need both Virginia and Kentucky to win. Furthermore, the Democratic leadership felt that if Johnson could not carry his home state he should not ask for renomination. But the old war horse had determined to run and President Van Buren could not forsake him. General Jackson, despite his friendship for the aging colonel, felt also that he was the weakest candidate. Johnson was obdurate, however, and would not withdraw. He would "go into the fight, show my scars and be reelected."

The convention again was held in Baltimore. Five states did not send delegates. Massachusetts sent one delegate to cast all its votes. Connecticut, Virginia, Delaware, South Carolina, and Illinois were not represented by delegates; New Jersey sent too many representatives and they divided their votes. The convention was unique in other ways. It marked the first time the Democratic party drew up a platform and the only time a convention refused to make a nomination. Van Buren was again nominated for President but the convention left the Vice-Presidential nomination to the states. The various state conventions met and named their candidates for that office. New Hampshire, New Jersey, Michigan, New York, Pennsylvania, and Ohio named Johnson.

Benjamin Harrison was elected. Van Buren polled only sixty votes for President while Harrison polled 234. It was an overwhelming defeat. Johnson polled forty-eight votes for Vice-President, L. W. Tazewell of Virginia received South Carolina's eleven votes while James K. Polk had one vote—that of an elector from Virginia. John Tyler of Virginia, running as Harrison's mate, was elected with 234 votes.

This defeat of Van Buren was a defeat for both the Whigs and Democrats, for Harrison lived only one month and Tyler, his heir, was more of a Democrat than a Whig. It was especially disappointing to Johnson. He had hoped to be President in 1844 and had looked forward to following Van Buren as Little Matty had followed Jackson. He was not completely through, however, for he went back to Kentucky and was again elected to the state legislature where he worked as earnestly as he had done in Congress, in the Senate and as Vice-President. The colonel still had hopes of being the Democratic nominee for President and indeed he developed considerable strength throughout the West, particularly in Illinois. Johnson went so far as to make a trip through the North to test out the strength of sentiment in his favor. He was a candidate for the United States Senate from Kentucky but was beaten by Crittenden. That defeat ruined any prospects of the White House. Again Jackson opposed his nomination and the old man who sat in the Hermitage exercised too much power for the colonel to overcome. In 1844, the convention again met in Baltimore and, under the two-thirds rule, nominated Polk of Tennessee for President on the ninth ballot. At one time in the balloting, Johnson received thirty-eight votes for President.

When the balloting for the Vice-Presidency was begun, 256 votes were cast for Senator Silas Wright of New York. This was almost the unanimous vote of the convention but Wright declined the nomination and, after two more ballots were taken, George M. Dallas of Pennsylvania received the nomination.

Johnson was again a candidate for the Presidency in 1848 but he could provoke little interest in his candidacy. He was sixty-eight and the party had seen too much of him. He could stay in the Kentucky legislature, however, and he continued to be elected up to the year of his death. Johnson was by this time half demented and a newspaper wrote of him that "He is totally unfit for the business of a legislature." He died November 18, 1850. He was then seventy, worn out, and disappointed—to have come so near and yet to have missed the Presidency.

There was a constructive side to the man's life. He was an earnest worker and an energetic member of any body to which he was elected. He made an effort to be a thoughtful legislator up to the day of his death. Big Dick Johnson was lovable and kind, and he was good to his slaves, many of whom he freed. He was loyal to his friends. He came very near to being a military genius, as has been noted, and, had the opportunity presented itself, it is probable he would have gone far as a commander.

Johnson never married. He kept his Negro mistresses openly in Washington and installed one Julia Chin in his magnificent home on E Street, along with their two children, Imogene and Adaline. He educated these girls and "had for them a tutor." He insisted that society should recognize them. They both married white men and he gave them liberal doweries. His mistress died during the cholera epidemic in 1833. After Julia's death, Colonel Johnson took other Negresses as his mistresses, and current gossip was that the colonel did not know the number of his offspring. He openly flaunted Washington society.

This was Richard Mentor Johnson, not altogether a nonentity but one whom history in the main has passed by, a legislator, military leader, a representative and a Vice-President of the United States, the first from the West.

CHAPTER X

John Tyler

THERE ARE SEVERAL ODD aspects to the career of
the tenth Vice-President. Among them is that he was elected
to that office largely because of the alliterative narcotic in a piece
of political doggerel, "Tippecanoe and Tyler too!" Another
singularity is that he was Vice-President for a month only, step-
ping into the shoes of the hero of Tippecanoe on General Harrison's sudden death. In addition, he occupied the White House
and the nation's highest office without the support of either the
Whigs or the Democrats, a tightrope performance perhaps more
difficult a century ago than it is in national politics today, although that is debatable.

On March 29, 1790, Tyler, the fifth generation of Tylers in
America, was born at Greenway, near Charles City Court House,
in the peninsula section of Virginia. His ancestors had come to
the Jamestown Colony in 1636. The fourth John Tyler was an
outstanding patriot during the Revolutionary War. He was an
intimate of Jefferson and was well acquainted with Patrick
Henry, Madison, and General Washington. When he retired
from the governorship of Virginia, he was succeeded by his
friend James Monroe. He stepped from the governor's chair to
a seat on the federal bench where he presided until his death in
1813.

The Tylers belonged to the first families of Virginia and they
claimed descent from Wat Tyler, the English rebel. The Randolphs, the Wyeths, the Campbells, Bollings, Lees, Lightfoots,
and Harrisons of Virginia, along with the Calhouns, Youngs,

Haynes, Marions, and Alstons of the Carolinas, whose sons and daughters went out through the South and the West to make a new nation, were friends of the Tyler family.

John Tyler, the fifth in line, was precocious. He was graduated from the secondary school of William and Mary College at the age of sixteen and was licensed to practice law two years later. Tyler explained later, "They neglected to ask me my age—and I forgot to tell them." He was of medium height, slender, with light-brown hair, blue eyes, and a "great charm of manner"; he never "took on flesh" and was always "slender as a reed" —say some of his biographers.

When Tyler was twenty-one, his friends sent him to the Virginia legislature where he gave a notable account of himself. He was the youngest member to sit in the Virginia House of Delegates. The War of 1812 broke out during his second year in the house and the young member formed a company of volunteers to defend Richmond. His career as a soldier was of short duration, as his company was not called upon to do any fighting and he was soon returned to the legislature.

Tyler was a member of the Virginia house for five years, and for two years sat on the Executive Council of the state. At twenty-six, he was elected to fill an unexpired term in Congress from the Richmond District.

In 1813, Tyler married Letitia Christian, a daughter of Robert Christian of Cedar Grove, Virginia. Christian was one of the leading Federalists of the state and, with Tyler's Democratic friendships, together with the Federalist support of the Christian family, Tyler was to prove a hard man to beat at the polls.

Just as Tyler had been the youngest member of the Virginia house, so he was the youngest member of Congress when he took his seat in 1816. He went to Washington for the second session of the Fourteenth Congress. Monroe was President and Daniel Tompkins, of New York, Vice-President. The "era of good feeling" was opening: the country had weathered the war and domestic improvements were under way throughout the young nation.

The last act by Madison had been to establish a National Bank at Philadelphia, an institution which was to bring about more internal dissension during the next twenty years than perhaps any single factor in the political history of the nation.

Tyler was a consistent foe of the Bank, as conducted under the charter of 1816, and when the time came to renew its charter he was adamant in his opposition. Almost his entire political life was spent in fighting the Bank and especially "Biddle's Bank." As a member of Congress he fought Nicholas Biddle and when he became a member of the Senate he continued his fight against "Biddle's Bank." He went so far as to resign his seat in the Senate rather than vote for a second charter for the institution. The Virginia legislature, however, had instructed him to vote for the measure, but rather than obey those instructions, which were repugnant to Tyler's sense of justice, he withdrew from the upper house.

Tyler was a leader in the movement to reprimand General Jackson for his actions in the Florida "invasion," and one of his greatest speeches was delivered on the issue of limitation of military authority. A Virginia representative had introduced a resolution condemning Jackson for his "invasion" of Florida and his hanging of the two Englishmen. Taking the floor, Tyler said, in effect, that although we may honor a man for his heroic acts, we cannot condone mistakes that a man may make merely because he has been a hero in the past, and that services in past wars do not extenuate a violation of the Constitution. Old Hickory took great offense and many years passed before he forgave the gentleman from Virginia for his vote to censure him.

Tyler was re-elected to Congress in 1819 and he was active in the Missouri Compromise fight, opposing the principle of legislating territorial boundaries in the matter of the slavery question. He asserted with prophetic insight that the time would come when the prohibition of slavery in any territory or state would eventually mean its abolition in all states where it existed, but that that abolition would come by revolutionary action.

Shortly after his fight against the Missouri Compromise, Tyler fell ill. He resigned his seat in Congress because, as he wrote, he feared for his life; he would "go home and recuperate." He spent the next four years in retirement.

In 1823, Tyler's neighbors persuaded him to be a candidate again for the Virginia House of Delegates. He was elected. Here he was at home. In 1825, the General Assembly elected him governor of Virginia. He was proud and happy, particularly since his father had been governor.

So popular was Tyler as governor that he was elected unanimously to a second term. In 1827, John Randolph's term in the Senate was to expire and Randolph had expected no opposition. Because of some of his eccentricities, however, he had become unpopular with many elements in Virginia. He was a sick man, and several historians have said that he was half insane. Governor Tyler's name was offered and he defeated Randolph by 115 to 110.

As governor, Tyler had refused to be an active candidate for the Senate but had said that if elected he would serve. He was criticized by some for running against Randolph, but one sees no reason for that criticism. Randolph had been over long in political life. He was a bitter antagonist in debate and was ruthless when crossed. From the day in 1795 when he gave the toast "To George Washington—may God damn him," to the day of his death, he gave no quarter. How could he expect any?

Tyler took his seat in the Senate on December 3, 1827. Earlier, in Congress, he had opposed John Quincy Adams and Henry Clay on their tariff proposals; in the Senate he continued to oppose them. He was against the Tariff of Abominations, and he fought side by side with Calhoun for States' rights. The National Bank Bill and Biddle's tactics in attempting to pass the bill were continuously before the Senate. He stood with Calhoun in the nullification threat and these two men were a tower of strength to the waning Southern influence. The people of Virginia agreed with their senator, and in 1833 he was re-elected by a large majority. On the organization of the Senate, Tyler was elected President pro tem of that body.

Tyler was firm in his convictions and he would not take dictation, not even from the legislature of his own state. It was during this term of office that Tyler resigned rather than obey the instructions of the House of Delegates with regard to the National Bank Bill. He was courteous in his remarks, he would not offend unnecessarily, he "was ever the soft spoken one," but he would not swerve from his conception of what was constitutional. It took a good deal of courage for Tyler to resign his seat, but he faced the situation squarely and returned to private life.

He was determined, however, to seek that office again. When a vacancy did occur his opponent was Senator Rives. After thirty-eight ballots, the House of Delegates was still unable to elect a senator. Clay and the Northern Whigs did not want Tyler in the upper house: he was a man they could not control.

Finally, in desperation, they offered a compromise. If Tyler would withdraw from the senatorial race, they, in turn, would guarantee him the Vice-Presidential nomination in 1840. He agreed, and Senator Rives was returned to the Senate.

In 1840, General Harrison was again the nominee for President on the Whig ticket and Tyler, who had always been a Jeffersonian Democrat, was nominated Vice-President. Van Buren was the Democratic nominee, running for his second term, with Richard M. Johnson again his running mate. The campaign was bitter, with Van Buren on the defensive and fighting a losing battle. "Tippecanoe and Tyler too" swept the nation. Van Buren polled only sixty electoral votes.

Harrison had promised Clay, Webster, and Thurlow Weed "anything to get the nomination." He had given these gentlemen his word that he would consult his cabinet before he made any change and finally that he would "not veto any message passed by the Congress." He was inaugurated President on March 4, 1841.

He died one month later of a cold apparently contracted while standing bareheaded during the Inauguration.

Tyler was playing marbles in a Richmond street when Daniel Webster's son came to inform him of Harrison's death. He had to borrow $500 from a business friend to make the trip to Washington. He took the oath of office at Brown's Tavern. He called Harrison's cabinet together and informed them that he was not bound by the general's promise to abide by their decisions and that while he would gladly consult with them, he was to be President and would make his own decisions. Clay made an effort to bring Tyler off his high horse, and old Adams from his seat in the house fumed and insisted that Tyler must call himself "Acting President" and that he could not accept the salary of President or live in the White House. But Tyler consulted with Chief Justice Roger B. Taney of the United States Supreme Court, who agreed with him that he was as much the President of the United States as though elected to that office.

When Clay realized he could not dictate to President Tyler, he made an effort to provoke the resignation of the entire cabinet. Most of the cabinet followed Clay's advice, but Webster would not withdraw as Secretary of State. The cabinet had resigned without notice; the President smiled one of the quiet smiles for which he was noted and accepted the resignation, much to the chagrin of Senator Clay. It was said that President Tyler selected his new cabinet "in a day." In the Treasury he placed Senator Forward of Pennsylvania; John McLean of Ohio became Secretary of War; Upshur of Virginia was appointed Secretary of the Navy; Wickliffe of Kentucky was made Postmaster General; and Legaré of South Carolina became Attorney General. Justice McLean was a member of the United States Supreme Court, however, and preferred to retain his seat. The President then appointed Senator Spencer in his stead as Secretary of War.

Tyler had appointed a strong cabinet. Each member was a man of experience and well qualified for his post. Webster remained in the cabinet as Secretary of State for two years, when Upshur was promoted from the Navy to that position and, when he was killed in the explosion on the U.S.S. *Princeton*, the President named Calhoun, the senior senator from North Carolina, to the State Department.

If Tyler had been fortunate in his cabinet selections, he never-theless had unending difficulties with Congress during the three years and eleven months he was President. He had been elected Vice-President as a Whig at a time when that party swept the country in a landslide. Its leaders had not foreseen the possibil-ity of his becoming President and felt that they owed no alle-giance to a President who had come to that honor by the accident of death and who was not even a member of the party.

Both houses of Congress passed the Bank Bill, and Clay chuckled over the position in which he had placed Tyler. The President promptly vetoed the measure and, try as he would, Senator Clay could not gather sufficient votes to override the veto. He ranted and he raved. He took to drinking more, and lost many friends. He could not "boss" Tyler and his influence began to wane. Clay had been a power in the House and the Senate for thirty years and he had felt that he would be the dominant in-fluence in the Harrison administration. Harrison had offered him the post of Secretary of State before he appointed Webster, but Clay had refused it, believing he would be more powerful in the Senate as administration "boss."

Under Senator Clay's direction, Congress passed another Bank Bill and again Tyler vetoed it; once more, with the aid of the Democrats and the anti-Bank Whigs, the veto was sustained. Clay succeeded in passing a high tariff bill and the President vetoed that as well. He had been elected as a Whig but he was always a Jeffersonian Democrat and never more one than during the years he was in the White House. It was when President Tyler vetoed the second Bank Bill that a mob stormed the White House.

Even in the face of his trials with Congress, Tyler's adminis-tration was successful. He resolved the Oregon boundary dispute; he quelled Dorr's Rebellion; he concluded the "Florida War" and had an act passed by Congress empowering the Army to occupy that territory; and finally he brought about the annexation of Texas. In April of 1844, the Senate had rejected the Treaty of Annexation by a vote of thirty-five to 160. In the election campaign of 1844, the annexation of Texas was the foremost point of issue and because the Democrats, led by Polk, won by such a large majority, Tyler felt it was the will of the people that Texas should be annexed. One of his last official acts was to sign the treaty "bringing into the Union, as a State, the Republic of Texas." (It is interesting to note that Tyler had voted for Polk as President.)

Tyler went back to Virginia and to private life. Letitia had died and he had married a young lady of "estimatable character," a Miss Julia Gardiner. "A Damosel," wrote Tyler of his second bride. Mrs. Tyler was the mother of seven children, as had been the first, and Tyler was the father of fourteen. There are many descendants of the fifth John Tyler living throughout the land to this day.

Tyler did little public work after his retirement from the Presidency. He studied; he did some lecturing; he was concerned over the imminence of the Civil War, and he did all in his power to prevent its outbreak. As late as 1860 he hoped that it could be prevented; he was a leader and president of the Peace Committee which met in February of 1861. It was too late, however. The Confederacy was formed; Jefferson Davis became its President; and Tyler, who believed that the United States was "a Union of several States," followed Virginia into the Confederacy. When seventy-one years of age, he declared himself a candidate for Congress in the Confederate States of America.

Tyler could always be elected in Virginia for whatever office he sought, and the elderly man, now past his three score and ten, took his seat in that body. He was active in its deliberations until his death on January 17, 1862.

So passed a man who had led a full life. He had been a member of the Virginia House of Delegates on three occasions, a member of the governing Council of the State of Virginia, a representative, twice governor of his state, United States senator, President pro tem of that body, Vice-President, President of the United States, and finally, in his old age, a member of Congress of the Confederacy. He had, at one time, even been a road overseer. He was elected to that position by neighbors who wanted to embarrass him; to their astonishment, he not only accepted the position but it was said of him that he was a "damn good one."

Tyler's administration was unfortunate in that he had a Congress which opposed him throughout his entire term of office; indeed its members had tried to jockey him into a position where impeachment proceedings might have been instituted. He was a President without a party. He was a Jeffersonian Democrat, sitting by accident as a Whig President. He had served as Vice-President only a month when, by reason of Harrison's death, he inherited the White House post. It may justly be said that his administration illustrated—once again—the danger of choosing a Vice-President out of sympathy with party policy and for the sake of appeasing a faction, or of gaining additional votes.

CHAPTER XI

George Mifflin Dallas

THE ELEVENTH VICE-PRESIDENT of the United States was an amateur and dilettante in politics, and he had a marked distaste for the rough-and-tumble of national public life. It is somewhat ironic then that despite this diffidence, or perhaps because of it, George Mifflin Dallas had a long career in high posts. One after another, political plums fell into his lap while he continued to profess—probably sincerely—his repugnance to either elective or appointive office.

The father of Dallas, Alexander Dallas, was an immigrant from Jamaica. His parents were Scotch and as a young man he had spent considerable time in England and Scotland where he received much of his education. He had made friends with Benjamin Franklin and Doctor Samuel Johnson while a boy, and they were impressed with his "intellect and manners." Alexander Dallas studied law and, in 1783, he went to Philadelphia, bearing in mind his early friendship with Dr. Franklin. Ten days after landing, he made application for citizenship but he had to wait for two years before he could practice law in his adopted country.

The young Scotch-Jamaican soon became a power in national politics. He was for thirteen years United States district attorney for Pennsylvania. Alexander Dallas made many friends. He was on friendly terms with Washington, Jefferson, Madison, Gallatin, and other men of prominence in the new nation. His influence increased steadily. He was Secretary of the Treasury during the closing months of Madison's administration and he was an able financier at a time when the monetary situation was critical. He formulated a successful tax program and was prudent in national expenditures. This was the man from whom George Mifflin Dallas, the son, was to inherit much of his ability and to whom he looked for advice. Seldom do men of eminence produce great men, but in this instance the father and son were both exceptionally able.

Dallas was born July 10, 1792. His father could afford to have the son tutored by the best of teachers. George Dallas attended Princeton University, from which he was graduated in 1810 at the head of his class. He studied law with his father and was admitted to the bar shortly before his twenty-first birthday.

During the War of 1812, Dallas served in the Army but he was not in combat. Young Dallas was appointed to go with Gallatin to Russia where the former Secretary of the Treasury under Jefferson—and a close friend of Alexander Dallas—was sent as a peace emissary between Britain and the United States. Dallas was employed as a confidential messenger, and was the bearer of important dispatches to Washington from the American peace commissioners at Ghent.

He began the practice of law with his father. In 1817, the father died of "gout in the stomach," which was probably appendicitis.

Dallas became mayor of Philadelphia ten years later. He was only thirty-five years of age, and the youngest man to hold that office. In 1831, he was appointed to the United States Senate to fill an unexpired term, and sat for two years, but he declined to be a candidate for re-election. He liked to practice politics, but did not care for the office. In the Senate with him, during his short term of office, was that strong coterie of men who so long dominated American politics, Clay, Calhoun, Webster, Benton of Missouri, and the other "strong boys," as they were called. Senator Dallas' father had been the author of Madison's Bank Bill and the son was always a "bank man." He voted and worked for the measure during his term of office; he supported President Jackson on the nullification controversy but nevertheless he retained his friendship with Calhoun.

On his retirement from the Senate, Dallas was appointed attorney general of Pennsylvania, a post he held for three years. In 1837, President Van Buren appointed him ambassador to Russia. But he found little to occupy his time at St. Petersburg and he wrote that he could see no justification "in even being there." He kept a diary and records the day-by-day happenings, mostly of a social nature. Dallas was a favorite at the Russian court and the envoy struck up a friendship with Czar Nicholas. He wrote in his journal that he saw "a lump of naked gold weighing 24 pounds" and mentions some interesting experiments "in animal magnetism." He remarked that he was offered the appointment as Secretary of the Navy by President Van Buren, and recorded his decision to reject the offer.

After two years Dallas asked to be relieved of his ambassadorship, and he returned to Philadelphia where he resumed the practice of law and the agreeable avocation of playing politics. He was an unswerving Democrat and, while he was not an abolitionist, he hated slavery.

James Buchanan and Dallas could never see eye to eye in politics and, while they were each staunch Democrats, they led different factions in party affairs, particularly in Pennsylvania state politics. In time they came to be fairly good friends and later Buchanan, when President, continued Dallas, then a Pierce appointee, as ambassador to Great Britain.

The Democratic convention of 1844 was held in Baltimore and nominated Polk for President. Senator Silas Wright of New York was offered the Vice-Presidential nomination by a vote of 258 to ten but he declined. After two more ballots, Dallas was nominated to run with Polk. In the election, Polk and Dallas polled 170 electoral votes against 105 for Clay and Senator Frelinghuysen of New Jersey.

In Polk's cabinet, Buchanan was Secretary of State. Robert J. Walker of Kentucky was Secretary of the Treasury; William L. Marcy was Secretary of War; George Bancroft had the Navy portfolio; Cave Johnson was Postmaster General; and John Mason of Virginia was Attorney General. This was a fairly strong and well-balanced cabinet. Most of its members had been in the Senate when Polk was Speaker of the House and they were personal as well as political friends of the Chief Executive.

As Vice-President Dallas had a strenuous time. These were the days of the Mexican War, the Wilmot Proviso, the California problem, and the eternal and everlasting tariff dispute. Dallas was a just presiding officer of the Senate and an excellent parliamentarian in view of his legal experience.

The Senate membership at this time was composed of many men with whom Dallas had served ten years before. Benton of Missouri was still there; Clay was absent—he had run for President and had not yet returned to the Senate; but there were Webster, Calhoun, Sam Houston, newly elected from Texas; Crittenden of Kentucky, and a new senator from Maine, Hannibal Hamlin. It was a strong body, perhaps one of the most competent in the nation's history.

Slavery was the chronic issue before Congress. Even this early there appeared no solution short of resort to arms.

In 1848, Polk refused a second term. He was one of the extremely few Presidents who had no desire for a second term.

Zachary Taylor and Millard Fillmore were elected in 1848 and

Dallas, now fifty-six, went back to his Philadelphia law practice and his social pleasures. In 1856, President Franklin Pierce offered Dallas the post of ambassador to Great Britain. That appealed to him and he took his wife and daughter to London, where he promptly established himself as a political as well as social favorite. There had, however, been some perturbation over the appointment. Pierce had been compelled to ask Great Britain to recall her ambassador Crampton, because of his brazen activity in enlisting men for the British Army. He had gone so far as to open a recruiting office in Washington to recruit Americans to serve in the Crimean War, and Great Britain acknowledged that he had exceeded his authority and recalled him. Somewhat to the surprise of the President, the British offered no objection to receiving Dallas as envoy.

Diplomacy was Dallas' strong point. He was a suave and ingratiating representative and accomplished much in his mission. He brought the Clayton-Bulwer Treaty to a successful conclusion and it was Dallas who finally convinced England that the right to "search and seize" American ships must cease.

That had been a critical question for more than a half century; it was the primary cause of the War of 1812. Ambassador Dallas bluntly told the British Foreign Office that the practice must cease—or there would be a "third war with Britain." The British lion could no longer bluff and when the white-haired and amiable gentleman from the States was through, the British realized that here was a man who meant what he said. The Foreign Office wrote an apology to the ambassador and since that time there has been no "search and seizure" of American vessels.

Dallas kept a diary while envoy to Great Britain just as he had while in Russia. The diary is interesting reading after ninety years. He tells of seeing the steamer *Great Eastern;* he received the first cable message; he attended prize fights; and he wrote of dining with Queen Victoria and her numerous "offspring." He watched carefully the political developments at home, three thousand miles away, and read the New York and Philadelphia papers. He was a spectator now and not a participant in politics but he was "always interested in the mail and the papers." He wrote of Abraham that "Lincoln is as absolute selfmade as our democracy could desire. He began life as a day-laborer and took to making fence-rails." He read Lincoln's Inaugural Address on March 17, 1861, thirteen days after its delivery, and was pleased over its "firmness and mildness . . . firm against the unconstitutionality of secession, mild in assurance and language." He wrote in his diary that "My poor country can henceforward know no security of peace until the passions of the two factions have covered the hills and valleys with blood and exhausted the strength of an entire generation of her sons."

President Lincoln had appointed Charles Francis Adams, descendant of the Quincy (Massachusetts) family, as ambassador to Great Britain. He relieved Dallas in May of 1861 and that gentleman, now almost seventy years of age, went back to his native Philadelphia to watch the Civil War from the side lines. He had always been an opponent of slavery but he was not and never had been an abolitionist for he could not abide the prospect of secession. He had no use for "Garrison and his rabble." He was a Democrat and had been a follower of Jefferson and Tyler but he was at no time in sympathy with the Secessionists. He saw with sorrow the breakup of the nation, knowing that he could not prevent or postpone the coming debacle.

He was nearing his seventy-third birthday when he died on December 31, 1863.

History has passed by George Dallas. He is remembered, and then only vaguely, because there is a city in Texas named for him. This writer once asked a group of Dallas school children what they knew of the origin of the name of that city and only one, a youngster of seventeen, knew that it was named after the eleventh Vice-President of the United States.

Dallas was primarily a successful diplomat; he was a compromiser, a negotiator. He could have been Secretary of the Navy and was offered the portfolio of Attorney General of the United States, but he was never overeager for political office. He played politics as an amateur. He cared little for political rewards. He was a conservative and a cosmopolitan; he was, in effect, the gentleman in politics and perhaps for that reason one more or less forgotten in American history.

CHAPTER XII

Millard Fillmore

THERE IS TODAY A well-defined formula that must be followed both for election to the Vice-Presidency and for the conduct of that somewhat amorphous office. There are, of course, several outstanding exceptions. First, the aspirant must come from a community as distant as politically feasible from the bailiwick of the White House candidate; second, he must be able to say convincingly (a neat trick indeed) that he advocates this and that measure, making certain first that these cancel each other out, leaving him free for an overnight study which way the political cat will jump; and third, so far as humanly possible, he must be singularly colorless and nondescript.

This is more of a feat than appears at first sight; a consistent adherence to that formula is, like walking a tightrope, a considerable tour de force, and rarely an accidental performance.

The formula is superbly exemplified by the career of Millard Fillmore, twelfth Vice-President and thirteenth President of the United States.

Fillmore was born at Summerhill, Cayuga County, New York, near Buffalo, on January 7, 1800. He was the second child and the first son of Nathaniel Fillmore, who had immigrated to New York from Vermont in 1788. Fillmore was the first Vice-President, as well as the first President, to be born in the nineteenth century, and thus began a new era. Prior to that time, American history had been made by the heroes of the Revolution and later by men who had been active before and after the War of 1812. Fillmore was a boy of twelve at the time of the start of the second war with Britain.

The father was a descendant of the English Fillmores who came to the colonies in 1704. They were average citizens and were patriots during the Revolution when many of their neighbors were Tories. When Nathaniel Fillmore settled in northern New York, he was in a community of men who had been often called Loyalists, although blunt George Clinton called them "dirty traitors to their country." He was a farmer and in the log house he built, his son Millard Fillmore was born.

Times were hard and a living was difficult to wrest. Millard Fillmore wrote in later life that his father was determined his sons should not suffer the hardships he had faced. He apprenticed them to tradesmen so that they might have a reasonable opportunity to make their way and might escape the hazards a farmer faces.

When Millard was fourteen, his father apprenticed him to a wool carder. The wool carder was a disagreeable man, so mean indeed that young Fillmore at one time actually planned his murder; he even selected the weapon to use. The weapon chosen was an ax, and he painstakingly planned how he would go about the killing. But he soon abandoned the idea. At nineteen he got together $30 and bought up his wretched apprenticeship.

Millard's education had been of a most sketchy nature but that did not prevent him from teaching school and, for the next four years, during which time he studied law, he taught in a country school near his home. When he took up teaching he possessed only an English dictionary—he had had no schooling since the age of fourteen. But schoolteachers were scarce; learning was limited; and opportunities were abundant. At twenty-three he was admitted to the bar of New York. He practiced law in East Aurora until 1830, when he moved to Buffalo. He remained there for forty-four years, became its leading citizen and one of its richest men.

In 1829, Fillmore met Thurlow Weed, the political boss who had displaced Van Buren and his regency. Weed persuaded the young lawyer to become a candidate for the state legislature and assisted his election on the "anti-Masonic ticket."

Fillmore had one major accomplishment as a member of the state legislature. He introduced and pushed to enactment an act to prohibit imprisonment for debt. Van Buren had introduced such a bill years before but he had made little effort to get it passed, and it was left to young Fillmore to attach his name to the bill which finally became law. With this bill to his credit, it was relatively easy for Weed to elect him to Congress.

Fillmore went to Washington as a representative from the Buffalo District when he was only thirty. He remained a member of the House for four years but he declined to stand for re-election. In 1836, however, Weed persuaded him to enter the race again, and from that year to 1842 Fillmore was a regular Whig in the lower house. He was chairman of the Ways and Means Committee during the 1840 session, but again refused to be a candidate in 1842. Fillmore returned to his law practice in Buffalo and in 1844 was a candidate for the Vice-Presidential nomination at the Whig convention, but he could muster only limited strength. He made an attempt to be elected governor of New York but was defeated by Senator Silas Wright, who had refused the Vice-Presidential nomination on the Democratic slate. Wright offered the Vice-Presidency to Dallas. Fillmore asserted that he was defeated for governor by the abolitionists and the "foreign Catholics."

In 1847, Fillmore was elected comptroller of the state of New York, but he resigned that post in 1848 to run for Vice-President.

President Polk had refused to be a candidate to succeed himself, and the Whigs were looking for a candidate with a war record. They remembered that with General Jackson the Democrats had re-established themselves, and that they themselves had been victorious with General William Henry Harrison. Accordingly, they picked old Rough and Ready Zachary Taylor as their candidate for the Presidency. Taylor, a hero of the Mexican War, had been a regular army officer since he was nineteen. Taylor, however, did not know whether he was a Whig or a Democrat—thus, in some ways, the ideal candidate. He had had no part in politics and indeed could not remember if he had ever voted. He was a slaveholder and maintained his residence in Louisiana, but that did not stop his nomination on the Whig ticket, or his support by such ardent slavery haters as Lincoln, Seward, Webster, Weed, and Frémont.

For his part, Clay did not particularly care for Taylor; in fact, he detested the idea of military men as Presidents—a prejudice, incidentally, which remains deeply rooted to this day. He had opposed Jackson and Harrison, and his support of General Taylor was only lukewarm. He insisted that if he were to support Taylor he must be permitted to name the Vice-President—he could endure, he said, "one Cotton man," but not two. To placate the aging senator, who had been disappointed so many times, Weed agreed to Clay's demand, and he was agreeably surprised when Clay advanced Fillmore, of Weed's home state, for the Vice-Presidential nomination.

The Whigs won, and in March of 1849 Zachary Taylor was inaugurated. Fillmore was forty-nine when he reached the Vice-Presidential chair.

As a representative, Fillmore had been an anti-Bank man and he would not follow Clay and Biddle in their efforts to foist that institution on the nation. As Vice-President he now had an opportunity to be of assistance to the man he had opposed in the years gone by, but who had made him Vice-President. He repaid the debt in part during the debate on Clay's last great compromise measure, the Omnibus Bill of 1850. He felt that his and President Taylor's election had put an end to all disunion, and as presiding officer of the Senate, he showed the still renowned senator from Kentucky the most exceptional courtesies. He invoked a seldom-used rule of the Senate by calling the members to order and threatening disciplinary action for unseemly and untoward acts derogatory to senatorial dignity. That action met with Clay's approval, and he was well pleased with his selection of Fillmore for Vice-President.

On May 9, 1850, Taylor died of a "stomach colic," which was probably appendicitis; and the day following Fillmore became the second Heir Apparent to attain the White House by accident. Taylor's cabinet resigned and Fillmore appointed one completely new, with Webster as the Secretary of State. Webster served in the State Department until his death, when Fillmore appointed another Massachusetts man of ability, Edward Everett, to that post. Crittenden, of Kentucky, the man who had long been Clay's colleague in the Senate, was Attorney General, and in the newly created position of Secretary of the Interior he placed Thomas McKennan.

Thomas Corwin of Ohio was Secretary of the Treasury; Charles Conrad of Louisiana was Secretary of War; William A. Graham of North Carolina became Secretary of the Navy; and Nathan K. Hall, a close friend of Fillmore's from New York, was made Postmaster General. This was a fairly strong cabinet, and its appointment was perhaps the one outstanding act Fillmore performed during his administration as President.

Clay's Omnibus Bill was enacted and Fillmore signed it in the presence of its sponsor. The Fugitive Slave Law, which ultimately was to cause so much furor, received the President's signature, an action for which the abolitionists damned him—as a result of which he lost much of his popularity in the North. But the President remained cool, though his approval of that measure was the final straw which robbed him of the Whig nomination in 1852. General Scott, another hero of the Mexican War, was nominated and went to defeat at the hands of Franklin Pierce, who went from New Hampshire to a post he did not particularly relish and which, like Polk, he refused to consider a second time.

In 1853, Fillmore returned to Buffalo to resume his role as the outstanding citizen of that city. He practiced law while planning a comeback. In 1856, while traveling abroad, he was again a candidate for President, this time on the Know-Nothing ticket, which was comprised of remnants of the anti-Masonic party, the die-hard Whigs and the generally disgruntled. He received the electoral vote of only one state, Maryland, and he realized at last that he was finished as a national figure. James Buchanan, of Pennsylvania, was elected and General John C. Frémont, running as the nominee on the newly formed Republican party ticket, was the runner-up.

Fillmore now joined the Republican party and in 1860 he voted for Lincoln, but four years later he bolted the party to follow the fortunes of General George B. McClellan, the Democratic candidate. He had not approved the conduct of the Civil War and he felt that a change in the administration was needed.

Fillmore was one of the four former Presidents who requested Martin Van Buren to call a meeting in an eleventh-hour attempt to prevent the Civil War. Nothing came of that move, but Fillmore and Tyler had held high hopes that something could be achieved by five men, all former Chief Executives (save Van Buren, the incumbent), to save the Union from the debacle they saw in the offing. The five were Van Buren, Polk, Pierce, Tyler, and Fillmore.

In 1855, Oxford University offered Fillmore an honorary degree but he refused it on the sensible grounds that neither his educational nor scientific knowledge justified the honor.

Fillmore's administration had shown few outstanding accomplishments, yet it was during his term as President that Commodore Perry paid his memorable visit to Japan, which opened the doors of that country to diplomatic relations with the rest of the world, and it was in 1851 that Wells, Fargo and Company organized a general express for the purpose of carrying mail and merchandise throughout the West.

From 1856, when Fillmore made his attempt to gain the Presidency on the American or Know-Nothing ticket, until his death in 1874, he was politically inactive. He was sympathetic to President Johnson's plans for reconstruction and was a defender of that Chief Executive against the almost successful efforts to convict him on impeachment charges, but he did not actively engage in that partisan farce.

Fillmore died on March 8, 1874. His death, it must be said, scarcely caused a ripple in the nation. He was honored in Buffalo, his home city, but he was forgotten elsewhere.

It is accurate to state that Fillmore was a political accident. He was a geographical candidate, and the men who made him President were remorseful afterward. He was a machine man and for twenty years a satellite of Weed and Seward in state and national politics. He was a fair presiding officer over the Senate and he appointed a strong cabinet when faced with the resigna- of the men Taylor had appointed. He was almost totally without color, not a singular characteristic among the majority of Americans practicing the art of government at a post once removed from the top.

CHAPTER XIII

William Rufus King

THE THIRTEENTH VICE-PRESIDENT is better remembered for his contributions to the foreign relations of the United States—he persuaded France and Britain against intervention over our annexation of Texas—than for his career in the nation's second highest office. He was the only Vice-President never to serve in that office.

William Rufus King was born in Sampson County, North Carolina, on April 7, 1786. The Kings were well-to-do planters, slaveholders, and prominent citizens of their community. For that period he received an excellent education. The family provided him with tutors and he later attended the University of North Carolina from which he was graduated in 1803. He was only seventeen years of age at that time.

Young King studied law with William Duffy, at Fayetteville,

and in 1806, when not yet twenty-one years old, he was admitted to the bar in his native state. When only twenty-two, he was elected to the North Carolina state legislature and served in the state Assembly for four years. In 1812, the voters of Fayetteville sent the then twenty-six-year-old assemblyman to Congress. He was one of the youngest representatives and, on becoming a member, he joined with Calhoun and the "War Hawks" in support of the War of 1812. All during that unpopular struggle, the War Hawks supported the administration and sponsored every movement to bring the war to a final successful conclusion.

King and young men of similar convictions became fervent admirers of General Jackson, and King remained a faithful follower of the general during all his political and social trials.

After spending six years as a member of Congress from North Carolina, King, then thirty-two, went to Russia and the kingdom of Naples as secretary of the American legation, with William Pinckney as the American ambassador. (This Pinckney was not the same who ran for President of the United States so many times as the forlorn hope of the Federalist party.)

King was in Europe for two years, and in 1818 he returned to the United States and settled in Dallas County, Alabama. Dallas County was called so after Alexander J. Dallas, who had been Secretary of the Treasury and acted as Secretary of War early in the nation's history.

King was a member of Alabama's Constitutional Convention and was one of the able and efficient men who framed her constitution. The records show that he did good work at the convention. The people of the new state appreciated his efforts and the legislature elected him as Alabama's first senator. In the upper house, King was a Jackson Democrat and his colleagues said of him that he never failed Old Hickory. He was quiet-spoken and was considered "not particularly able" by Calhoun. Although never an outstanding member of the Senate, he was President Pro Tem during 1837-1841 when Richard M. Johnson was Vice-President. He presided over the Senate during a great part of its sessions in those years, and in every instance he voted for what he believed was Jacksonian policy. He was actively opposed to the Bank bills and supported Jackson on the Tariff of Abominations as well as on the Nullification Act, differing in this instance with Calhoun.

When Tyler became President, he appointed his friend and colleague from Virginia, Representative Henry A. Wise, as ambassador to France. Wise was a member of Tyler's "kitchen cabinet," and the Senate, being strongly anti-Tyler and opposed to friends whom he was attempting to place in positions of trust and honor, refused to confirm the appointment. The President then sent the name of Senator King to the Senate as ambassador. King, then President Pro Tem of the upper house, was promptly confirmed.

It was a fortunate appointment. King was well received in Paris. He was polished and spoke French fluently. He convinced the French government that the intentions of the United States in the matter of the annexation of Texas were "honorable." President Tyler had had grave fears that there would be difficulties with both England and France, and he was gratified when King reported that neither France nor England would object to the annexation of the republic.

King returned to the United States in 1845, and the next year was again a candidate for the Senate, but was defeated.

In 1848, however, he was once more in the Senate, this time because of Senator Bagby's resignation and his appointment by the Alabama governor. He was a strong supporter of Clay's Compromise of 1850, the Omnibus Bill, which was to be Clay's last effort to avert the disunion which he knew was not far distant.

Senator King also lent his efforts to the Fugitive Slave Law and was again President pro tem of the Senate during the administration of Fillmore. There was no Vice-President at the time, and King presided over the Senate ably enough and was well liked by his colleagues. It was during this session of the Senate that the long and acrimonious debate over the Omnibus Bill took place. It fell to King's lot to see the last days of the "Big Three" in the

Senate. He had been a friend of Calhoun at all times except when that gentleman differed with General Jackson; he had been opposed to most of Clay's efforts and had little confidence in the senator from Kentucky, but he supported him in his last compromise; he had often listened to Webster but could never agree with him. Alabama was too far from Massachusetts and "Big Blustering Dan" was too flamboyant for the "quiet and meek Mr. King," to quote a contemporary.

The three men were superior in ability to King but due to his conciliatory attitude they elected him President pro tem of the Senate on three occasions, and he held that post for six years.

In 1852, King supported Buchanan for President. He felt that the "wry-necked," elderly Pennsylvanian was entitled to the nomination. He felt that Buchanan had earned the nomination because of his long and faithful service to the Democratic party. He was much disappointed when Pierce received the nomination and, as a sort of sop to the Buchanan element, the Vice-Presidential nomination was given to King.

Senator King was then sixty-six years old. He was in a state of advanced tuberculosis. He resigned from the Senate and went to Cuba to recuperate but he could not overcome the effects of his long illness. When the day drew near for the inauguration of the newly elected Vice-President, it became evident that he would not be able to go to Washington for the ceremonies. A special act of Congress was passed by which he was permitted to take the oath of office in Cuba. He was sworn in as Vice-President at Havana, and returned home soon afterward to King's Bend, Alabama, to die on April 18, 1853.

When the time came for the Senate to hold its memorial service in commemoration of the man who had presided over its members for six years as President pro tem—yet who had never attended a session of the body as Vice-President—there was embarrassingly little to be said. He had been a member of Congress as a representative and senator for twenty-nine years; he had been secretary of the United States legation at Petrograd and Naples; he had been ambassador to France, yet no one could remember any outstanding legislation he had sponsored or, indeed, any act of major importance in his diplomatic career. The senators spent their time vaguely stressing his long service in Congress, his "kindliness of spirit," and his "gracious manner." There was little else they could say.

He was one of the many who had sat in the seats of the mighty but he was never one of the great, or near-great. Ironically, perhaps, he is remembered chiefly because he never attended a meeting of the Senate as Vice-President, and because he took the oath of office outside the United States. Certainly these are painfully negative achievements.

CHAPTER XIV

John Cabell Breckinridge

JOHN CABELL BRECKINRIDGE, the fourteenth Vice-President and a defeated candidate for the Presidency, would almost certainly have won his way to the White House had he lived at almost any other time in the nineteenth-century history of the United States. He was head and shoulders above most of his political contemporaries, a man of outstanding legal and administrative talents, with an educational equipment few men of his day could match. As it was, because of the momentous decades in which he lived, as well as because of his deep convictions, he felt compelled to turn soldier, and it is one of the exceptional achievements of this exceptional layman that he became one of the greatest generals of the Confederacy.

The descendant of an illustrious family, one of its ablest members, Breckinridge was born on January 21, 1821. The family home was outside Lexington, Kentucky, and despite his wanderings he always thought of Lexington as his home. John Breckinridge, his grandfather, had been Attorney General in Jefferson's cabinet, a senator, and at one time a candidate for Vice-President. The father of the future Vice-President was a well-known lawyer in Kentucky at the time of his death when only thirty-five. The son John Cabell was then three years old.

The young Breckinridge received a good education, first at the Lexington schools, then at Centre College, where he was graduated, and finally at Transylvania University. Transylvania was a university of front rank and numbered among its alumni men of standing throughout the nation—Clay, Richard M. Johnson, Stephen Austin (the President of the Republic of Texas), and a number of governors, senators, and congressmen.

For a time Breckinridge was also a student at Princeton, and in 1843 he was admitted to the bar. He had talked over his plans with his friends as well as with former Governor Owsley, in whose office he studied law, and they advised him to practice in a city in which he was not reared. He took their advice and started to practice in Frankfort but soon decided to go farther west. He went to Burlington, Iowa, and for two years hung his shingle there. The year 1845 saw him back in Lexington on a visit, which became permanent, and for the next thirty years Breckinridge lived in Kentucky.

In 1846, he was given a commission as a major in the Kentucky Battalion and saw service during the Mexican War. He had little active duty and his name only appears as counsel for General Pillow in the latter's dispute with General Scott.

Three years later Breckinridge was elected to the Kentucky legislature. He was strongly in favor of Kentucky's new constitution, and a staunch defender of slavery. On both these issues he disagreed with his Uncle Robert and, in 1851, when he sought a seat in Congress from the strongly Whig district, Robert Breckinridge electioneered for John's opponent, General Leslie Combs. The Ashland District, named for Senator Clay of Ashland, was normally a Whig district by some 1,500 votes, but the thirty-year-old Breckinridge overcame that handicap and was elected to the House of Representatives by a majority of more than five hundred. Old Robert Breckinridge and the Whig crowd were astounded. To think that a young blade of thirty would rout the old war horse was too much for them.

When Breckinridge came up for re-election in 1853, the Old Guard brought out ex-Governor Robert Letcher to teach him a lesson. But the sharp-witted young representative was too much for the slow-thinking Letcher. In debate "he tore the old man to pieces," and Lucille Stillwell, Breckinridge's biographer, writes that the former governor "almost larded down," he perspired so much. Letcher accused Breckinridge of having once stolen some watermelons. Breckinridge answered that he only needed the vote of every man who had ever stolen watermelons to elect him. He received them, for he again beat the Whigs and went back to Congress for another term.

Clay died in 1852 and Breckinridge, as the representative from the district, delivered the oration at the memorial service. His speech can be described as one of the great orations of the time.

In Congress Breckinridge was a leader among the younger men and he soon became known as a master in debate. He had a political argument with Representative Frank Cutting of New York, and Cutting challenged him to a duel. Breckinridge answered, naming rifles at sixty feet. He was a crack shot but older members of the House persuaded the hot heads to patch up their differences.

When Breckinridge's second term expired, he declined to run for re-election and went back to Lexington to repair his fortunes. President Pierce offered him the post of ambassador to Spain, but the representative, now thirty-three, wanted no diplomatic career.

Breckinridge practiced law for the next two years and in 1856 was a delegate to the Democratic Convention which nominated Buchanan. There had been no Vice-President for four years (King had died before he could begin his term) and the Democrats were eager to nominate a young and able man. Buchanan was aging and the party leaders remembered that two Presidents had died in office in the last fifteen years. They wanted someone who could carry the burden if the necessity should arise.

Who better, they reasoned, than the former Kentucky representative, the man the Whigs could never beat, the man who carried Clay's own district? The delegates flocked to Breckinridge and he was nominated for Vice-President, with crocheted, wry-necked Buchanan as the Presidential candidate. Buchanan said, "I am too old, my friends are all gone, I have no one to reward— my enemies are dead, I have no one to gloat over." Breckinridge was thirty-five, the youngest man ever nominated for the office of Vice-President.

Breckinridge made an active campaign. He spoke throughout Indiana and Pennsylvania and his oratory won the people of those states. When the votes were counted, Breckinridge had carried Kentucky by 6,000 votes and Buchanan had defeated General Frémont for the Presidency.

Breckinridge went to Washington in 1857 as Vice-President, to preside over the Senate, the majority of whose members were old enough to have been his father and many of whom were men of prominence before he was born. He made an agreeable impression on the senators. He was dignified beyond his years and he had no preconceived ideas as to his importance. In his inaugural address he promised fair treatment to one and all, irrespective of political party; he would do his duty, he said, to the best of his knowledge.

Breckinridge was an able Vice-President. He presided over the Senate at a time when shrewd men of the nation knew that the Union was dissolving. He and they tried to save the nation. They tried valiantly to hold together the ship of state. The dissolution was inevitable. Compromises were offered but the Dred Scott decision, the Kansas bloodshed, and John Brown's capture of Harpers Ferry were the last straws in a long struggle which could only be brought to a conclusion by a bloody civil war.

Breckinridge was also a popular Vice-President. He was affable, gracious, and an effective public speaker. He had been a popular choice and, an exception to the rule, not merely a geographical appointment; in 1859, nearly a year and a half before his term as Vice-President expired, the Kentucky legislature elected him to the United States Senate "if and when he is no longer Vice-President." The history of the United States does not show such an honor ever before or since paid a man by the citizens of his native state.

Vice-President Breckinridge presided over the Senate at the time of its removal from the old dark chamber to the present spacious quarters. He delivered the farewell oration made in the old chamber.

In 1860, the National Democratic Convention met in Charleston. The party was hopelessly divided and nothing was accomplished. The Northern element was strong for Senator Stephen A. Douglas of Illinois while the Southerners were unanimous for Breckinridge. The Charleston convention had offered Breckinridge the nomination but he refused as he had hoped that the party might get together. The convention later met in Baltimore and the seceding Southern members again offered him the nomination. He answered that, although he was not a candidate, he would accept in the hope that he might be able to save the Union.

The Republican Convention nominated Abraham Lincoln of Illinois, with Hannibal Hamlin of Maine as Vice-President. The Northern Democrats placed Douglas, the "Little Giant" who had been Breckinridge's friend and crony in Washington, in nomination and the Know-Nothings nominated Bell of Tennessee as a forlorn hope.

The campaign of 1860 was bitter and hectic. Secessionist sentiment was in the air and, with the Democrats badly split and with Bell to draw from their support, it was evident that Lincoln would be elected. Breckinridge made an active campaign, however, and carried the South. In the electoral vote Lincoln received 180 votes, Breckinridge seventy-two, Bell thirty-nine, and Douglas twelve.

Breckinridge had declared in his campaign speeches that he had no secessionist ideas. "Kentucky will cling to the Constitution while a shred of it remains. I am an American citizen, a Kentuckian who never did an act or cherished a thought that was not full of devotion to the Constitution and the Union." He believed in the abstract principle of secession but he did not approve it in the crisis at hand.

South Carolina seceded from the Union; Major Robert Anderson surrendered Fort Sumter; and the Civil War was under way.

Breckinridge was a member of the Senate, by virtue of his election in 1859, and he returned to Washington to fight to hold the Union together. He talked with Lincoln. The President was friendly but could offer no solution. Texas, Alabama and, in the end, all of the states south of Kentucky withdrew from the Union, and Breckinridge saw the nation dissolve.

He refused to vote for war measures and he opposed the policy of sending an army to invade the South. He pleaded with Kentucky to remain neutral and he made one of the greatest speeches of his career justifying his appeal and his stand. On September 21, 1861, Kentucky voted to remain in the Union and ordered all Southern sympathizers to leave the state. On October 2, the legislature asked Breckinridge to resign. He fled the state and was appointed a brigadier general in the Confederate Army. On December 2, the United States Senate declared him a traitor. In answer to the Senate's charge, Breckinridge said, "I exchange with satisfaction a term of six years in the Senate for the musket of a soldier."

He had helped to organize the Provisional Government of Kentucky (Confederate) and in October he was in the field as a brigadier general under General Albert Sidney Johnston. He proved to be an able commander. He had as much active service as any one man could in the next four years. He was at Shiloh with General Johnston when that great soldier was killed, and served as a major general at Vicksburg. He was at Murfreesboro with General Braxton Bragg, and his commanding officers complimented him for his skill in covering Bragg's retreat.

Breckinridge fought on every major front and was the idol of his men. In the struggle around Washington, Breckinridge's division won the battles of Martinsburg and Manocacy. He strongly advised going into Washington and taking over the Capital but he was overruled by the war council, its argument being that the small army General J. B. Early had at his disposal could not hold the city even if he captured it. General Breckinridge insisted that even though Confederate troops could not hold Washington, and even if every man were lost in taking and holding it "even for a day," the psychological effect would be so great that the South could afford the loss.

Breckinridge had had but little military experience before his entry into the Confederate Army. At twenty-five, he had been a major in the Mexican War but he saw little active service and, when he became a brigadier general with the Confederate forces, he knew little or nothing of a soldier's life or the privations of a campaign. But his instinctive ability to influence men and his indomitable will, his energy and his daring, made him a great leader in the army.

When Lee had surrendered at Appomattox Court House, Breckinridge went south with General Johnston and was his adviser at the Confederate surrender to Sherman. Jefferson Davis had appointed Breckinridge in February, 1865, as Secretary of War, and he made every effort to hold the army together. When he realized that the Confederate cause was doomed, Breckinridge turned his attention to the soldiers. He obtained every dollar of "hard money" he could lay his hands on, and paid the troops. Privates drew the same amount as did officers.

Breckinridge saw Lee surrender, but he would not surrender himself. He was with General Johnston at his conferences with General Sherman, but he would not surrender himself. He went to Washington, Georgia, with President Davis and his cabinet, when that gentleman attempted to escape in women's clothes. Then Breckinridge took Old Joe, his body servant, and a few young officers and set out for Cuba. They arrived there after weeks of wandering and after crossing the path of Judah P. Benjamin, the Jewish secretary of state who also would not surrender. (Benjamin afterward reached England and was for many years a leading member of the British bar.) They starved and suffered incredible hardships. For a time they had been pirates and had captured a ship manned by Union deserters. With this sloop they reached Cárdenas, Cuba, and from there made their way to Havana. In Havana, Breckinridge was treated with marked respect and received the courtesy believed due the Secretary of War of the Confederate States.

From Havana, Breckinridge sent funds to Jefferson Davis' lawyers to assist in his defense and it may be noted that the president of the Confederacy was not convicted of treason.

Breckinridge took passage to England and sent for his wife. They lived in London until 1868 when they went to Toronto, where they lived in a small cottage.

President Ulysses S. Grant had voted for Breckinridge for President in 1860, and was strongly in favor of granting him a pardon. He approached the cabinet and the Senate on the pardon but so much opposition developed that he was forced to withdraw the proposal. He complained that "it would seem the President has no influence." In 1869, however, General Breckinridge was advised that he was free to return to the United States. He was met at Cincinnati by a great throng which "serenaded him in the rain." He and Mrs. Breckinridge returned to Kentucky and to Lexington where the general was received as a conquering hero. It was said then that "Kentucky did not join the Confederacy until after the War."

Breckinridge settled down to mending his fortunes, and was soon engaged in law practice. He became a corporation attorney and was elected vice-president of a local railroad. He soon prospered.

Had his citizenship been restored, Breckinridge could have been elected to any office within the gift of the people of his state. His home eventually became a shrine.

In May of 1875, he developed a liver ailment. He consulted his physician who advised an operation. The general submitted to the operation, which was unsuccessful, and another was performed from which he did not recover. On May 17, 1875, Breckinridge died at the age of fifty-four. There is a monument to him in Lexington where he lived and where he died.

Breckinridge was a man of outstanding ability. He was far above the stature of most Vice-Presidents. He was a persuasive orator. He and millions of other thoughtful Americans held to the sincere conviction that their view was the morally right view. And from the standpoint of sheer ability, among Vice-Presidents, Breckinridge has had few peers in American history. Had he lived at any other period of the nation's progression or, for that matter, had he chosen the Union side of the Civil War, a safe prediction is that he would have achieved the White House.

CHAPTER XV

Hannibal Hamlin

THE FIFTEENTH VICE-PRESIDENT was a full-blown example of the perennial officeholder but certainly one above mediocrity. For sixty-five years he remained in the main stream of American history—he was a difficult man to dislodge from office, and the only one who really succeeded in that effort was Andrew Johnson. Had Johnson failed, Hannibal Hamlin would have succeeded the assassinated Lincoln.

Hamlin was born at Paris Hill, Maine, on August 27, 1809. He was the fifth generation of Hamlins who had lived in New England since James Hamlin went to the Massachusetts Bay Colony in 1639.

Cyrus Hamlin, father of Hannibal, was a down-East Yankee, a sturdy citizen, and a staunch admirer of General Jackson. The son attended the village schools in the vicinity of his home and was a student at Hebron Academy, but he did not go to college. He had hoped to matriculate at Bowdoin, the college from which

Franklin Pierce, Longfellow, and so many of New England's leaders had been graduated, but the Hamlins were unable to send their son there.

For a time he was a member of a surveyor's crew, and at twenty he and a young friend purchased a small newspaper at Paris Hill. Hamlin could not set type but his partner taught him enough so that he was able to edit *The Leader* for six months. The newspaper had paid its former editor a salary of $1.50 per week, on which sum Hamlin lived at the best boardinghouse in town.

When he was twenty-one, however, Hamlin began the study of law with the firm of Fessenden and Deblois. The Fessendens were one of Maine's best families; they had been representatives, senators, and leaders in the state, and one of them was Secretary of the Treasury under Lincoln.

In 1833, Hamlin was admitted to the bar, and three years later he was sent to the state legislature at Augusta where he served four terms. He was again a member of the Assembly in 1848, during one of the periods between his service in Congress and the Senate. He was Speaker of the house of the state legislature during three of his terms and was to find his legislative experience good schooling for his future career.

As a member of the Assembly, Hamlin was a conservative Democrat of Jacksonian type. He was a political behind-the-scenes worker, not a speaker. He believed little was accomplished by oratory, that speeches never changed ideas.

In 1842, Hamlin was elected to Congress and served in the House for two terms. His record in Congress was that of a conservative, machine Democrat. Slavery was becoming the paramount issue and he was a strong antislavery man. He was later to become an abolitionist although he hated the abolitionists for what he regarded as their impracticability. Hamlin's first reaction to slavery was that it was wrong, but that it was an institution which could not be abolished by law. He held that emancipation must come by education and tolerance. This was the British point of view, incidentally, and it was by this method that England sought to solve the same problem.

In 1848, Hamlin was back in the Maine legislature and from the Assembly he went to the United States Senate to fill a vacancy. He was re-elected in 1851 for the regular six-year term. After 1848, he was to be in and out of the upper house for the next thirty years.

Hamlin went to the Senate when its membership was probably the strongest in its history. He sat with Clay, Calhoun, and Webster. He knew Thomas H. Benton, Alexander H. Stephens, the cripple who was a giant mentally and who was vice-president of the Confederacy at the time Hamlin held the same position in the Union. He knew Polk, Tyler, Dallas, and old Buchanan. He voted against the annexation of Texas.

On February 38, 1844, the tragedy occurred aboard the U.S.S. *Princeton* in which Secretary of State Abel P. Upshur was killed. Hamlin was in Congress at the time and had been invited to make the trip on the warship but while on the wharf, waiting to board the craft, he was called back to a conference and so avoided that fateful expedition. A new gun was to be shown the guests aboard the U.S.S. *Princeton* and when it was fired an explosion occurred, killing several of the crew and Secretary Upshur. President Tyler had stepped below decks for a moment and escaped the explosion. In other circumstances, the nation would have been in a quandary since there was no Vice-President and, with Secretary Upshur dead, a controversy would have arisen then over the line of succession.

Hamlin followed his habitual practice in the Senate, in the legislature and in the House of Representatives—he made few speeches and did most of his work on committees and in caucuses. He was chairman of the Committee on Commerce and was regarded as a hard-working member.

In 1852, Pierce and King were the Democratic candidates for President and Vice-President. Hamlin supported them and stumped on their behalf throughout New England with great fervor. But when Buchanan came to run for President, Hamlin bolted the regular Democratic and was instrumental in forming the Republican party. Slavery had become the all-important issue and he could not tolerate the Democratic viewpoint. The result was that he left the Senate to become a candidate for the governorship of Maine, to which post he was elected as a Republican. His election on the Republican ticket opened a period in which the Republicans were to control the state for more than seventy years.

Hamlin was governor of Maine for only a month, resigning again to become a member of the Senate. Why he resigned his seat in the Senate, ran for governor and then resigned that office to run for the Senate, he never fully explained.

From 1856 to 1861, Hamlin was an active antislavery leader in the Senate. He was strongly pro-Union and, while he had many close friends among the Southern members, he could not abide their political opinions. He had great admiration for the Vice-President and called Breckinridge the "courtly Kentuckian," yet Hamlin was to preside over the Senate when the former Vice-President was expelled from that body for treason.

In 1860, the Republican Convention was held in Chicago. William H. Seward confidently expected to be nominated to head the ticket but the West, in a surprise move, nominated Lincoln. The convention then began looking for a suitable Vice-Presidential candidate. Geography was the important factor. Lincoln's strength lay in the West and party leaders needed an Eastern man to balance ticket—the old formula.

Hamlin of Maine was the answer. Senator Hamlin had, of course, helped to organize the Republican party. He was a conservative, an antislavery man and yet he had never been coupled with the abolitionists. But his record in the Senate was good and the party felt that Hamlin would strengthen the ticket in areas where Lincoln was little known.

Hamlin wrote that he never met Lincoln until after the Chicago convention. Lincoln had been a candidate for the Senate but had been defeated by Douglas. He had been in Congress only one term. Hamlin was under the vague impression that he had heard Lincoln make a speech once in Congress but that he had never been introduced to him. Lincoln agreed.

The campaign of 1860 was bitter and its results are well-known. Douglas was snowed under while Bell, the Union candidate, a relic of the old Know-Nothings, carried some of the border states and polled thirty-nine electoral votes. The "courtly Kentuckian," Breckinridge, carried the South with seventy-two votes, and Lincoln was elected President with one hundred eighty-four.

The campaign had brought into the open charges that Hamlin had Negro blood. He was called a Mulatto, and most of the South referred to him as a "black nigger." Hamlin was of swarthy complexion and perhaps had some of the appearances of Negro color, but it was never proved that he had any Negro antecedents.

Elected to the Vice-Presidency, Hamlin resigned his seat in the Senate and on March 4, 1861, he was escorted to the Vice-President's chair by Breckinridge and took the oath of office as the fifteenth Vice-President of the United States.

The Union was rapidly breaking up; Southern senators were resigning and friendships of a lifetime were being severed. During the first year of Hamlin's term, twenty-six Southern senators left Washington, some with gladness and some with sincere sorrow. Hamlin's office was a difficult one. He came to know and hold great respect for Lincoln. He was consulted by the President over the make up of the cabinet and he was given the privilege of naming the New England member of the official family. He recommended Gideon Welles as Secretary of the Navy and that appointment was made. Hamlin was later sorry that he had asked for that appointment for Welles did not work well with the administration.

The Vice-President became a favorite with Lincoln and the President read Hamlin the Emancipation Proclamation one evening in the early fall of 1862 before its release to the public. Hamlin was deeply affected by the President's decision to free the slaves, and he took this opportunity to urge the enlistment of Negroes in the Army.

Lincoln made many changes in his cabinet during his first administration, and he made it a point to discuss the changes with

Hamlin. Hamlin had been instrumental in persuading Seward to become Secretary of State in the cabinet, and Lincoln appreciated the Vice-President's efforts. Lincoln had been reluctant to offer the State portfolio to Seward but offered him the appointment, which was accepted.

In 1864, Lincoln and Hamlin were both eager to succeed themselves. George B. McClellan, who had been an unsuccessful commander of the Union Army and who had fought the drawn battle of Antietam with Lee, was the Democratic candidate. His campaign was one of criticism of Lincoln's conduct of the war. A year before, McClellan might have been elected on such a platform but Grant was now in command and the South was weakening fast; thus, the people would not flock to McClellan's support. Hamlin was looked upon as the logical candidate to run again with Lincoln, but once more political expediency and geographical selection played a part and Andrew Johnson of Tennessee, a war governor, was chosen as Lincoln's running mate. The votes of the New England states were assured and it was thought by leading members of the Republican party that Johnson could save some of the border states. The fact was these states were safely in the Republican fold regardless who the Vice-Presidential candidate was, and the party found itself saddled with what the opposition described as a "drunken liability," rather than a conservative Maine Yankee. Again the matter of Hamlin's purported racial background was brought to the fore, and used effectively against him, particularly his advocacy of Negro enlistment in the Army.

The nomination of Johnson was one of the gravest political mistakes a party ever made. Regardless of Johnson's ability or otherwise, or his personal habits, he was a heavy liability. His nomination was nothing less than stupid. He was known to be erratic, and the Republican leaders should have known he was the last man to couple with Lincoln. They began to realize that during the campaign; it was further impressed on them when he was Vice-President and it became a certainty when he succeeded Lincoln as President.

Hamlin was bitterly disappointed, but he went along with the ticket and campaigned throughout New England for Lincoln and Johnson.

Hamlin, the discarded Vice-President, went back to Maine to practice law and, shortly after Johnson became President, he was appointed collector of the Port of Boston. It appears that the appointment was given Hamlin because of his shabby treatment by the party. The leaders had realized their mistake and wanted to atone in some way. The New England leaders persuaded President Johnson to give Hamlin the collectorship and, as the position was the most renumerative within the gift of the federal government in New England, Hamlin accepted. There was a salary of $10,000 attached to the post, in addition to commissions and fees which made it worth $30,000 to $40,000. It was a sinecure, which Hamlin had no difficulty persuading himself to accept.

Hamlin remained in the position of collector for only little more than a year. He could not stomach Johnson and felt that he was doing himself a disservice by serving under him. He resigned and returned to Maine, where he became the president of a small railroad, and again practiced law.

In 1869, he was sixty years old and he felt that he would like to sit again in the Senate. He offered himself as a candidate to the Maine legislature and that body elected him by a vote of seventy-five to seventy-four over Senator Mollison. There were cries of fraud by the Mollison supporters as there were 150 eligible and present to vote, but only 149 votes were cast, one ballot being returned blank. Hamlin was declared elected, however, and in 1869, he returned to Washington where he remained for the next twelve years.

The Senate had changed since Hamlin had been there last. The Reconstruction era was under way. Grant was in the White House. When Hamlin returned to represent Maine in the Senate he joined the radical group. He favored harsh treatment of the Southern states and, while willing to accept individual Southerners back as "citizens," he was opposed to a general amnesty.

Hamlin was friendly with the carpetbagger senators from the South, and developed an intimate friendship with the Negro senator from Alabama, Hiram R. Rush. This again inspired the charge of Hamlin's colored blood.

As a senator in the period of 1869-1881, Hamlin developed a strong friendship for President Grant. They became cronies and Senator Hamlin served as a political adviser to the general. On the other hand, he was never friendly with President Hayes and fought the President's Civil Service Bill until it finally became law. Hamlin could see no merit in Hayes' efforts to streamline the federal officeholding procedure, and was a supporter of the old method of giving all offices to deserving party members. But the Senate was not a party to the salary grab and refused the $5,000 extra compensation voted.

In 1881, he was seventy-two and no longer interested in re-election. He thought it would be pleasant to round out his service with a diplomatic post. The old politician again became a job seeker. He was appointed to the Madrid ambassadorship by President Garfield, and spent two uneventful years in Spain and in touring Europe. There was little to do and the elderly envoy enjoyed himself visiting museums throughout Italy and Spain.

Hamlin was seventy-five when he tired of political life. He had never ceased to grieve over missing the renomination with Lincoln. Hamlin felt that he had been double-crossed by his New England friends and that Lincoln had wanted him as his running mate but had been persuaded to keep out of the Vice-Presidential fight by Hamlin's so-called friends.

The onetime representative, senator, governor, Vice-President, and minister to Spain returned to Maine to spend the last eight years of his life in retirement.

He had known the Presidents of the United States from Jackson to Harrison. On July 4, 1891, when he was eighty-two, he walked down to his club, smoked a couple of black cigars, and played some cards with his cronies. There he toppled over in his chair and died.

Hannibal Hamlin was a mixture of New England honesty and

practical politics. He was an able senator in a quiet, unassuming manner. He possessed some oratorical ability yet seldom spoke publicly. He preferred to play the game as a conservative wire-puller.

CHAPTER XVI

Andrew Johnson

ANDREW JOHNSON, sixteenth Vice-President and seventeenth President, presents to the historian a moving study in courage. His entire career proves him to have been a man of extraordinary qualities, for all his little schooling, his idiosyncrasies and irascibility. It is an appalling travesty that one of the most highly principled Presidents is remembered by posterity chiefly because of his trial for impeachment, the only Chief Executive to suffer that ordeal (although an effort was made to remove Washington), and because of his occasional overfondness for alcohol, a predilection by no means exceptional in his day.

Johnson was born in Raleigh, North Carolina, on December 29, 1808. His father was Jacob Johnson, who had been a captain of militia and who was janitor of the local bank as well as the church sexton. Andrew had no knowledge of his grandparents.

When he was ten, "Andy" was apprenticed to a tailor whose name was J. J. Selby, and became his "bound boy." By this "binding," Andrew was to be a servant to his master until he was twenty-one; in return, Selby was to teach him the trade of tailor and to feed and clothe him.

Andrew remained with Selby until he was seventeen, at which time he became embroiled with a widow. In company with a friend, he "stoned the home" of the lady in question. She reported them to the authorities and they left town "between sundown and sunrise." Johnson fled to Laurens Court House, South Carolina, where he set himself up as a journeyman tailor. He remained in South Carolina for a year and then returned to Raleigh. It would appear that he had again been in trouble with a woman. He went home believing that his escapades had been forgotten but he learned that he was regarded by police as a runaway and that Raleigh had not forgotten his indiscretions.

Again he left town in haste. This time he set out for the West, accompanied by his mother and stepfather—she had remarried after the death of her first husband.

Johnson wrote that he drove to Greenville, in Eastern Tennessee, in a cart "drawn by a blind pony." Andrew and his stepfather walked the entire distance while his mother rode in the cart. Johnson said in later years that on this trip he killed a bear with a shotgun.

It was in Greenville that Johnson finally settled, and it was there that he lived for almost a half century.

Up to this time, Johnson had had no schooling. It is possible that he knew his ABC's and that perhaps he could read a little, but it was Eliza McCardle, whom he married in 1827 when nineteen—and his bride seventeen—who taught him to read and who inspired him with a passion for more knowledge.

Eliza was the daughter of the village shoemaker; she was a "personable young woman" and certainly the future President was fortunate in finding such an intelligent helpmate. They were married, incidentally, by the local justice of the peace, Mordecai Lincoln, who, Johnson wrote, was a kinsman of the Emancipator.

Mrs. Johnson was responsible for such knowledge and learning as Andrew Johnson ever possessed. She read to him while he plied the needle in his tailorshop. She was patient and methodical. She not only taught her tailor-husband to read and write but she also instructed him in mathematics and in rhetoric. She evidently was a proficient teacher because ultimately Johnson obtained a broad grasp of history and many of the classics. His speeches show a remarkable breadth of learning, particularly of the Roman orators, and of ancient history in general.

In Greenville, Johnson became the leader of and the spokesman for the workingman against the plantation owners. One of the most admirable traits of Johnson was his consistent sympathy for and interest in the welfare of the underprivileged.

In Greenville, in 1835, Johnson's wife persuaded him to run for the state legislature. At this time, when only twenty-three, he was mayor of the town. He was easily elected over his Whig opponent. In his new post he showed himself as unquestionably opinionated, and he was in constant hot water. Two years later he was defeated for re-election, largely because of his hostility to the plantation owners, but in 1841, he was again elected to the legislature, defeating Brooks Campbell, to whom he had lost in 1837.

By this time, he had become more knowing politically. He had learned to compromise in some degree, how to give and take and trade, and he remained in the lower house of the legislature, and subsequently in the state senate, until he felt ready to make a run for the national Congress. In national politics, he was always a Democrat but he opposed Polk when his fellow Tennessean was the Presidential candidate and he was, in a large way, responsible for the loss to Polk of his home state in the elections of 1844.

Johnson had been a Van Buren elector but he had opposed Polk because of his friendship for Hugh White, who was also a Presidential candidate, and for John Bell, who was to be a candidate against Lincoln in 1860 on the American party ticket. These two men had been intimates of Johnson in the legislature, and he would not forsake them for Polk even though they were staunch Whigs.

In 1841, when Johnson had advanced to the state senate, the Whigs had a majority of two in the legislature, and the Democrats a majority of one in the Senate. There were two vacancies in the United States Senate. White's term had expired and Felix Grundy had died. The election of a successor to these two had to originate in the Senate, and Johnson knew, of course, that in a joint ballot the Whigs would come up with a majority of one. For two years, as the leader of the Senate Democrats, he kept the state of Tennessee from representation in the upper house of Congress. It would appear that this was a shortsighted move and that a compromise might have been made. One compromise was offered by a Senator Laughlin, by which the two opposing parties would each receive one senator at Washington, but again Johnson prevented an election.

In 1843, Johnson's term in the state senate expired and he went back to Greenville with Congressional ambitions. He was now thirty-five, he had become a moderately prosperous businessman and he was the leading citizen of his community. He had four children, a large house, and a newly purchased farm. He was becoming portly and admitted that he "was drinking a lot of corn whiskey." It is interesting to note that Johnson was a slaveholder and owned several Negroes who were his household servants and field hands; indeed, he owned slaves as late as 1860.

For all his other activities, Johnson's vocation remained that of a tailor. Often during his political career he would return home, sit on his bench, and make clothes for his fellow townsmen in Greenville. Later, when he was governor of Tennessee, he made a suit of clothes for the governor of Kentucky and that official, returning the courtesy, made Johnson a shovel and a pair of tongs—the Kentuckian had been a blacksmith.

In 1843, Johnson began to feel that his past political services had entitled him to promotion, and he entered the race for Congress in the First Congressional District. He was elected, and for the next decade he was a Democratic member of the House of Representatives. Johnson was hard-working; he was a Jacksonian Democrat; and his maiden speech in the House was a plea to refund the fine that had been assessed against Old Hickory for declaring martial law in New Orleans in 1815. His colleagues agreed that Johnson, the erstwhile tailor, had made an eloquent speech.

Johnson was opposed to the high tariff and was a supporter of Calhoun on that issue as well as on the vote to annex Texas. The question of that annexation was one of great moment during Johnson's first term in office, and Calhoun's masterly strike in persuading President Tyler to affix his signature to the treaty of annexation signaled the doom of Van Buren as a political leader.

If there is one piece of legislation which would lend substantial prestige to Johnson's career in Congress, it is the Homestead Act. Johnson offered this bill to Congress many times, only to see it repeatedly voted down, but he persisted until it finally became law. The measure has remained in substance the same as drawn by Johnson more than a century ago. The bill offers to anyone who is the head of a family 160 acres of land, provided that he occupy it and cultivate it for five years. Buchanan vetoed the measure as late as 1857, and for many years it was considered as extremely unpopular legislation.

Johnson was re-elected to Congress continuously for five terms. In his ten years as a representative, he remained a particularly painful thorn in the flesh of the Whigs. They could not defeat him in his First District, so they did what they regarded as the next more effective thing. They gerrymandered the district so that he was no longer a resident of his original district. They appear to have acted hastily, however, for while they acquired a new representative, the state of Tennessee found itself with a new governor—the displaced member of the lower house. It was a particularly gratifying victory for Johnson because Gustavus Henry, whom he had defeated for the governorship, had led the fight to gerrymander him out of his House seat.

In many ways, Governor Johnson was politically far in advance of his times. He proposed that Tennessee should offer certain amendments to the Constitution of the United States. Among these were that United States senators should be elected by the voters of the state, not by the legislature; that the Electoral College should be abolished and that the President and the Vice-President should also be elected by direct popular vote; that a different method should be found for the selection of the Justices of the United States Supreme Court, and that the appointments to that bench should go to alternating political parties. These were interesting and pertinent reforms, and the first has long since been adopted.

There was a good deal of the progressive and liberal thinker and political student about Johnson for all his temperamental shortcomings.

In 1854, Johnson was re-elected governor although the Know-Nothing candidate gave him considerable opposition. The Know-Nothings, otherwise the American party, had come into prominence at this time under the leadership of former President Fillmore, and for a time it was a substantial threat to the major political factions. It was strictly "American"—anti-Catholic, anti-Jewish, antiforeign birth and foreign influence, and it found its followers chiefly among the middle class. Like all "anti" movements, it influenced a large number of voters and for a time it had numerous following but, like most movements lacking a constructive program, it never became a salient factor in the political life of the nation.

The Know-Nothings attacked Johnson's personal life, but he nonetheless succeeded in his re-election.

It was during this second term that Governor Johnson engineered the purchase of the Hermitage, General Jackson's old home, by the state of Tennessee. The price paid for the 500-acre estate was $48,000, and the governor had hoped that the site might be used as a western branch of West Point. On one occasion the House Military Affairs Committee reported favorably on that Johnson proposal.

In 1857, Johnson refused to be a candidate for re-election as he had received the promise of political leaders of the state that he could have the United States senatorship. The Tennessee legislature elected him to that office in October and, on December 7, 1857, Johnson—now fifty, portly, and unquestionably a two-fisted drinker—returned to Washington as the junior senator from his state.

In the thirty years he had lived in Greenville, the tailor had done very well by himself.

The Senate, the final one before the dissolution of the Union, was wracked by dissension from the day it met until the hour it adjourned. The Dred Scott decision had been handed down; the

Kansas-Nebraska Bill was under furious debate; and John Brown was hanged for treason. The breach was widening daily. Senator Johnson was a Union man, as he had always been. He frequently clashed with President Buchanan, protesting that the Chief Executive showed undue partiality to the Southern senators and that instead of seeking to unite the Union he was widening the gap between the opposed factions.

Johnson now reintroduced his homestead measure, and he pushed it through to passage in both houses. Buchanan vetoed it, however, and its tireless sponsor had to await a more propitious time to see it finally become law.

In 1860, there were four candidates for President. Lincoln of Illinois was nominated by the Republicans at their convention in Chicago. (Four years later Lincoln ran on the so-called Union ticket with the Democrat, Andrew Johnson.)

Douglas was the nominee of the Northern wing of the Democratic party while Breckinridge was the standard-bearer of the Southern Democrats. Bell, who had so long been a member of the Senate from Tennessee, was nominated by the American party. Johnson received Tennessee's twelve votes in the Democratic convention which in the end nominated Breckinridge. It is interesting that Johnson voted for Breckinridge in that election.

The campaign that followed was perhaps the most bitter ever waged in the history of the nation, not even excepting in acerbity the Adams-Jefferson campaign in 1800. Scurrilous accusations were cast at every candidate. Lincoln's character was assailed; he was accused of being a "moral reprobate," an "infidel," and of illegitimate birth. Hamlin, his running mate, was called a Mulatto. Breckinridge was called a "destroyer of the Union." Douglas was lampooned by some newspapers, while Bell's association with the Know-Nothings was shouted from the housetops.

Lincoln was elected by a small plurality of the popular vote.

Johnson now faced a serious situation in his home state. An election was held on June 8, and it disclosed that a substantial majority favored secession; the majority was in excess of two to one. But the doughty Johnson refused to abide by the vote of his constituents. "I have always been a Democrat," he said on the floor of the Senate, "and I expect to die a Democrat"—but he was irrevocably a Union man. He would not resign his seat in the upper house, and threats were made against his life, but he could not be swayed. Johnson's own district was in sympathy with his views: they were Union sympathizers but they were outvoted by the more populous Western section.

The Civil War was in progress. Tennessee was overrun by both Confederate and Union soldiers and the state was a battleground from Chattanooga to Memphis. There was to be more actual fighting in Tennessee during the four-year conflict than in any other state with the exception of Virginia.

In 1862, Lincoln believed that in view of the success of the Union forces in capturing Nashville, a military governor should be appointed to take command of that state. He appointed Senator Johnson a brigadier general and made him military governor of Tennessee. He held down that difficult post for three years, at much personal risk, and gave the state an efficient administration. He raised and equipped twenty-five regiments for the Union Army. His son Robert commanded a regiment, a son-in-law commanded another, and his son Charles was an army surgeon.

Johnson now ordered an election to send a Congressional delegation to Washington, but the House of Representatives would not seat its members, and for three years Tennessee was without representation at Washington. The governor remained, in that period, the sole federal officer in the state.

He persisted in his efforts to bring Tennessee into the Union and in 1865 he saw his efforts rewarded at last when the state voted to rejoin the Union and W. G. Brownlow was elected governor. Meanwhile, Johnson the year before had been elected Vice-President and he relinquished the military governorship.

The Republican party had met in Baltimore on June 7, 1864, and had unanimously nominated Lincoln for a second term. Hamlin thought that he was entitled to the renomination as well as Lincoln, but political expediency played its usual potent role and Johnson was named as the Vice-Presidential candidate. That act was a grievous mistake by the party and every man who had had a part in committing it soon came to the realization that the convention had selected a political tartar.

Vice-President Johnson was friendly with Lincoln; he had a deep respect for the long, lean, and homely man from Illinois who was carrying a burden such as no man ever carried as President, with the possible exception of Franklin D. Roosevelt during World War II. It is asserted by some historians that had Lincoln lived, Johnson would have made a good second-in-command. But with the rest of the Republican leaders, he could not see eye to eye. Johnson was a Democrat and, while he was earnestly devoted to the war effort and was willing to make every sacrifice for the Union, he had no sympathy with most Republican policies. He displayed that hostility in the campaign of 1864. He could vote for and support the President, but he could not bring himself to temporize and subscribe to Republican policies.

George B. McClellan was the Democratic candidate and he based his claim to succeed Lincoln on the conduct of the war. But Lincoln's personal popularity and General Grant's successes in Virginia made the outcome of the election a certainty.

On March 4, 1865, Lincoln was inaugurated and Johnson spoiled an otherwise perfect day by being as "drunk as a boiled owl" at his own inauguration. There were too many witnesses to permit of any doubt that he was intoxicated. Apologists have said that he was overtired, worn, and excited over the day's events. But certainly Johnson had been too long in public life to allow himself the indulgence of becoming unduly excited over the prospect of being sworn in as Vice-President. He had been in the House and the Senate, and for three terms had been governor of Tennessee.

But that day he simply drank beyond even his own prodigious capacity and made an unholy spectacle of himself.

That scandal alienated the few supporters among the Republican leaders he might still have had, and he entered office under the most unfavorable circumstances. Six weeks to the day after he had disgraced himself in public, Andrew Johnson, however, was President of the United States. John Wilkes Booth assassinated Lincoln on April 14, 1865, and for the third time in the nation's history the Heir Apparent succeeded to the Presidency.

Johnson made his greatest political mistake in retaining Lincoln's cabinet. Its members owed nothing to the new President, and were openly antagonistic to him; they were Republicans; he had always been a Democrat, and he had voted for Lincoln only because he was his running mate. Had he seen fit to have asked for the cabinet's resignation immediately on becoming President, it is conceivable that he might have escaped four years of chronic wrangling.

As President, Johnson made an effort to follow Lincoln's policies in his treatment of the Southern states. His was a mollifying attitude. He wished to make it easy for the Southern states to re-enter the Union and for the Southern people to rehabilitate themselves.

Johnson clashed repeatedly with his cabinet, and most often with the Secretary of War, Edwin M. Stanton. He asked Stanton to resign. The secretary refused and dared the President to remove him. Johnson was as strong-willed and obstinate as Stanton and did expel him, appointing General Grant to his place. There was, in fact, a precedent for discharging Stanton. Adams had summarily discharged Timothy Pickering and made his act stand. But Grant showed little backbone when the real struggle for power came and deserted President Johnson.

The quarrel with Secretary Stanton was the starting point of the impeachment movement. There were only twelve Democratic members in the Senate and the Republicans proceeded to formulate plans for the conduct of the government without consulting the President, feeling certain they could carry out their program. The reconstruction period was under way, and Thaddeus Stevens of Pennsylvania and Charles Sumner of Massachusetts led the "Radicals" in the revolt against Johnson. He, in turn, was as bitter as were these men and he could be equally vituperative. In his speech on the Tenure of Office Bill, the President widened the breach, and in his efforts to lighten the load of the Southern states he broke with Congress. Then it became evident that there was no healing. He took matters into his own hands and by proclamation re-established civil government in Virginia, North Carolina, and Mississippi and a short time later in Texas, Alabama, and South Carolina.

In 1867, Congress passed an act "for the more efficient government of the Rebel States," which undid all of that which Johnson had done for the establishing of the civil government in the foregoing states. The President vetoed the bill but it was passed over his head. Then Congress passed the Freedmen's Bureau Act which Johnson also vetoed and which Congress again passed over his veto.

The President took the case to the people. He made a tour of the nation explaining his side of the argument but he found little sympathy. Feeling was too high and the North still remembered the four-year struggle, the assassination of Lincoln, and the trial of Jefferson Davis which was occupying much space in the papers.

Johnson returned to Washington and to unremitting dissension. No agreement was possible and impeachment was being freely talked of both in the House and in the Senate. In January, 1867, Congress passed a bill depriving the President of his powers as commander in chief of the Army. This was accomplished by providing that all orders to the Army must come from General Grant. The act was palpably unconstitutional. The proponents knew it to be so, but the war was on in earnest and they were out to unseat Johnson.

The measure was tacked on the General Appropriation Bill and the President, of necessity, approved it but with a written protest.

One day in the spring of 1868, Representative Cavode, of Pennsylvania, stood on the floor of Congress and moved that "Andrew Johnson, President of the United States, be impeached of high crimes and misdemeanors." From that day until the Senate adjourned after its abortive effort to remove Johnson,

Washington was the scene of a great national drama. The city was a caldron boiling over with excitement, and the majority of the people was in favor of impeachment.

Impeachment had been discussed before in the history of the nation. There had been an effort made to impeach Washington during his second term of office and but for the fact that not enough members could be found to sign a petition for impeachment, history might have recorded such an ordeal for the first President.

But there had never before been an impeachment and the country was wildly excited. Leaders in the effort to remove the President were Senators Bingham, Stevens, and John Logan, as well as Sumner, Benjamin Butler, and Henry Wilson, who later was Vice-President. These gentlemen prepared the certification papers which the House of Representatives overwhelmingly approved. The trial began March 3, 1868, with Chief Justice Benjamin Franklin Wade sitting as judge and the Senate as the jury. There were eleven charges but only three were brought to a vote.

As counsel, President Johnson had five of the country's ablest lawyers. The Attorney General, Henry Stanberry, resigned his office to defend the President and the other senior counsel was the great William Evarts.

Article I charged the President with illegally suspending Secretary of War Stanton.

Article II charged the appointment of a Secretary of War without the consent of the Senate.

Article III charged the President with preventing Secretary Stanton from resuming his office.

It was on these three charges that Johnson was tried and on these only that a vote was ever taken.

President Johnson denied all the charges and more than 1,200 pages of testimony were taken and long days spent in argument. Wagers were made that the impeachment would succeed but when the ballot was taken the outcome was in question until almost the last name was called. The final vote showed thirty-five votes for conviction, nineteen against. (A two-thirds vote is required for conviction.) One additional vote against Johnson would have meant his political eclipse, yet this man lived to sit in the same body and with the men who had impeached him.

When the result was announced, Secretary Stanton resigned his post in the cabinet, which left Johnson with a very dubious victory. Stanton had been a power in Lincoln's administration, and had hoped to dominate Johnson. The two men were much alike in temperament and such a clash was inevitable. But the whole performance was a disgrace to the nation.

The impeachment trial and apprehension over who would become President in the event of Johnson's expulsion brought about the passage of the law which states the order of succession in the event of the death or the incapacity of both the President and the Vice-President. This act was passed in July, 1868. By its passage the order of succession after the Vice-President was the Secretary of State, the Secretary of War, the Secretary of the Treasury, the Attorney General and the Postmaster General.

It was during the administration of Johnson that Alaska was purchased from Russia for $7,200,000 and that the Emperor Maximilian was deposed as Emperor of Mexico and executed by the people of that nation. Johnson had taken a firm stand in the Maximilian affair and the manner in which he handled that delicate situation, not only with Mexico but with Louis Napoleon, was noteworthy.

Late in his term of office President Johnson issued the General Amnesty Proclamation which restored to citizenship most of those Southerners who had supported the Confederacy. This move by Johnson went far toward restoring normal political conditions and gave to the South a degree of self-government. Many of the leaders of the Confederacy applied personally to Johnson for pardon and were, by executive order, restored to citizenship; among those were Alexander H. Stephens, who had been vice-president of the Confederacy, and many former senators and representatives.

In 1868, Grant was elected President and Johnson went home to Greenville. For thirty years he had held office in his state, in the halls of Congress, as Vice-President and as President.

He could not get politics out of his blood, however, and in 1872 he was again a candidate for office, this time for the newly created position of congressman at large from Tennessee. He ran as an independent candidate and was opposed by both the Democratic and Republican nominees. Johnson was defeated but in 1875 he faced those who had sought to unseat him seven years before. That was a profound satisfaction to the sixty-seven-year-old former President. He took his seat in the Senate in January of 1875, but on July 31 he went into a sleep from which he did not awaken.

So died a remarkable and interesting man. Andrew Johnson had lived life to the fullest. He had many failings; he was erratic, domineering, and obstinate; and he was an intemperate drinker, but he lived in a section of the country where men made liquor by the barrel and drank it as water. His morals were the morals of his times. Evidence that his constituents did not hold his mode of life against him is the fact that Tennessee was always enthusiastically for Johnson and that its citizens almost never refused him office when he sought it.

Several modern-day biographers of Johnson have sought, if not to whitewash him, at least to portray him as a man of deep faith in the people and of an almost fanatical devotion to the Constitution. Earlier studies of Johnson have so emphasized his partisan contest with the House of Representatives, as well as his fondness for spirits, that most Americans, it seems to the writers, only remember that Johnson escaped conviction by the narrowest of margins—the one vote; and the impression has appeared to grow that his acquisitive interest in alcohol had something to do with the impeachment proceedings, which of course is untrue.

He had certain glaring defects of character, noticeably a consuming shyness, which he sought to hide by a manner that was often brusque and boorish and often tasteless; that inevitably earned him more enemies than had he had some of the urbanity that, say, usually accompanies a less haphazard education than was Johnson's. But he was a man of strong convictions, and his figure and character stand out sharply against the succession of Vice-Presidential lightweights.

CHAPTER XVII

Schuyler Colfax

THE CAREER OF SCHUYLER COLFAX follows such an unhappily familiar formula in American political life that, except for the pertinent dates and the names of his contemporaries, he seems to step directly from the newspapers of tomorrow's early editions. Perhaps the most singular aspect of the adult life of the seventeenth Vice-President is that he was sufficiently agile to survive three major mistakes, any one of which was sufficient to wreck the public career of far more able and conscientious men.

Colfax, Vice-President during Grant's first administration, was inevitably saddled with the label of the "Great Joiner." He joined everything in sight, on the political horizon, that had any potential votes by way of backslapping, or even a single vote. His birthplace was a two-storied house in 'way downtown New York, now given over to small factories and import-export houses, but then a fashionable neighborhood and the residential section in which lived the well-to-do and professional businessmen of the city. He was born on March 23, 1823.

Colfax's ancestors were prosperous merchants. His paternal grandfather was General Colfax of Revolutionary fame, and he belonged to those Schuylers who were long the leaders of the New York upper crust.

The father of the future Vice-President died in October of

1822, and the son was born the following March. His mother had been a Miss Hannah Stryker and, before she was eighteen, had been married three years and was the mother of two children, a daughter Mary, who died in infancy, and the son Schuyler. Mrs. Colfax, a few years after her husband's death, married George M. Matthews, a young Baltimorean who was three years younger than his bride.

Thus, Schuyler Colfax's stepfather was only fourteen years older than himself. They were close friends for many years, and Matthews was more of an older brother to his stepson than a stepfather.

He attended the public schools of New York until he was eleven, when his grandfather, General Colfax, directed that he learn something practical to do, and he accordingly became a clerk in the store of his stepfather. In the public schools, the boy had studied Latin and French and, it is recorded, was exceptionally studious for one of his years.

In 1836, when he was thirteen and in his second year of a clerkship apprentice, his family moved west. They settled in Indiana, near South Bend, and for fifty years thenceforth Colfax was South Bend, and South Bend was Colfax. There he studied law for three years but was not admitted to the bar.

His stepfather was elected county auditor by the Whigs, and he became a figure of local political importance. The county auditor was a member of the county board of supervisors, and for eight years Schuyler was his stepfather's assistant. His mother encouraged him in his political aspirations, and she appears to have had more influence upon him than the woman he married when he was twenty-one, Evelyn Clark, the daughter of a neighbor.

In 1845, Colfax and a young friend, A. W. West, established the *St. Joseph Valley Register* for which Colfax served as editor. That weekly newspaper was to serve an influential role in South Bend and St. Joseph County for many years. Colfax exploited it to advance his political ambitions, and it was his personal organ during the seven terms he spent in the House of Representatives.

Early in his political career, Colfax embraced the Whigs. He was a Whig as long as there was a Whig party, save for the time that (he said) he was "almost" led into the ranks of the Know-Nothings. He was present at the accouchement of the Republican party, and was a member for the remainder of his life.

It was during the middle of the nineteenth century that fraternal organizations and their masquerade flummeries began to appeal powerfully to many Americans in what is now the Middle West. With an acute eye to the main chance, Colfax joined the Independent Order of Odd Fellows, the first of a long series of adroit fraternal affiliations. Early in adult life he developed an itch for political office. Before he was twenty-five, he was appointed clerk of the state senate, and in that post became ambitious for election to Congress. In 1848, he was a delegate to the Whig Convention where he made an address that gave his hearers and himself the idea that he was a powerful orator. (Unfortunately, that speech is lost to history.)

The same year, Zachary Taylor had been elected President, and a few months later Colfax was a delegate to the Indiana Constitutional Convention where he worked zealously to draft a new constitution. He then believed the time ripe to make a try for the House of Representatives and, in 1851, he announced himself a candidate through the columns of his newspaper. He was defeated but two years later he won. He had learned to become an assiduously good mixer, he was a generally well-liked newspaperman, and he was, as remarked before, an incorrigible "joiner." For fourteen years he remained in the lower house of Congress, and for three years was Speaker—incidentally, now the Heir Apparent where a Vice-President does not exist or is incapacitated—but during that long period not a constructive piece of legislation bears his name. The future Vice-President was a spectacularly inarticulate representative.

In 1855, Colfax was elected a delegate to the national convention of the Know-Nothings. That might have seemed then an anomaly—a staunch Whig (Republican) flirting with the opposition American party—and Colfax was never able to explain his attendance at the convention. He lamely explained that "I had no knowledge of my election as a delegate," but he attended the convention, sat as a delegate and took a leading part in its deliberations. But it has been noted that Colfax was a strenuous and somewhat unselective "joiner." He withdrew from the convention when he found that his influence with its leaders was negligible.

In Colfax's first term in the House, the membership was so evenly divided that it spent two months electing a Speaker. Two years later, when he was once again up for election, the same situation obtained and, to enliven matters, there were charges of bribery and corruption among the members. One Representative asserted that he had been offered $1,500 for his vote for the speakership, and when that was publicly disclosed a newspaper correspondent was arrested and jailed throughout the entire session of that Congress because he would not reveal his source of information.

Colfax, meanwhile, was mending his political fences back home and gradually becoming a power in the Middle West: he was displaying a remarkable talent at compromise. He had been appointed chairman of the Post Offices and Post Roads Committee of the House. That chairmanship gave him the opportunity to dispense patronage, and he exploited that opportunity to jockey himself into the speakership. It was disclosed later that he had accepted bribes from contractors, and it was proven later that he had accepted $4,000 from an envelope manufacturer presumably for awarding contracts to him on behalf of the Post Office Department. This was not established until long after his tenure of office as chairman of the joint committee—when he was again in trouble, this time over the Crédit Mobilier earthquake.

In 1860, Lincoln was elected President. Colfax had hoped to be Postmaster General, but Lincoln gave the cabinet appointment to another Indianian, Caleb Smith. Smith had been a Whig war horse in the difficult years, and he had been promised the appointment even during the administration of Zachary Taylor, some fourteen years before; and Lincoln felt that Smith was entitled to it for political services performed. Lincoln discussed the appointment with Representative Colfax, and explained that he was young—Colfax was then thirty-seven and Lincoln fifty-one—and urged that in time he would go far with the new party.

Colfax returned to Indiana to run for re-election, and was nearly defeated. His past flirting with the Know-Nothings, his support of Bates for the Presidency over Lincoln before the convention, and his failure to play "regular" with the Indiana delegation in the lower house, were almost too much for his friends to overcome. But he was returned by a small margin and, once in Congress, his seniority gave him a commanding lead for the speakership. In December, 1863, Colfax was elected to the speakership and thereafter re-elected three times. He wrote that at one time Lincoln offered him a cabinet post, and that he refused the invitation; his papers omit, however, to cite the post offered him, and there appears little substantiation, on the historical record, for that assertion.

The speakership is a powerful job in the House, and the man who is elected to it can, under many circumstances, swing legislation affecting millions of Americans, particularly financial measures which under the Constitution must arise in the lower branch of Congress. Colfax took that enormous responsibility indifferently; only occasionally did he step to the floor and make himself heard, and then patently not to offend anyone. He was equivocally opposed to the readmission of the Southern states to the Union, an issue in which he was not the only if-but-and-when member of Congress at that time.

Colfax was unquestionably involved in the Crédit Mobilier fraud. Oakes Ames, entrepreneur of that railroad loan to the Union Pacific and other carriers, perhaps only inveigled him into taking twenty shares of stock. Details of that scandal were confused in the eventual investigation, the report of which was a sort of Mexican standoff. But it was established, in any event, that Colfax had banked more money than he could account for. James A. Garfield, later elected President, was also embroiled in that unsavory scandal, and after the investigating committee of Congress charged Garfield with perjury its report remarked, laconically, that Colfax's testimony "is impossible to believe." Shortly after that inquiry, the matter of Colfax's acceptance of $4,000 from the envelope contractor was revealed.

But Colfax was never brought to trial.

In 1868, it appeared inevitable that Grant would be elected President. The issue was that only of a Vice-President. The Republican convention met in Chicago again, in May, and nominated Grant unanimously. The candidates most frequently discussed and supported for Vice-President were Ben Wade, Henry Wilson, Hamlin again, and Colfax.

In some ways, Colfax was the logical candidate. He had been a supporter of the martyred Lincoln; he had been a loyal member of the party; he had been a strong Union man during the Civil War; he had voted for Johnson's conviction; and he was a veteran campaigner. At that time, the envelope-bribe scandal had not been disclosed and the Crédit Mobilier affair was still unrevealed. Geographically, however, Colfax was not well situated. Grant was from Illinois, and many of the delegates preferred an Eastern running mate for the Presidential nominee. Hamlin had been treated shabbily in 1864, and the leaders of the Republican party had not forgotten the mistake they had committed in passing him over for Johnson. They recognized Colfax's right to the Vice-Presidency but were a little chary after their experience with Johnson. Once more party expediency was the deciding factor, however, and on the fifth ballot Colfax was nominated with a vote of 224 ballots.

Mrs. Colfax had died some years before and on November 18, 1868, Vice-President-elect Colfax married Ellen Wade, a niece of General Benjamin Wade, and a social leader in Washington and Ohio society.

Colfax was then forty-five years of age. He was Indiana's favorite son, had refused the governorship a few years before, and now he had hopes of succeeding to the Presidency.

As Vice-President, Colfax had a strongly Republican Senate

behind him and his duties were agreeable enough. Reconstruction was in progress, the Southern states were being readmitted to the Union and his association with President Grant was amicable. In 1871, Grant offered Colfax the portfolio of Secretary of State, asking him to resign the Vice-Presidency. Colfax refused—he was well pleased at being Vice-President and there was always the possibility of falling heir to the White House. He was not yet fifty and he believed, in all logic, that his chances of becoming President were better as Vice-President than as Secretary of State.

He felt that Grant might not be a desirable candidate in 1872; if so, who was in a better position to succeed to the Presidency than the Vice-President? This reasoning was almost valid: Grant was not altogether satisfactory to the party leaders and many of them favored Colfax as his successor. But the Colfax sentiment did not gain enough momentum and, when the convention met, Grant was renominated by the Republicans, with Henry C. Wilson as his running mate.

Grant had learned of Colfax's plans to succeed him and he knew that Horace Greeley wanted to defeat him, even if he had to run himself. Greeley had hoped to act as a stalking-horse for Colfax and, at the last moment, to throw his strength in the convention to Colfax. Their plans never matured and Colfax found himself without the Vice-Presidential nomination and defeated as well for the Presidential nomination.

Colfax had made a grave political error in 1870 by announcing his retirement from political life. He had hoped for a public clamor that he withdraw that decision but to his embarrassment it was not forthcoming and the voters took him at his word. His luck had run its course. He had become arrogant with newspapermen—a cardinal sin, coming from one of their own fraternity—he was obsessed with the conviction that it was his destiny to be President, and he had listened to poor advice from Horace Greeley and the New York *Tribune* coterie.

Many students of the time are of the opinion that it was this last factor, more than any other, which brought about his involuntary retirement, and that had he bided his time and been willing that Grant finish out two terms, which party precedent provided, he would have been considered the Heir Apparent and would probably have had the Presidential nomination in 1876. Colfax would have been only fifty-three and in all likelihood could have been elected. He had been a political figure for thirty years but at forty-nine, when most men are only coming into their political prime, he was finished. There is no telling, however, for the envelope scandal broke shortly after and people were realizing that there had been too many accusations of corruption and bribery brought against Colfax.

Under a cloud, Colfax returned to South Bend to become a Chautauqua lecturer. He had almost purchased an interest in the New York *Tribune*; Greeley had died, and the owners of the *Tribune* had offered the editorship to Colfax. The deal nearly materialized but Colfax could not raise sufficient capital and an alternative contract did not please him. In addition, the second Mrs. Colfax was adverse to living in New York. Thus Colfax spent the next twelve years as a platform lecturer. He lectured on Lincoln and on behalf of the temperance movement—Colfax was a total abstainer. He was a favorite orator at lodge conventions, Fourth of July picnics, and the like, but he could not again win over the voters. He was asked to run for Congress in his home district but declined. He had betrayed Grant in 1872, he had been involved in the Crédit Mobilier scandal, he had been caught in the envelope deal, and he did not have the courage to begin once more.

He had had a few attacks of vertigo and was advised to discontinue his barnstorming. He would not obey the doctors' orders, however. One cold morning in January, 1885, he stopped at a town in Minnesota and sat down in the railroad station to wait for a train. There he died. The date was January 13.

The United States has furnished many politicians of the Schuyler Colfax mold. He was a good husband and father, a temperate man, loyal lodge member and the most prominent citizen of the community in which he lived. He was inordinately ambitious. He was not always above taking advantage of his position to feather his own nest. He made three cardinal mistakes: he bolted his party and then jumped back into the Republican fold; he attempted to double-cross his chief, President Grant; and he became involved in two malodorous financial scandals.

CHAPTER XVIII

Henry C. Wilson

THERE WERE TWO OUTSTANDING aspects in the career of Henry C. Wilson, eighteenth Vice-President. One was his uncompromising opposition to slavery, although in that he was not alone, of course. But in the second he was entirely alone and fully a half century ahead of his day: he demanded an eight-hour day for New England labor and he was an advocate also of collective bargaining. His neighbors and colleagues believed that Wilson, a small shoe manufacturer, was obviously demented.

On February 16, 1812, one Jeremiah Colbaith was born at Farmington, New Hampshire. He was one of many children whose father was a day laborer in a sawmill. The family was desperately poor and at times there was acute want. There was scarcely enough food and at ten years of age Jeremiah was "bound out" to a farmer for the period of his minority. He was to have food and clothing, and one month's schooling each year. His master was kind to him and young Jeremiah served out his apprenticeship. He wrote that he went to school one month each year and read every book he could borrow during the rest of the year. During the eleven years of his apprenticeship, he read literally thousands of books.

Jeremiah was an industrious apprentice. He served his master well, and when he was twenty-one he was given six sheep and a yoke of oxen, which he promptly sold for $85. He went to his home and received permission from his parents to change his name—for what reason has never been explained. He then went to the state assemblyman from his home district and persuaded that official to introduce a bill which would change his name from Jeremiah Colbaith to Henry C. Wilson. (Presumably the "C" stands for Colbaith.)

Work was difficult to find; the country was in the throes of a depression; and Henry Wilson at last went to the local shoemaker and asked him to teach him to make shoes. In three months he was sufficiently skilled to go into business for himself.

Wilson was a prodigious worker. He would labor long hours and study longer ones. He prospered and in time owned a small shoe factory. He worked hard himself but was a considerate employer. He taught school between the period of learning the shoemaker's trade and starting his own factory, and he took time to make a trip to Virginia and to Washington. In Virginia, Wilson saw the slave markets, and the sight engendered a hatred for slavery which remained with him throughout his life. .

In time, his shoe factory employed approximately one hundred people, and Wilson was particularly considerate of them. He believed in shorter working hours than was the practice then. He advocated an eight-hour law at a time when the factory help in New England labored twelve hours daily. Wilson believed in collective bargaining years before that principle was considered even by the majority of labor. He had been poor; he had been a "bound boy" and had served out his apprenticeship, and he did not forget the trials of the people with whom he was raised. His was not merely a political friendship for labor. He practiced what he preached.

By reason of his reading and his association with others, Wilson developed an interest in politics. In 1840, he was elected to the Massachusetts legislature. He married the same year.

Wilson spent nearly ten years in the legislature as a Whig. During this period he was twice defeated but he persisted and eventually always returned to the legislature, first to the lower house and then to the senate. A staunch Whig, he opposed the annexation of Texas and, in 1848, when Zachary Taylor was the party candidate for President, he bolted and joined the Free-Soilers along with Millard Fillmore and many other Whig leaders, who did not like Taylor's attitude on the slavery issue. Old Rough and Ready was himself a slaveholder.

In 1848, Wilson purchased the Boston *Republican* and served as its editor and publisher until 1851; he converted it into a Free-Soil organ. He was interested in his newspaper work and, like many other politicians then and now, he used the paper as a means of political advancement.

As a state senator, Wilson was largely instrumental in electing the abolitionist Charles Sumner to the upper house at Washington. At this time, he was President of the state senate and his influence was such that he was able to throw the necessary strength to Sumner. Sumner and Wilson were for many years friends and political associates. Later they sat in the Senate together and, when Senator Brooks assaulted Sumner on the floor of the Senate with a cane, Wilson strongly criticized that attack, calling it "a cowardly move from the rear." Senator Brooks challenged his colleague for those words. Wilson said that he would not fight but that he would not retract a word he had said. Friends quieted the matter but Senator Wilson never apologized. (Senator Sumner said that the terrible beating Senator Brooks gave him over the head affected him permanently and that he was never the same afterward.)

In 1854, Wilson joined the Know-Nothing party. This was about the time that Colfax was flirting with the same faction and Wilson as well as Colfax were to regret their association with the secret society which called itself the American party. Wilson was severely criticized by Sumner and his friends for that move; but a year later, when he was a candidate for the United States Senate, it was a member of the American party in the Massachusetts legislature who nominated him to be Sumner's colleague at Washington. Wilson was elected.

At the Capital, Wilson became a leading antislavery senator. When Lincoln was nominated for President at Chicago, in May of 1860, Senator Wilson stumped the New England states in his support. Hamlin, Lincoln's running mate, was a close friend, and the two campaigned throughout the Northern states where Douglas was strongest. Lincoln and Hamlin were elected and Wilson was made chairman of the Senate Military Affairs Committee. In that post he again proved himself a "terrible worker," to cite his associates. He was at his desk day and night and Secretary of War James D. Cameron congratulated him on his devotion. In forty days he recruited 23,000 men in his native state. General Scott said that Wilson, as chairman of the Military Affairs Committee, did more than all the chairmen during the preceding twenty years.

With the war over and after the assassination of Lincoln, Wilson broke with Andrew Johnson. He was active in the movement to impeach Johnson, and was bitterly disappointed when conviction failed. He was the author of the bill creating the Freedmen's Bureau and was an active leader of the radical element in the Senate.

Senator Wilson made a trip through the South to study conditions, and he returned to Washington with an entirely different viewpoint. From that time he was more conciliatory in his attitude toward the Southern states. The change in Wilson's attitude was remarkable in that he was no longer a leader of the Radicals but had become a conservative senator and, indeed, a friend of the South.

In 1872, when President Grant was up for re-election, there were two candidates most often spoken of as his running mate. They were Vice-President Colfax and Wilson, the junior senator from Massachusetts. The incumbent always has the edge in matters of this kind and, under ordinary circumstances, Colfax could have counted on renomination. But Colfax, as has been noted, had not played fair with President Grant. He had sought the

Presidential nomination himself and, as a result, had incurred the displeasure of the President. There was the unexplained Crédit Mobilier affair and the $4,000 which Colfax had accepted while chairman of the Committee on Post Offices and Post Roads from an envelope contractor. To these disadvantages could be added the fact that Senator Wilson was a better candidate geographically than was Colfax. These three factors were too much for Colfax to overcome, and it was soon evident that Wilson would be the nominee.

The convention met and General Grant was nominated overwhelmingly. Schuyler Colfax was advanced as a candidate to succeed himself while the New England delegates offered Wilson.

Wilson won easily and the Republicans snowed under Horace Greeley in the November election. Grant and Wilson polled 286 votes with the Democratic votes scattered among a half dozen candidates.

In March, 1873, Wilson was inaugurated as Vice-President. But he was now an ill man. He was burned out, and he had been the "terrible worker" too long. For a half century he had not slowed down and Nature was beginning to demand payment.

The Senate was no longer the able body it had been for so long. There was scarcely an outstanding man in its membership. The strong men were gone. James G. Blaine was Speaker of the House; Joe Cannon of Illinois came into Congress; and Alexander H. Stephens of Georgia, who had been Vice-President of the Confederacy, was once more a member of Congress. The bitterness engendered by the war was being slowly forgotten. But a sick man was Vice-President, a man with a will but with an exhausted body. On November 22, 1875, Wilson was stricken with paralysis while presiding over the Senate. He was taken to his offices adjoining the Senate chamber, and there he died. He was sixty-three. The Vice-President had worked himself to death.

Little reliable material is available on Wilson's early life. Of his many children there are no records except for one son, who was a lieutenant colonel in a Negro regiment during the Civil War. He was the friend of every man who ever worked for him, or who worked for a living. He was far in advance of his time in his thinking on labor problems, and he was an outstanding chairman of the Senate Military Affairs Committee during the critical years of the Civil War.

CHAPTER XIX

William Almon Wheeler

THE EXPERIENCE OF BEING acutely hungry at one time in his young manhood cast a pall over the career of William A. Wheeler, the nineteenth Vice-President. That experience seemingly engendered some kind of complex which, among other consequences, gave him a marked distaste for the uncertainties of politics, although he was to hold a number of high elective posts. But there would seem to be, throughout the life of this rather obscure American, the haunting fear that at any moment he might again be hungry, and in his papers he several times refers to that obsession—certainly an odd one in a gentleman who became fairly well-to-do.

Wheeler, the least known of all the obscure Vice-Presidents, whose running mate, Rutherford B. Hayes, had to ask his wife in 1876, the year of the election, "Who is Wheeler?" was born in Malone, New York, on June 30, 1819.

He was the only son of an accomplished lawyer, Almon Wheeler, the descendant of a Puritan family of some distinction. The Wheelers had been citizens of substance in the New England colonies for two hundred years. One Thomas Wheeler founded the town of Fairfield, Connecticut. He had come from Concord, Massachusetts, where he had settled in 1637. The future Vice-

President's two grandfathers had served in the Revolutionary War.

Almon Wheeler, father of William, died when the boy was seven years of age. He was beginning to make his name as a leader at the time of his death, but he left his family without means of support. The young mother and widow, born Eliza Woolworth, was forced to take in boarders, most of them students of Franklin Academy, a small school in Malone.

The youth attended the academy and from there he went to the University of Vermont where he spent two years during which time he came perilously close to starvation. He wrote that for six weeks he lived on bread and water and that he was always hungry. After two years of that struggle he left the university and returned to Malone to study law under Asa Hascell. Wheeler had developed an eye ailment in Vermont which prevented him from studying at night.

Wheeler was an earnest law student. Back in Malone, he had enough to eat and made progress in his studies. In 1845, he was admitted to the bar and the same year he married Mary King, a young woman who was to be a great help to him in his later career. But his hunger and hard times at the University of Vermont were to affect his entire life. He became a hypochondriac and on many occasions expressed the desire to retire from public life and "go back to Malone and die." It was Mary King who persuaded him to stay in politics, and it was Mary also, who whipped up his enthusiasm to the point where he would start on another climb up the ladder which she, and not her husband, wished him to climb.

Wheeler was a marked success as a lawyer, so much so that he could retire from his practice and become the manager of one of the banks in Malone. In addition, for fifteen years he was a trustee for the stockholders of the Northern Railway. He was elected district attorney of his home county in 1846 and remained in that office for three years. In 1850 and 1851, he served in the New York State Assembly, and he was a state senator from

1858 to 1861, during which time he was president pro tem of that body.

In 1863, his wife persuaded him to run for the House of Representatives. He had been an efficient district attorney; he had been a loyal Whig and, later, an unswerving Republican, a conservative and hard-working member of the Assembly and the senate and, of more importance to the people of the district, an honest man at a time when simple morality in political life was a somewhat unique virtue.

In 1863, Wheeler was elected to the lower house of Congress by a substantial majority over his Democratic opponent. But he was not then interested in a political career and refused to be a candidate for re-election.

In 1867, New York held its third State Constitutional Convention. Wheeler was sent as a delegate and was elected president of the convention. He did the same meticulously good job which he always did when entrusted with almost any undertaking. His duties as presiding officer of the convention were difficult; he had much committee work to do, and the new constitution of New York in the end was, more or less, a Wheeler constitution. These duties preoccupied Wheeler until 1868, and the next year he was again in Congress. He was appointed chairman of the Committee on Pacific Railways, but was not at any time implicated in the Crédit Mobilier scandal. Oakes Ames vainly attempted to "give him some railroad stock" but he indignantly refused to be a party to any suspect deals and, as has been noted, he was scrupulously ethical at a time when Congress was rampant with graft. When the notorious salary grab bill was passed, Wheeler took his additional salary, converted it into United States bonds, and canceled the certificates.

When Wheeler returned to Congress in 1869, Roscoe Conkling attempted to make him Speaker of the House, to replace James G. Blaine, but he would not be a candidate. Then Blaine promised him the chairmanship of the powerful Committee on Appropriations, a promise he did not keep.

In 1874, Wheeler was appointed chairman of the committee

to investigate the Louisiana elections, and his finding, embraced in the "Wheeler adjustment," settled a dangerous situation that had brought that state to the brink of rebellion. The "adjustment" is the only piece of legislation which bears Wheeler's name.

Wheeler was no orator but he was a good parliamentarian. His experience as president pro tem of the New York state senate and his two years as president of the New York State Constitutional Convention stood him in good stead later when he became Vice-President.

In 1876, the Republican party wanted harmony above all. There were many candidates for the Presidency with Blaine outstanding. The Democrats nominated the brilliant Samuel J. Tilden of New York and named Thomas A. Hendricks of Indiana as his running mate. The Republicans could not agree on Blaine and, in the end, nominated Rutherford B. Hayes, a former governor of Ohio and a Civil War major general; a compromise candidate was Wheeler of New York, and it was then that Hayes asked, "Who is Wheeler?"

Hayes and Wheeler were given 185 electoral votes, Tilden and Hendricks 184. By that narrow margin Wheeler won the Vice-Presidency.

President Hayes appointed two strong men to his cabinet. William Evarts of Massachusetts became Secretary of State and John Sherman of Ohio was appointed Secretary of War. Hayes had hoped to appoint Joseph E. Johnston, the former Confederate general, as Secretary of War, but pressure was brought to bear on the White House against that selection and Hayes compromised by making David Key of Tennessee, also a former Confederate officer, but not so well known as General Johnston, the Postmaster General. Carl Schurz was appointed Secretary of the Interior in reward for his help in the Hayes campaign.

Wheeler presided over a Senate which was again largely comprised of strong men. Blaine had moved over from the House; there were George Hoar of Massachusetts, who was to be a power for many years, Wade Hampton of South Carolina, George Vest of Missouri, John S. Logan, later a candidate for Vice-President, and John Sherman, who resigned his cabinet post to sit again in the Senate. In the House were such men as Garfield, William McKinley, Thomas Reed of Maine, John S. Regan of Texas, who had been Postmaster General of the Confederacy, and Joe Cannon. Men who were to be in power in the nation for forty years were now arriving on the scene.

President Hayes evacuated the troops from the remaining Southern states. He ran into much opposition on the part of the "Stalwarts" in the Republican party, yet, in short time proved to them that he was a man of strong convictions and was determined to re-establish civil government in the states which had seceded. In these labors Hayes was greatly aided by the Vice-President, who had become close to his chief. After Mrs. Wheeler died, in 1876, the Vice-President spent much of his time with the Hayes family.

Wheeler was a staunch supporter of President Hayes in his efforts at civil service reform. He exerted what influence he had in the House and the Senate toward passage of the Civil Service Reform Bill, and again he and President Hayes found themselves aligned against the group known as the Stalwarts. Blaine, Ben Wade, Benjamin Butler, Hannibal Hamlin—all of the Old Guard —were opposed to reforms of any kind and particularly in the ranks of the civil service. The upshot soon was that Hayes and Wheeler were men without a party. The Senate became so violently opposed to its presiding officer that certain senators booed when the Vice-President appeared in their chamber.

Feelings were such that in 1880 Hayes would not consider re-election. For his part, Wheeler had not cared for the Vice-Presidency at the outset and, now that his wife was dead, he wanted more than ever to return to Malone.

The Republicans nominated Garfield for President and Chester A. Arthur, whom President Hayes had removed as collector of the Port of New York, as Vice-President. Once more Ohio and New York carried the Republican party to victory. Hayes went back to his Ohio family to bask in reflected glory as a former President; Wheeler took himself back to Malone.

On June 4, 1887, he died. When his will was probated, it was found that he had left the bulk of his estate to various missions. He had no children, no family, no cronies, and the few intimate friends he possessed were in business and church circles. He had wanted to die for twenty years. The truth is that he never recovered from the sufferings he underwent at the University of Vermont. He never forgot that he had been hungry there. The experience affected his entire outlook.

Wheeler had refused to be bribed when such men as Garfield and Colfax were strongly suspected of accepting railroad stock for their support of certain legislation. Wheeler had refused to be party to the salary grab, he went through life without desire for self-aggrandizement, and virtually every move he made to advance himself was at the suggestion and the influence of his devoted Mary. He was never eager for political preferment and yet he became Vice-President. He was one Heir Apparent who had no desire to succeed to the throne.

CHAPTER XX

Chester Alan Arthur

THE TWENTIETH VICE-PRESIDENT, the only elective office held by Chester A. Arthur, and one from which he jumped to the White House by reason of Garfield's assassination, was perhaps less fitted for the nation's second highest office than anyone before him or since. It is one of those seriocomic incidents of national politics in the United States that he could win the post of Heir Apparent only two years after he had been removed, as unfit for the office, from the lucrative collectorship of the

Port of New York. Aside from that, his chief place in American political history is that of personifying the spoils system.

Arthur was the third Vice-President to succeed to the Presidency by death of the incumbent. He came to the Presidency, as had Andrew Johnson, as a result of an assassin's bullet, which this time struck down Garfield, on July 2, 1881, only four months after his inauguration. Garfield did not die until September 19, and for two and a half months the country was without a President. Arthur could not act as President as long as President Garfield was alive, although too ill to serve.

Arthur was born in Fairfield County, Vermont, on October 5, 1830. He was the fifth child and the eldest son of William Arthur, a Baptist preacher who had resigned from the Episcopal church. The father preached throughout northern Vermont and Quebec, holding pastorates on both sides of the border. This led to a charge, made in 1880, that the future President was not a United States citizen, that he had been born in Canada during one of the periods his father held a pastorate in the Dominion. The charge was made by a New York lawyer and it is altogether possible that there is truth in the claim that Arthur was born outside the United States (which would have made him ineligible for the Presidency). The lawyer, one Hinman, wrote in a pamphlet that an Arthur son was born in Canada and that that one was Chester Alan. He also stated that that son took the date and place of birth of a younger brother who had been born in the United States and who had died in infancy. Hinman asserted further that Arthur made a trip to Canada as late as 1880 to cover up the evidence. The New York *Sun* denied the charges, the family insisted that Chester had been born in northern Vermont and, in the end, the American public showed itself indifferent.

As a child, Chester Arthur shuttled from place to place with his itinerant preacher-father until he arrived at Schenectady, New York, where he attended Union College. Before this he had attended Union Seminary, in the little town of Union, New

York. It was there that the American institution known as the college fraternity came into existence. He joined Psi Upsilon and was, at one time, its national president. He was graduated from Union College in 1848. He had partly paid his way through school by tutoring and, during his last year at Union, he was paid $18 a month to teach in the winter.

From 1848 to 1853, Arthur taught school and studied law; and in 1853, he began to practice law. He went to New York City and became the junior member of the firm of Culver, Parker, and Arthur. The firm engaged in general practice and the young Arthur had the usual number of routine cases. His firm served as defense counsel in various runaway-slave cases and Arthur gained some notice in these suits and in corporation work.

Arthur was a tall, heavy-set man, well over six feet four inches in height. He developed a fondness for extreme clothes. He was a good mixer and a tireless political worker in Whig ranks. He supported General Scott in 1852, when that candidate was roundly defeated by Franklin Pierce for the Presidency. In 1856, Arthur joined the newly formed Republican party and picked a loser when he supported John C. Frémont against Buchanan.

In the period 1854-1860, Arthur established himself as an attorney and a tireless worker in New York Republican circles. Thurlow Weed was the boss and Roscoe Conkling was becoming the boss who would soon succeed him. Edwin D. Morgan was governor and young Tom Platt was gaining in strength and was soon to be elected the junior senator from New York. In 1860, Arthur worked diligently for Morgan in his campaign for re-election as governor and, when Morgan began his second term, he looked around for young men to appoint on his purely orna-mental staff. He picked Arthur, then thirty, as engineer in chief for the state. Arthur was not an engineer and he had no technical training which could possibly have qualified him for the post but he accepted the appointment and wore the resplendent uniform that went with the post; the spoils system was ever thus. Arthur never refused any political position or honor offered him.

The election of 1860 was a disappointment to him. He had hoped to see Seward as President and was much discomfited when Lincoln was nominated. He supported Lincoln and Hamlin, however, and went down the line with the Republican party. But in 1864 Arthur would not vote for Lincoln and said that he would rather be a Copperhead than vote for Honest Abe's re-election.

Arthur took no active military part in the Civil War. Governor Morgan appointed him assistant quartermaster general of the state forces under Cuyler Van Vechten and, when Van Vechten resigned, Arthur fell heir to the post. He did good work in that capacity and was known as an honest administrator, refusing bribes in the form of money, saddles, uniforms, and equipment. During his service as quartermaster general he was active in the defense of New York harbor.

With the war over, Arthur resumed his New York law practice. He was favorably known politically, he joined the leading clubs of the city and was becoming so prosperous that he could afford to purchase a home in the more fashionable part of the city. In 1859, Arthur had married a Miss Herndon, the daughter of a naval officer and a Virginia girl. The Herndons were Southern sympathizers; and brothers and cousins of Mrs. Arthur were in the Confederate service. This circumstance made matters awkward for "General" Arthur, and he had some explaining to do, particularly in view of his strong anti-Lincoln sentiments. Arthur weathered the criticism, however, and tied himself closer to Roscoe Conkling, the red-haired, rabid, and bitter senator who was about to succeed to the mantle of Weed.

Arthur became a member of the Republican Central Committee and eventually its chairman. He worked with Conkling and, when the collectorship of the Port of New York became vacant, Conkling persuaded President Johnson to appoint Arthur to that lucrative post. Next to the President's salary, the compensation of the collector of the Port of New York was the highest-paid government position. His income was based on fees and, during a part of his term as collector, he made more than $40,000 a year.

There were more than nine hundred employees in the department when he assumed the collectorship, and he appointed almost a hundred more. He paid his political debts by appointing friends and thus created a political machine which he expected would keep him in office. Bribery was rampant and while Arthur, as collector, was never convicted of receiving bribes, his lieutenants were notoriously unscrupulous. Little work was done by the majority of the employees and in 1878, when President Hayes's investigating committee made its report, it stated that the "Collector was in the habit of coming to his office never before noon."

In 1876, the Conkling machine, with Arthur as the second in command, was strongly opposed to Hayes's nomination and gave only grudging support to the campaign. Hayes was nominated against its wishes and Wheeler, an upstate man was given the nomination as Vice-President. Since Wheeler was not a New York City man nor one of Conkling's satellites, the irascible Conkling would not support President Hayes during his administration.

Hayes believed in civil service reform and one of his first efforts was to achieve it. He appointed a committee to investigate federal job holders. Its members' first point of attack was on the Port of New York, then with more than a thousand employees. The report was explosive and it caused consternation in the Republican organization in New York City. The entire setup of the collector's office was criticized. Arthur was declared unfit to hold the office and his removal was recommended, along with that of his chief assistants. The office was declared to be full of deadwood. Arthur offered to abide by the committee's recommendations and did discharge some two hundred employees but the committee would not recede from its findings as to Arthur. Conkling came to his rescue and appealed to John Sherman, the Secretary of the Treasury. Sherman was adamant, refusing to intervene, so Conkling and Tom Platt, his upstate henchman, went to Hayes. The President, like Secretary Sherman, could not be influenced and the Conkling machine took a beating. The battle was vicious. Conkling was persistent. He asserted that he alone should control New York City appointments and the collectorship of the Port of New York belonged to him as the head of the New York organization. But one cannot defeat the President if he has courage, and after the smoke cleared Arthur was removed as collector.

His chief assistant was also removed but they both immediately staged a political comeback. The assistant collector, Alonzo B. Cornell, was elected governor of New York and in 1880, two years after he was discharged from the collectorship, Arthur was elected Vice-President.

In 1880, there were three outstanding candidates for President. General Grant was anxious to sit again in the Presidential chair. Blaine, a great orator, whose Catholic mother had inadvertently been the cause of his loss of the Presidency on another occasion—and who would again be a factor in his defeat—was seeking the nomination, with many pledged delegates. Sherman, of Ohio, an able man who had been both senator and Secretary of the Treasury, was the third of the three leading candidates. Garfield was Senator Sherman's manager.

The public had forgotten the Crédit Mobilier scandal and General Garfield was very popular with the ex-soldiers as well as with the rank and file of the Republican party. Blaine had made a strong bid for the Southern delegates by his friendly attitude toward Jefferson Davis, and he had hopes of sufficient strength to win the nomination. In the convention, Grant had three hundred Stalwarts who stood by him throughout twenty-eight ballots. At one point he lacked only seventy votes of a majority. Then his opponents joined forces and on the thirty-sixth ballot Garfield was nominated with 399 votes; Grant received 306, Blaine forty-two and Sherman three votes.

Grant had been nominated by Conkling in an eloquent speech, if one filled with vitriol. It brought Grant's followers to their feet in a prolonged cheer but did not gain a vote. Conkling was always a poor loser and when the convention, in a mollifying humor, offered the Vice-Presidency to him or to one of his choice, he disdainfully refused for himself, and he would not offer a substitute. The Ohio crowd then offered the nomination to Arthur. For once in his life, he refused to abide by Conkling's advice and became the Republican nominee.

The Democrats nominated General Winfield Scott Hancock. General Hancock was an able man but he could not arouse enthusiasm among the voters.

Garfield and Arthur were elected. The Republican party was still in the saddle. They had been in power for twenty years and were to have another four years before Grover Cleveland, a New York Democrat, defeated Blaine in 1884.

Garfield and Arthur were a peculiar combination as President and Vice-President. Garfield represented what were called the half-breeds in the party; they were men who would compromise as compared to the Grant and Conkling Stalwarts. Arthur was a Stalwart and a lieutenant of Conkling's in the Stalwart organization. Garfield had been a member of the House and was definitely implicated in the Crédit Mobilier scandal.

For his part, Arthur was entirely unfit for the office of Vice-President. He had never sat in the House or the Senate and had never been elected to any office. He had held the appointment as collector of the Port of New York and had been removed for "inefficiency." He had been active in the Conkling organization and had aligned himself first with the notorious Weed gang and later with Senator Conkling. It was said of him that he belonged to Weed and Conkling. He was associated with men of little reputation and people came to suspect that he was tarred with the same brush as were his intimates.

As Vice-President, he led the fight for the Conkling appointees and when President Garfield was shot by Charles J. Guiteau, a crazed office seeker who cried, "I am a Stalwart of the Stalwarts," the finger of suspicion was again cast on Arthur and the Stalwarts. Guiteau was convicted of murder. He had only his brother-in-law as counsel and many historians have held that an insane man was hanged.

When Arthur succeeded to the Presidency he brought with him no experience to qualify him for that office. He had been no more than a moderately successful lawyer. The one good account he had given of himself was as quartermaster general of the state of New York, and that had been twenty years ago. His nomination had come as a sop and because the Ohio crowd felt that a New Yorker was needed to balance the ticket.

President Arthur fell heir to a swarm of office seekers. They demanded that he scrap all of President Hayes's civil service reforms. Senator Conkling insisted that all New York appointees be made by him and that he should be consulted by Arthur on the composition of his cabinet—this despite the fact that Conkling had not been returned to the Senate. Arthur made an effort to be a leader but he had a Democratic majority against him in the House of Representatives, with John G. Carlisle as Speaker, and his own majority in the Senate was so small (only two at any time) that he could hope for little assistance from the upper house. He was unsatisfied with the cabinet appointed by President Garfield; it was unusually weak. He replaced Garfield's men with appointees of his own choosing as the opportunity offered. He appointed a Stalwart as Secretary of the Treasury, Charles J. Folger of Geneva. Blaine, the one strong man in the Garfield cabinet, was replaced as Secretary of State by Frederick Frelinghuysen of New Jersey. Benjamin Brewster, an elderly attorney who had been in the government service since 1846, was made Attorney General.

Altogether, it was a mediocre cabinet appointed by a mediocre President.

Former President Grant intervened in the situation. He became a sort of "lord high commissioner" and was so "bossy" with Arthur that the harassed President was placed between the devil and the deep-blue sea. With Conkling to please and Grant to mollify, he never knew which way to turn. The only cabinet member on whom they could agree was Robert T. Lincoln as Secretary of War. Lincoln was a son of Old Abe and they dared not replace him. He was a moderately able Secretary of War and remained in Arthur's cabinet, even though he had been appointed by Garfield.

An interesting event in Arthur's administration was his offer to Conkling of a place on the Supreme Court. Conkling refused. Thereafter, Arthur felt that he had repaid the old man for any debt he might have incurred. Arthur became more independent, and there was a noticeable decrease in Conkling's influence over him, but the change came too late, since the damage had been done.

During Arthur's administration there occurred the Star Route scandals in the Post Office Department. A former carpetbagger senator from Arkansas, one Damey, had been active in the campaign for Garfield and Arthur. He had spent a great deal of money, particularly in the pivotal state of Indiana. Damey joined in a fraud with the Second Assistant Postmaster General. They stole hundreds of thousands of dollars through falsification of Star Route contracts and the ensuing scandal reflected seriously against the President. Arthur was friendly toward Damey, he had sat with him at a dinner in New York, and had made a laudatory speech on Damey's behalf. From newspaper accounts of the time, it might be inferred that President Arthur was under the influence of liquor when he made the speech—it was long, rambling, and incoherent. The President was never accused of receiving any of the stolen funds and Damey was never sent to prison for these thefts, although there were two trials and the administration was openly accused of protecting Damey.

On the credit side of the ledger of Arthur's administration may be put his labors for a large Navy. He interested Congress in re-establishing the Navy, which had so long been neglected that there were only twenty seaworthy vessels.

During the later part of his administration, Arthur became converted to Hayes's conception of civil service reform, and in 1883 he signed a bill strengthening the original act. This move divorced him once and for all from Conkling and the Stalwarts. The year before he had been faced with an off-year election. A governor of New York was to be elected and the President joined in the campaign against Cleveland, who had succeeded Millard Fillmore as the first citizen of Buffalo. Cleveland was elected and in 1884 he was the Democratic nominee for President. The Congressional election of 1882 disclosed a strong Democratic swing. It began to appear that Republican supremacy was to give way to the Democrats, who had so long been only the opposition party.

In 1884, Arthur made strenuous efforts to enter the Republican convention with a sufficient number of delegates to nominate him. With the one hundred votes which the administration controlled in the South, it looked for a time as though he might muster sufficient strength to be nominated. But the tide was against him and, on the first test vote in the convention—that for temporary chairman—Blaine's candidate, Powell Clayton, of Arkansas, was the loser. The South was not yet fully in control of its own politics and as late as 1884 there were a few Negro representatives and one Negro senator from the South.

On the first ballot for President, President Arthur received 278 votes but on the fourth ballot Blaine was nominated with 541 votes, with Arthur receiving 207. Only fifty-seven votes from all Northern states went to the President. John A. Logan, the Grand Army man, was Blaine's running mate and they went down to defeat by Cleveland and Hendricks. Cleveland carried New York by slightly more than one thousand votes.

Arthur was bitterly disappointed.

When Arthur was defeated, he turned his efforts to winning a seat in the Senate. But he could not rally the support of the party organization. Its members claimed that he had not kept faith with them, that he had not given his support to Blaine in the campaign, and that had he shown the proper enthusiasm New York would have gone Republican and Blaine would have been elected. It was shown that seven members of the Arthur family had not voted for Blaine and the "organization boys" would accept no excuses for such dereliction in party regularity.

After Cleveland was inaugurated, the ex-President returned to New York and resumed the practice of law. He was suffering from Bright's disease and on November 18, 1886, he came to the end of his career.

Perhaps the weakest of all Presidents, Arthur suffered continuously from the men with whom he associated. He was a machine politician and one of little ability to command votes. He held only one elective office—the Vice-Presidency. Arthur did not possess oratorical ability; he made few speeches and their merit was their brevity. He could not dissociate himself from Roscoe Conkling and the influence of Damey.

Perhaps the best that may be said of him is that he returned to private life with a fair measure of the respect of a singularly indulgent and gullible public, despite his unsavory record as a political spoilsman on a wholesale scale. In a vein of irony, perhaps lost upon its audience, the New York *World* obituary on Arthur dealt at length with his prowess as a salmon fisherman to the exclusion of his career in public office—presumably on the charitable principle that of the dead, say nothing but good.

CHAPTER XXI

Thomas Andrews Hendricks

THE FIFTH VICE-PRESIDENT to die while in office was Thomas Andrews Hendricks, the twenty-first Heir Apparent.

He was born near Zanesville, Ohio, on September 7, 1819. His father was William Hendricks who came of a substantial Pennsylvania family. His mother was a Jane Thomas, and an uncle had been a representative and twice a United States senator. The Hendricks were staunch Presbyterians and the family life was the typically devout one lived by families in a region then regarded as part of the "Far West."

In 1820, the parents of the future Vice-President moved to Indiana, first to the town of Madison and two years later to Shelby County, where Thomas Hendricks spent the next sixty-four years of his life.

The father became a well-to-do resident of the county. He was able to send his son to Hanover College, after the youth attended Greensburg Academy. He took the regular four-year course at that little Presbyterian college and was graduated in 1841, when he was twenty-one. He had made a reputation as a debater in school and wanted to study for the bar.

In 1843, he began the study of law at Chambersburg, Pennsylvania, where his uncle, Thomas Hendricks, was an instructor, and two years later he was admitted to the bar at Shelbyville. The same year he married Eliza Morgan.

In 1848, Hendricks was elected to the Indiana Assembly as a Democrat. The twenty-nine-year-old attorney showed ability in a day when political skill was often measured in terms of oratory. He was a supporter of the Democratic program nationally and locally. He was appointed chairman of the Committee on Banking and that assignment stood him in good stead in 1850 when he was elected to the State Constitutional Convention; Indiana's constitution had become outmoded and a convention was held to redraft that instrument.

Despite his youth, Hendricks was a leader in the work of the convention and emerged from it a recognized force in the state Democratic party. He was opposed to allowing Negroes to enter the state, but was not proslavery. He wrote the banking plank in the new constitution.

In 1851, Hendricks was a candidate for the House of Representatives and he was elected the year following to the full term. In 1854, the Whigs and the Know-Nothings combined on a fusion candidate and Hendricks was defeated for re-election.

In 1858, President Pierce appointed former Representative Hendricks as Commissioner of the United States General Land Office and he served in that capacity until 1859. This was a key post in the federal service and Hendricks proved himself a capable incumbent. But he resigned the commissionership after a year and returned to practice law in Indianapolis.

In 1860, he was a Douglas Democrat and campaigned throughout Indiana for that ticket. The break in the ranks of the Democrats brought about Lincoln's election and the defeat of Hendricks for the governorship. He had been unanimously nominated as the Democratic candidate for that post but Henry Lane defeated him on this occasion.

In the period 1851-1884, Hendricks was constantly active in Indiana politics. He was a candidate for Congress three times, he was the Democratic nominee for governor three times, he was United States senator in 1863-1869, and he was twice the Democratic nominee for Vice-President. On all these occasions Hendricks' nomination was unanimous. This is a unique record in American political history. In addition to these honors at the hands of his party, Hendricks in 1880 refused the Democratic Vice-Presidential nomination.

The Civil War was going adversely for the Lincoln administration in 1863 and, with Hendricks' personal popularity as an added factor, he was able to defeat the Republican senatorial incumbent by a small majority. Indiana was normally a Republican state but Hendricks alone was able to carry it for his party.

In the upper house, Hendricks soon became the Democratic leader. He was an astute politician, particularly effective in debate, and he led the small band of Democrats at a time when only twelve of them were in the Senate. He supported the war effort and when Vice-President Johnson succeeded the assassinated Lincoln, he led the battle on behalf of the Chief Executive and was the backbone of the defense for Johnson in his impeachment trial (although Johnson, of course, was a Republican). William Evarts, who had been one of the counsel for Johnson, gave Senator Hendricks great praise for leading the fight to clear the President of the charges. Evarts was later elected to the Senate from New York and, on the death of Vice-President Hendricks, he delivered the eulogy at the memorial services in which he said:

"No man appeared better in his composure of spirit, in his

calmness of judgement, in circumspect and careful deliberation, with which, avoiding extreme extravagences, he drew the line which should mark out fidelity to the Constitution, as distinguished from addiction to supremacy of party interests and party passions."

In the Reconstruction period, Senator Hendricks took the position that the Confederate States had never been out of the Union and that they should be treated as states of the Union now that the war had ended. He contended that the leaders of the secession were such as individuals only, and that any punishment meted out should be to them as individuals and not to the states in which they lived. He was opposed to the Emancipation Proclamation, however, and argued in the Senate that freedom of the slaves should come progressively through education and tolerance. He opposed the Thirteenth Amendment (abolishing slavery) to the Constitution on the grounds that the time was unpropitious. When the Fourteenth Amendment was offered (prohibiting abridgment of citizenship rights), Hendricks led his small band of Democrats against its adoption on the argument that the states which were most interested in the amendment, the South, were not represented and that a vote should be held only when those states were represented in the Senate.

He generally upheld President Johnson in his Reconstruction program and insisted that it would have been Lincoln's had he lived.

In 1868, Hendricks was strongly supported by many Democrats for the Presidential nomination. His record was consistent and he had held the Democratic minority together through extremely difficult years. He was not nominated, however, but was again the unanimous choice of the Democrats for governor of Indiana. This time he came within less than one thousand votes of election, and in 1872 he was again the Democratic nominee. In that election he was victorious. He had garnered the temperance votes as well as the always strong Democratic minority.

Hendricks was the first Democratic governor to be elected in the North after the Civil War.

In 1872, Greeley ran against Grant and after the election, but before the Electoral College met, Greeley died. There were sixty-two Democratic votes and forty-two of them were cast for Governor Hendricks, a purely complimentary gesture but an indication of Hendricks' popular standing with the party.

Hendricks was a fairly able, popular, and strong-minded governor of Indiana, and in 1876 he was again favorably mentioned for the Presidency. The nomination, however, went to Tilden of New York. Governor Hendricks was nominated for Vice-President by acclamation and the "crime of '76" then took place, in which the Democrats asserted that the election had been stolen by the Republicans by means of an electoral commission appointed on a strictly partisan basis.

In 1880, when the Democratic National Convention met to nominate candidates, Hendricks was once more in the race for the Presidency, but he was passed over, and again the party offered him the nomination as Vice-President, which this time he refused.

His law practice was profitable and, when well enough, Hendricks was in court. But in 1880 he suffered his first paralytic stroke and he was a long time recovering sufficient strength to allow him to resume his activities. But by 1884 he was champing at the bit like a veteran firehorse, and he entered the lists for the fourth time, seeking the Presidential nomination.

He had polled forty-two votes for President in 1872; he had been the Vice-Presidential nominee in 1876 and had refused it in 1880; and now, in 1884, Hendricks, at the age of sixty-five, and a little uncertain on his feet, made one more effort. But this time it was Grover Cleveland, the governor of New York, who won the grand prize, and for the third time Hendricks was offered the Vice-Presidency.

Finally, he accepted.

Cleveland, partly by reason of his political astuteness, and Hendricks, because of his persistency, defeated Blaine and John A. Logan.

Hendricks was no longer a well man, and he was to serve as

Vice-President for less than nine months. He had failed to recover his strength and during 1885 he spent much of the time at his home in Indiana. But he went to Washington and stood up with Cleveland at the Inauguration. Then Cleveland proceeded immediately to expel virtually every Republican officeholder.

Cleveland and Hendricks had received 219 electoral votes, and Blaine and Logan 172: for the first time in almost a quarter century, the Democrats were able to dispense patronage. Thomas Bayard, the veteran senator from Delaware, became Secretary of State; Dan Manning of New York was Secretary of the Treasury; William Endicott of Massachusetts was named Secretary of War; William C. Whitney of New York was appointed Secretary of the Navy; the Attorney General was former Senator Augustus Garland of Arkansas—the only native of Arkansas ever to sit in the cabinet; the Postmaster General was William Vilas of Wisconsin, and the Secretary of the Interior was Lucius Lamar, an able Mississippian. Congress had provided for a new cabinet position, and accordingly President Cleveland appointed Norman Coleman of Missouri as Secretary of Agriculture.

Cleveland had picked a strong cabinet. Its members were men of experience and strong party adherents. They were no more compromisers than was the President, and the exodus of Republican officeholders became a long procession. The President consulted Vice-President Hendricks on the appointment of the cabinet but it was essentially a Cleveland cabinet. But Bayard and Garland were close friends of Hendricks and it is probable that he suggested those appointments.

On November 24, 1885, Vice-President Hendricks went to a reception in his honor. He complained of fatigue but seemingly enjoyed himself. He returned home late and showed symptoms of illness. He passed into a coma and on the afternoon of the next day he died.

Hendricks was at all times a partisan politician and a conservative, but he was a clear thinker and an excellent political manager. He was "one of the boys," but he was never accused of dishonesty. He led a minority in the Senate at a time when party feelings ran high. If any one man can be credited with saving Andrew Johnson from expulsion, it is Hendricks. His chief speeches were made during his hopeless fight against the Reconstruction Acts. He fought them when he knew that the cause was hopeless. He advised caution and pleaded for conservatism at a time when there was no caution in the halls of Congress and it appeared that all men were extremists.

It is accurate, if not charitable, perhaps, to say that Hendricks stood out in his time at Washington because he was a man of conventional morality and honesty in an era of outstanding corruption and looseness, after the Civil War, that recalls the aroma of the Harding administration. Probably given his career at any other less bizarre period of American history, Hendricks would have been lost in that special hell of oblivion that has been the reward of virtually all Vice-Presidents. But to say of a man that he was honest, at a time when fraud and malfeasance were commonplace, is scarcely the most eloquent political epitaph.

CHAPTER XXII

Levi Parsons Morton

THE TWENTY-SECOND Vice-President, and incidentally the longest-lived, was an Heir Apparent of marked intellectual powers, and of greater financial and economic grasp probably than any of his predecessors or successors. Indeed, he was so far superior to President Harrison, under whom he served, that the contrast was embarrassing, if not downright painful.

He was born at Shoreham, Vermont, on May 16, 1824, and he was ninety-six when he died on his birthday, May 16, 1920. He lived through the Presidential terms of Monroe, who had been an aide to Washington during the Revolution, to that of Woodrow Wilson. His first Presidential vote was cast for Zachary Taylor and his last for Charles Evans Hughes, sixty-eight years later. Not until he was fifty-four years did he enter active political life, and he was elected to office two years later.

Morton was the last of the Yankee-type merchant-bankers, and he became one of the wealthiest men of his time.

Two of Morton's forefathers had been passengers on the Mayflower and there were others who came to America later. Morton once said that the Mortons were all in the colonies before 1650. They had settled in Massachusetts and gradually drifted into what is now Vermont where the Reverend William Morton was a Congregational minister when Levi was born. The Parsons in his name was in memory of a missionary ancestor, and his parents had hopes that Levi would become a missionary or, at least, would enter the ministry.

When he was nine, his father moved to Springfield, Vermont, where the son attended school. From Springfield the family moved to Massachusetts and the youth remained at his studies until he was eighteen. Thereafter he was self-educated. He obtained work in a grocery store where his salary was a munificent $50 a year. He added to this sum by serving as sexton of his father's church. When he was nineteen he went to Hanover, New Hampshire, as a store manager, and he spent a prosperous and happy six years in that college town. While managing the store, Levi boarded with one of the Dartmouth College instructors. In the period between his nineteenth and twenty-fifth birthday, Levi Morton learned the mercantile business.

Morton made money early and engaged in a little speculation. When he was only twenty-five, he had accumulated about $13,-000. He left Hanover for Boston where he became associated with James M. Beebe and Company, leading merchants of the city. He made rapid progress and became so well known that one of the largest New York mercantile firms, George Bird and Company, invited him to become a partner. Bird wanted to withdraw from active participation in the business and, in 1855, Morton went to New York as head of the newly organized firm—at the age of thirty-one. Bird's two nephews, F. B. and W. F. Grinnell, were the junior partners and the reorganized firm was known as Morton, Grinnell and Company, "Wholesale Dry Good and Commission."

Levi now invested $100,000 of his money in the firm. As head, he was a driver and a hard taskmaster. He demanded that each employee work as hard and as long hours as himself and the other partners.

The firm prospered. In 1856, Morton married Lucy Young Kimball whom he had known for thirteen years. She was thirty, thrifty, and politically ambitious for her husband. She sought to persuade him to enter politics but he was not ready and devoted himself to his mercantile interests until 1861, when misfortune struck his company.

The firm had had many dealings with Southern merchants. Collections became so bad, however, that the partners found themselves facing bankruptcy. In 1861, the firm suspended business but settled the claims of creditors on a 50 per cent basis. When the bankruptcy proceedings were concluded, Morton and the Grinnell brothers reopened the business and in less than two years had grown so prosperous that Morton gave a banquet to his former creditors and at each creditor's plate placed a check in full payment.

By 1863, he was the most prosperous merchant of the city. The banking field looked promising, and for the next fifty-seven years Morton was a power in that sphere as head of the Morton Trust Company. His firm made loans, handled bond issues and trust affairs and did considerable business with the federal government in financing the closing months of the Civil War.

Morton opened an English branch of his bank and had as his associate one of England's great financiers, Sir John Rose. The association was successful and by 1873 Morton was recognized, along with J. P. Morgan, as America's leading banker. General Grant had been elected President. Lucy Morton had died and, in

1873, he married Anna Livingston Read Street, a social leader who was deeply interested in the politics of the day.

The Morton firm assisted in the settlement of the Alabama Claims. Its head had become a power in the financial world of both England and America.

Then the political virus assailed him. In 1876, he ran for the House of Representatives from the silk-stocking district of upper Fifth Avenue. He was defeated but threw a scare into the Democratic opposition and in 1878, when he was fifty-four, the banker went to Washington as a member of the lower house. He was a regular Republican and a member of the Tom Platt machine. A man of great wealth, he not only served on finance committees but he could go up and down Wall Street collecting campaign funds. As a member of the House, he made few speeches but he supported President Hayes in his civil service reform movement. He was a friend of General Grant and in 1880 when the general made his unsuccessful effort to obtain the nomination for a third term, Morton was one of his ardent supporters. That year Morton was a candidate for re-election. When Grant failed to receive the nomination, Morton supported Garfield and was active in gathering campaign funds among his banker friends.

The newly elected President was appreciative but would not appoint Morton as Secretary of the Treasury, as the banker had earnestly hoped. Garfield feared unfavorable comment if he appointed a Wall Street banker to the Treasury portfolio. He offered to give Morton the post of Secretary of the Navy. This he refused and requested instead an ambassadorship, "perhaps England or France." This compromise pleased Garfield and his appointment as ambassador to France was offered and accepted.

Morton had been approached before to run for Vice-President with Garfield—a proposal he rejected. The nomination went to Arthur and, seven months after Garfield's inauguration, Arthur was President because of an assassin's bullet. As long as he lived, Morton regretted the refusal he gave to the offer by Garfield's friends, and one may only speculate over the results had the able Morton succeeded Garfield instead of the mediocre Arthur.

Ambassador Morton enjoyed his duties in Paris although he felt somewhat embarrassed when he found that the embassy was situated over a grocery. The government would allow only $800 a year for embassy rent. But he soon established himself in a palatial home, and became a popular envoy. He made friends with men of affairs, he entertained lavishly and was well liked by the French people as well as by the political leaders of the young Third Republic.

In 1881, Morton had made his first bid for election to the Senate. He had failed and, a loyal machine man, he had bided his time. In 1885, Senator Laphan's seat became vacant; the senator had not been a marked success and Morton believed that he could be elected. But William Evarts, a distinguished lawyer, entered the race just when it appeared that Morton's election was assured. Evarts did not suffer from association with the Conkling-Platt machine, and again Morton was defeated. Evarts received sixty-one votes, Morton twenty-eight, and Chauncey Depew three. A young reformer named Theodore Roosevelt had been active in Evarts' campaign.

When Cleveland was elected President, Senator Thomas Bayard of Delaware became Secretary of State. He persuaded the President to appoint his friend, Robert McLane, as ambassador to France. Morton, now sixty-one, came home to be Vice-President. He had been in public life only seven years and looked forward to being President of the United States. Twice he had sought election to the Senate. He was to try a third time and again to be defeated.

Morton was not dependent upon political office for a living. He returned to New York, took a residence on Fifth Avenue and proceeded to build a country home at Poughkeepsie, one of those rococo mansions in vogue in the eighties, resplendent with gingerbread ornaments, turrets, bay windows and chimneys. (He established a purebred dairy and said, "I serve milk alternately with champagne—one costs the same as the other.")

It was in 1887 that Morton made his third unsuccessful try for the Senate. This time he polled thirty-five votes against forty-four for Senator Miller and twelve for Hissock. The voting continued for sixteen ballots. The Miller supporters could not hope to obtain a majority and neither could Morton, with the result that the Morton followers bolted to Hissock, who was elected by a vote of fifty to forty-three for Miller. Morton had been a representative; he was to be governor of New York and a Vice-President, but he always failed of election to the Senate. He had always shown himself to be a regular party man, however, and in 1888 he was offered the nomination as Vice-President. He remembered what his refusal had meant to him eight years earlier, and this time he did not hesitate.

Daniel Webster had been offered the Vice-Presidency. Henry Clay could have had the nomination rather than Millard Fillmore, and Zachary Taylor's death promoted Fillmore to the White House. Morton was not going to reject the offer again. On four occasions the office of President had gone to men who were second choices because the party's first selection had refused to be the nominee as Vice-President.

Benjamin Harrison was the Presidential nominee on the Republican ticket. Grover Cleveland was a candidate for re-election and his running mate was Allen G. Thurman of Ohio. General Harrison was an accomplished orator. He carried the speaking burden during the campaign. In the election, Harrison and Morton polled 233 electoral votes, and Cleveland and Thurman 161.

In 1889, when Morton was inaugurated Vice-President, he was sixty-five, a well-preserved American of broad experience. The Yankee lad, who had been a grocery boy, at $50 a year, was now Vice-President and one of the nation's richest men.

Harrison's cabinet had the perennial Blaine as Secretary of State. William Windom, who had been Secretary of the Treasury under Garfield, was again in the Treasury Department. John Wanamaker of Philadelphia was Postmaster General, and Morton's friend, Benjamin Tracy, of New York was Secretary of the Navy. This was a representative cabinet, stronger than most.

As Vice-President, he showed himself a capable parliamentarian, although without any law experience, and was counted by the Senate as an outstanding success. Thomas Reed was Speaker of the House and ruled that body with an iron hand. But Morton refused to be a dictator; he voted only a few times since the Republican majority was large enough to carry through most of the legislation the party wanted.

In 1892, President Harrison was unanimously renominated, and the New York caucus named Whitelaw Reid instead of Morton as its choice for Vice-President. It appears that labor played a part in the caucus; for example, the influential Typographical Union favored Reid over Vice-President Morton. Reid was nominated as Harrison's running mate, while the Democrats, for the third time, nominated Cleveland with Adlai E. Stevenson of Illinois as their Vice-Presidential candidate.

Again Morton proved himself to be an organization man. He went down the line for the ticket, but in 1892 conditions were reversed and Cleveland won by an electoral vote of 277 while Harrison polled 145. In that election the Populist party had a candidate, James B. Weaver, who polled twelve votes.

Morton left the Vice-Presidency on March 5, 1893. He was sixty-eight, hale, the father of five daughters, all children of his second wife. He had a beautiful home on Scott Circle in the northwest section of Washington.

In 1894, the Republican party of New York presented him as its candidate for governor. He was then seventy but he was an active candidate against David Hill, the Democratic boss of the state, and defeated Hill by a large majority, one of the largest off-year majorities ever given a candidate for governor. His plurality was more than 150,000 and his majority over all candidates was almost 75,000.

On January 1, 1895, when nearing seventy-one, Morton was inaugurated governor of New York. For twelve years the Democrats had been in power and the hungry Republican organization stormed Governor Morton's office for patronage. Civil service was theoretically in force in the state of New York but the organization could always discover ways to circumvent it. That is, its leaders had been able to do so in the past. This time an honest Yankee merchant was governor and the organization raid was defeated. Throughout his entire term, he had fought the politicians even while playing politics; he would trade with Yankee shrewdness but he could not be controlled. Senator Platt, the Republican state boss, would suggest appointments which the aging Morton made, or did not make, as his fancy suited. He did not owe the organization as much as the organization owed him. He had provided the campaign funds too many times, and he made it a point to know where the money was spent. The campaign for governor had cost Morton $19,790 from his own pocket.

As governor, Morton was at his best. He was growing old but he was mentally alert. He was strong of will and determined. He had demonstrated his ability many times as a merchant and banker, but never before had he had a real opportunity to display that ability in his political career, he had never had any illusions as to the powers allotted to the Vice-President. He signed the Raines Law, regulating the sale of liquor throughout the state, and he brought about the passage and signed the bill creating the City of Greater New York. He signed that measure against strong opposition. The mayors of both New York and Brooklyn were opposed to the creation of the enlarged city and brought pressure against the governor to prevent his approval of the bill, but once more the old man showed his Yankee determination. In a few years, the entire state came to approve his action and most of those who had been rabid opponents were loudest in their praise of the consolidation law.

When the Presidential election year of 1896 arrived, there were two active Republican candidates in the field. Both had been governors of their home states. William McKinley had a war record but, on the other hand, Morton had been Vice-President. The factor in McKinley's favor was that he had Mark Hanna as his political mentor and manager. Hanna was a wealthy man and astute. He possessed a faculty for strategy on the grand scale. Campaigns in the past had been managed by a diversity of managers. One man would handle the East, another the South, and so on, thus dividing authority and responsibility. Hanna organized the campaign on a national scale; he had a preconvention campaign fund and spent it lavishly before and at the convention. In New York City he organized McKinley-for-President clubs. He regimented the delegates and kept them in line on every vote at the convention. So great was his control of the convention that on the roll call for the Presidential nomination, McKinley polled 661 votes to fifty-eight for Morton.

Again Morton was offered the Vice-Presidential nomination, and once more he refused.

No other man in the United States history has been offered the nomination three times. Thomas Hendricks had the nomination unanimously at two national conventions and could possibly have had it a third.

As a regular party man, Governor Morton took an active part in the campaign. He was a philosophical loser. He had run for the Senate three times, each time to be defeated, yet he had always lined up behind the standard bearer of the party. This time was to be no exception.

But the governor was tired. He was not eager to be a candidate again for governor of New York and, when the offer of the nomination came, he refused it. He had been an able governor, he had missed being President, which was his one great desire, and now he was content to return to banking.

From 1896 to 1920, Morton displayed little active interest in national politics. He retired to his country home at Poughkeepsie.

The elderly gentleman who had been a poor parson's son, had climbed to the Vice-Presidency and was one of the wealthiest, most respected citizens of the nation, died on his ninety-sixth birthday, on May 16, 1920.

It is idle but nonetheless provocative to speculate on what might have resulted had Harrison died in office, and Morton had succeeded to the White House. He had much the same social and geographical background as Coolidge, who was also a Vermonter, with much the same hardbitten Yankee shrewdness, but beyond that down-East commodity the analogy does not extend. In simple intelligence and social vision, he was as superior to Coolidge as he was to the wheel horse Harrison. With his firsthand knowledge of the economic forces at play in his time, together with a sense of finance that went beyond the till, Morton might conceivably have lessened the catastrophic effects of the panic of 1893 if Harrison had been gathered to his fathers early in his Presidential term—or even if the Vice-President had been able, under the law, to give the nation the benefit of his special talents.

Among the few Vice-Presidents of manifest ability, Morton personified unhappily one of the major follies of the Constitution: that by explicit stipulation the Vice-President, so long as the Chief Executive betrays any sign of sentience, is restricted to functions well within the capabilities of an average high-school sophomore who had spent a few minutes with Robert's *Rules of Order*.

CHAPTER XXIII

Adlai Ewing Stevenson

IN 1892, GROVER CLEVELAND was a candidate for President of the United States. He had been elected in 1884, defeating Blaine. In 1888, General Benjamin Harrison of Indiana had defeated President Cleveland for re-election, but in 1892 Cleveland was a candidate for the third time. He turned the tables on Harrison and, breaking all precedent, he returned to Washington, after an absence of four years, as President for a second term. General Grant had made the same attempt and Theodore Roosevelt was to make a like effort twenty years later.

Cleveland, the slow-moving and hard-headed former governor of New York, was again President from 1893 to 1897.

During this second term, Cleveland had as his Vice-President (and the twenty-third in line) his former First Assistant Postmaster General, Adlai E. Stevenson of Illinois. Stevenson had been assigned the politically agreeable task of ousting 40,000 Republican fourth-class postmasters when Cleveland was serving his first term and when, in 1892, he was nominated for the third time, he was pleased to have Stevenson as his running mate. Stevenson's record was unequivocal, there had been no tinge of scandal on his record, and he was an effective vote getter. (There were the 40,000 postmasters throughout the land who remembered that they owed their jobs to him.)

Stevenson was born in Christian County, Kentucky, on October 23, 1835. The Stevensons came from North Carolina and had been prosperous planters and slaveholders. The mother of the twenty-third Vice-President was Eliza Ewing; and his father was John T. Stevenson, whose father, in turn, had been a patriot during the time when the Marions and the Campbell clan were clearing North Carolina of the Tories.

Stevenson was seventeen when his family moved to Bloomington, Illinois, and he lived in and around that small city for sixty-two years. He attended the local academy; he taught at a country school for a short period and afterward spent two years at Centre College at Danville, Kentucky. The college was a favored seat of learning in the middle nineteenth century. The President of Centre, Dr. Lewis W. Green, was an educator of considerable scholarship, and he had a daughter, Letitia, who later became Mrs. Stevenson. The union of the Greens and the Stevensons took place in 1866 by which time Stevenson had become a prosperous attorney and served also as a master in chancery.

Stevenson spent two pleasant years at Danville but, when his father died, he was forced to leave college and help in the support of the family. Again he taught school and also studied law. He was a conscientious student and in 1858, when twenty-three, he was admitted to the Illinois bar. For ten years Stevenson practiced in the small community of Metamora and he became well known around the circuit. During this period he was state's attorney and master in chancery. His state's attorneyship gave him valuable experience in criminal law. In 1866, he returned to Danville to marry the college president's daughter.

During the period from 1858, when he began his law practice, until 1874, Stevenson was active in politics as a regular Democrat. In 1858, Lincoln and Douglas staged their celebrated debates throughout Illinois. When the pair appeared in Bloomington, the young Stevenson met the Little Giant and became a staunch admirer of the Senator. In 1860, he spoke throughout Illinois on behalf of Douglas in the Presidential campaign.

Stevenson was a strong Union man during the Civil War but he would not change his affiliation with the Democratic party. He organized the 108th Illinois Regiment and, while not himself active in the field, he gave all the assistance in his power to the success of the Union cause. In 1864, he voted for George B. McClellan for President and, although he was friendly with Grant, he would not support him for the Presidency.

In 1874, Stevenson entered the race for the House of Representatives and, with the pendulum again swinging toward the Democrats, he was elected. In 1876, he ran for re-election but was defeated. Two years later he was returned to the House but once again was defeated in 1880.

In Congress, Stevenson was a consistent advocate of a low tariff and a "soft-money man." He did yeoman service for the party and was a popular House member. He was an ingratiating man to meet, and he made friends who were to be of help to him when he was to run as Vice-President. His defeat in the election of 1880 was by a margin of only 242 votes; he then returned to Bloomington and practiced law until 1884, when he met Grover Cleveland, the Democratic candidate for President.

He admired Cleveland, as he had admired Douglas twenty-five years before, and he made an active campaign for him throughout Illinois and for Hendricks, of Indiana. The President appreciated Stevenson's assistance and, in making his appointments, he named Stevenson as First Assistant Postmaster General. The Republicans had been in power for twenty-four years, and

Cleveland proceeded to take over in sweeping fashion. He ousted every Republican officeholder that he could and instructed Stevenson to clean out the Post Office Department. The records show that Stevenson did a thorough job. He performed the purge to the President's satisfaction and Cleveland then nominated him to the Supreme Court of the District of Columbia. But the Senate, which was again Republican, would not confirm the appointment, and in 1889 Stevenson returned to his law practice in Bloomington.

In 1892, Stevenson headed the Illinois delegation to the Democratic Convention, which for the third time nominated Cleveland. Cleveland's first running mate had been Hendricks, and his second had been Allen G. Thurman of Ohio; the third Vice-Presidential candidate to run with him was his former First Assistant Postmaster General.

Again the political tide turned and General Harrison and his running mate, Whitelaw Reid, were defeated. Cleveland and Stevenson polled 277 votes while President Harrison's electoral vote was 145.

Stevenson proved to be no more than a run-of-mine Vice-President. There had been many like him before and since and will be afterward, a fact due in some part to the constitutional limitations of the office.

The Vice-President was fifty-seven when he took office. He was well acquainted in Washington, where he had spent eight years before, and many of the senators over whom he presided had been his friends when he was in the House and in the Post Office Department. He was friendly with the President and made it a policy not to embarrass Cleveland by openly disagreeing with him over the money issue.

Cleveland's cabinet during his second term as President was a strong one. He had not held too closely to geographical considerations. John G. Carlisle, who had been an eminent Speaker of the House, was Secretary of State. Daniel S. Lamont of New York was the Secretary of War. The Attorney General was Richard Olney, a distinguished lawyer from Massachusetts.

Cleveland's close friend, Wilson S. Bissell, was Postmaster General. Hilary A. Herbert, a former Alabama representative, was Secretary of the Navy, and Hoke Smith of Georgia was Secretary of the Interior.

The cabinet members believed with their leader that to the victor belong the spoils, and the exodus of President Harrison's appointees was spectacular. In 1892, as he had done in 1884, Cleveland threw them out in droves. But from 1861 to 1893 there had been only one Democratic President, and there were Republicans in federal offices who had fossilized there. Cleveland had rid himself of as many as possible when he was serving his first term in the White House, and in the four year period, 1893-1897, he completed the exodus with relish.

As Vice-President, Stevenson saw the tariff problem and the monetary question become the dominant issues in American politics. The tariff had been a hotly debated question for almost a century. Old John Randolph had said of the Tariff of Abominations that the "only consolation is that there will be many more tariff bills passed." He was right: there have been many tariff bills enacted, and there will be many more.

During the last years of the nineteenth century, the United States developed into a great manufacturing nation, and industrialists howled for protection for their products. The Republicans became the high-tariff party while the Democrats advocated tariff for revenue only.

By 1896, the country was right for another high-tariff law, and the gold-standard supporters were demanding that a firm stand be taken on the money controversy. Cleveland had been a candidate for the Presidency three times; he had served two terms; and he decided against seeking the office once more. There developed strong sentiment among the Democrats for a free silver plank in the party platform. That agitation came mostly from the Middle West and the mountain states, and when the convention met in St. Louis the fight became so bitter that the gold standard men withdrew and a silver-tongued orator from Nebraska, who had served one term in the House, hypnotized the convention into nominating him for President. William Jennings Bryan was thirty-six, his "Cross of Gold" address swayed the convention, and for the next twenty-three years he was to be the dominant figure in the Democratic ranks.

In March of 1897, Cleveland returned to Princeton to reminisce and fish, while Stevenson returned again to his law practice in Bloomington.

Stevenson supported the Democratic ticket, as he had since 1856, when Buchanan was the party candidate. He had no interest in the Republican administration but he was much pleased as well as surprised when President McKinley appointed him to the Monetary Commission which went to Europe in the hope of establishing international bimetallism. The commission was unable to accomplish anything but Stevenson was its most active member, although the lonely minority member.

In 1900, Bryan again carried the Democratic banner and this time the party brought back Stevenson, the seventy-five-year-old war horse, as the Vice-Presidential candidate. The platform was no longer free silver but the issue now was imperialism, and again McKinley was elected. His running mate was Theodore Roosevelt of New York.

In 1908, Illinois Democrats brought Stevenson out of retirement to pit him against Charles Deneen for the Illinois governorship. So strong was his following, so loyal were his friends and so forceful in speaking was the elderly man that he came within 22,-000 votes of election in a year when the fortunes of the party in the state were at their lowest.

Again the aged veteran of many political battles returned to Bloomington. There he died on June 14, 1914. He was seventy-nine. He was perhaps among the near-great of a nation which has produced a few great and many near-great. An honorable, conscientious, affable and well-liked man was Adlai E. Stevenson—an able vote getter, a man who laid no claims to being Presidential caliber, who was content with the obscurity of the Heir Apparent.

CHAPTER XXIV

Garret Augustus Hobart

THE TWENTY-FOURTH Vice-President, one of the most eminent lawyers of his day and one of the wealthiest, was also the sixth to die in office. (One is tempted to write that the second highest office in the land, while not one involving any hazards of death from overwork, does present the risk of sudden or lingering demise from pernicious boredom.)

Garret A. Hobart was born on June 3, 1844, at Long Branch, New Jersey. His parents were the sixth generation of Hobarts descended from one Edmund Hobart, an Englishman who immigrated to Chatham, Massachusetts, in 1633. Hobart was thus the seventh generation of American stock, descended from substantial men and women, many of whom were influential citizens of their respective communities. He was reared at Long Branch, where his father was a well-to-do businessman, attended the Long Branch schools and, when sixteen, entered Rutgers College. He was a precocious youth and in 1863, when he was graduated, was an honor man in his class. He took special honors in mathematics and English and, in 1864, the future Vice-President began teaching school. At the same time he studied law and in 1866 he was admitted to the New Jersey bar. He had studied with one Socrates Tuttle who took in the young man as a partner.

Hobart, studious and diligent, soon became a leading member of the state bar. He was city attorney of Paterson, New Jersey, and in 1872 was elected to the state assembly. He was speaker of the assembly when only thirty, and in 1876 was elected to the state senate. During the Presidential campaign of that year, Hobart campaigned for Hayes: he was an ardent Republican in national and state politics. Five years later, he was chosen as president of the state senate. He had campaigned for Garfield throughout New Jersey and he was becoming known as one of the leading Republicans of his state.

In 1884, Hobart was a candidate for the United States Senate, but that was the year that Cleveland swept the country and he was defeated together with his party. He was then forty, an able lawyer, and he had built up a sizable fortune from his law practice. Hobart possessed an unusually keen business sense and he was a director in several Paterson banks; eventually, he was interested in more than sixty corporations.

State Senator Hobart was five times a delegate-at-large to the Republican National Convention, and for eleven years was chairman of the New Jersey Republican Central Committee. In 1895, he successfully managed the campaign of his friend, Governor John W. Griggs, who was the first Republican in many years to head the state, and when the Republican National Convention met in 1896, Griggs suggested Hobart as a Vice-Presidential possibility.

The New Jersey delegation went to the national convention without definite instructions to vote for Senator Hobart as Vice-President, but with the understanding that if the opportunity offered, its members would advance his name.

The convention was strongly hard money in sentiment, and nominated McKinley over Levi Morton. Morton had been Vice-President under Harrison, it will be recalled, and he had refused to run for that office again. The convention then turned to New Jersey and Governor Griggs cited Hobart as the logical candidate. Hobart was a gold-standard advocate, and he was a successful attorney, and a wealthy one, who could be of financial assistance in promoting the campaign in the East; he was not nationally known but he had been able to swing New Jersey to the Republican fold for the first time in twenty years. He had never held federal office, but his reputation was the best and shrewd Mark Hanna felt that he would perfectly balance the ticket with "Billy" McKinley.

It was a Republican year. The Democrats were divided on the money question while the Republicans offered a solid front. In addition, it should be remembered that the greatest of all campaign managers, Hanna, was determined to elect McKinley; and as a Presidential campaign manager, the Ohio millionaire remains without a peer in the history of American politics—not excepting James A. Farley.

The Republicans that year could not fail. McKinley and Hobart were elected over Bryan and Thomas E. Watson.

Hobart had been active in the campaign but he made few speeches other than his acceptance address in which he argued that an "honest dollar, worth one hundred cents, cannot be carved out of fifty-three cents worth of silver plus a government fiat." The statement was effectively used in the campaign.

As Vice-President, Hobart became a close friend of McKinley. The Chief Executive valued Hobart's business abilities as well as his legal acumen. The President consulted with Hobart on matters of procedure and used him as a sort of auxiliary Attorney General. With the outbreak of war with Spain, in 1898, McKinley included Hobart in cabinet meetings.

McKinley had appointed John Sherman, grown gray in the nation's service, as Secretary of State. Lyman Gage of Illinois was Secretary of the Treasury; Russell A. Alger was Secretary of War; Joseph McKenna of California was the Attorney General; and John Long was Secretary of the Navy. A young politician from New York, Theodore Roosevelt, finally won the post of Assistant Secretary of the Navy.

During the war with Spain, Vice-President Hobart presided over the Senate with fairness and dignity. He was an expert in parliamentary law and he was well liked by the large Republican majority in the upper house. As usual, the Vice-President had little to do. He had no part in the food scandals which forced Alger out of the cabinet and brought in Elihu Root as Secretary of War. Vice-President Hobart voted against independence for the Philippines—the only vote of importance he cast during his term as Vice-President (the incumbent of that office votes only in the case of a tie).

Hobart presided over the Senate during its sessions from 1897 to 1899. He was known intimately to but few of its members, since he had never sat as a member of either the House or the Senate. He was generally esteemed, however, but he had few close friends in Washington. At times he would drive to the White House to be with the President and his semi-invalid wife. McKinley admired his intellectual abilities but he also frankly respected Hobart for his wealth. The President had never been well off and he was continually in need of funds. McKinley had long been in debt, and once was almost a bankrupt, and when he began the campaign for the Presidency, Hanna paid his debts so that he might run free from imminent bankruptcy.

During the summer of 1899, Hobart was in poor health. He returned to his home in Paterson to recuperate but he failed rapidly and on November 21 of that year he died, at the age of fifty-five.

Garret Hobart was one of three wealthy men who were Vice-President—the others were Dallas and Morton. Like those two, Hobart played at politics as an avocation. He was one of the most successful lawyers of his time, an organizer of and counselor to many enterprises. He was a leader in many civic and church activities in his community, and his name usually headed the list of benefactors of hospital and charitable campaigns.

McKinley was re-elected in 1900 with Roosevelt as his running mate. With McKinley's assassination, Roosevelt fell heir to the White House. Had Hobart lived, American history might have taken another turn. As it was, he was merely another Vice-President.

CHAPTER XXV

Theodore Roosevelt

THE EMINENCE OF A LATER Roosevelt has somewhat overshadowed much of the dynamic qualities and the mental vigor of the twenty-fifth Vice-President and twenty-sixth President of the United States. In the view of much of posterity, "Teddy" is rather cloudily recalled as the flamboyant commander of the Rough Riders and as a big game hunter, both of which were comparatively inconsequential episodes in his long career in the public service. Generally overlooked is the fact that Americans are in his debt for much enlightened legislation today in the fields of civil service reforms, conservation of national resources, government regulation of corporations, colonial policy, improvements in the Army and Navy—and perhaps for his greatest achievement—the daring and drive with which he pushed through the construction of the Panama Canal.

Roosevelt, who was Vice-President under McKinley for less than seven months, and President for more than seven years, was born in New York City on October 27, 1858. This branch of the Roosevelts had been Americans and New Yorkers for more than two centuries. There were many of them and they intermarried so often that many of them had difficulty knowing what kin they were to one another. They had come from the Netherlands in 1644 and had lived in and around New York since that time. They seldom migrated to other parts of the country; the father of the future Vice-President and President was the seventh generation of Roosevelts who had known New Netherlands as their home. This Theodore Roosevelt was a well-known and well-to-do citizen of the city. He had married a Martha Bullock of

Georgia, and of that union there were two boys and two girls. The second child and first son was called Theodore.

He was a puny, weak-eyed and asthmatic youngster whose childhood was preoccupied with natural history and who "prepped" for Harvard. He entered Harvard when he was eighteen and in 1880, when he was twenty-two, he was graduated with honors. Due to his weak eyesight and his asthma, he had been unable to engage in college sports, although he did do some boxing, which eventually cost him an eye.

Theodore's father had been appointed Civil Service Commissioner by President Hayes, but influence was brought to bear on the Senate by Roscoe Conkling and the then young Tom Platt, and the Senate refused to confirm the appointment. The next year the elder Theodore Roosevelt died and young Teddy was left a considerable fortune, in addition to a small annuity, which came to him monthly. It was perhaps well for the young man that he could spend his annuity only as it came to him. He took $50,000 of his inheritance, however, and went to the Dakotas where he invested the entire amount in a cattle ranch. The open life on the range and the life he led while there did much for his health.

For two years, Roosevelt more or less played at being a rancher. He soon lost almost all his capital and when the novelty of the range palled, and with his money gone, he returned to New York City.

In 1882, Roosevelt was elected to the New York State Assembly where he remained for two years. He was a frequent speaker on a number of subjects, although his voice was then high-pitched and prone to break at the peak of oratorical fervor. Young Roosevelt was lively "copy" for the newspaper reporters, and he was by no means shy of publicity. He could be interviewed on any subject and he quickly became a source of interest, color, and caricature to the press.

In 1884, Roosevelt was a delegate to the Republican National Convention, where he made an effort to block the nomination of Blaine. He was a strong supporter of George Edmunds but when

Blaine was nominated, Roosevelt supported him and saw him defeated at the hands of Cleveland. With reference to his support of Blaine after his strenuous effort to prevent his nomination, the New York *World* commented that "it was a most remarkable performance in the crow-eating line."

Roosevelt was a candidate for mayor of New York City that year and was third in a field of three candidates. He was grievously disappointed that the people of New York apparently did not take his candidacy seriously.

Roosevelt had done some writing before his entry into politics. He had written *The Naval History of the War of 1812* and *Thomas Hart Benton,* and during the period 1884-1886 he devoted much time to writing history, to articles on hunting and to works on natural history. His lifetime literary output was tremendous.

Mrs. Roosevelt was wealthy and with her husband's small competency and such royalties as he received from his writing the family lived in ease and comfort, if not in luxury. Mrs. Roosevelt was and is a woman of marked ability, and it was her business acumen that carried the family through such financial difficulties as arose. Roosevelt's valet once said of him that it was to Mrs. Roosevelt that he always went for any consultations on business matters, and that "Mr. Roosevelt had no business sense."

In 1888, Roosevelt supported Harrison for the Presidency and, when he and Morton were elected, he importuned both gentlemen to appoint him to some federal office. He frankly wanted a "big one," but he was willing to "take anything offered." President Harrison obligingly appointed him civil service commissioner, the same post to which President Hayes had appointed his father twelve years before. With this appointment, the Roosevelts moved to Washington. They kept open house and came to know the Republicans well. Roosevelt made much of his rather unimportant job but at this time he was never quite within the inner circle.

In 1892, the Democrats returned to power. Cleveland was inaugurated on March 4, 1893, and he did not get around to ridding himself of the civil service commissioner until a year later. The Roosevelts then returned to New York and Mayor William L. Strong appointed Roosevelt to a seat on the Police Commission. For two years he was Police Commissioner of the city, a resounding title but then a relatively unimportant post. It was written of him that he was "overzealous (and) accomplished little."

In 1896, he supported McKinley for the Presidency and when he was elected over Bryan, Roosevelt immediately presented himself for the expected reward and asked to be appointed to a federal post again. This time he had the potent support of Senator Henry Cabot Lodge and the Platt organization. Lodge, who had a genuine liking for the thirty-eight-year-old Roosevelt, persuaded Hanna to allow McKinley to appoint Roosevelt as Assistant Secretary of the Navy.

John D. Long of Massachusetts was McKinley's Secretary of the Navy. Long was a political appointee and was more interested in the political aspects of the secretaryship than in his cabinet duties. This suited Roosevelt perfectly. He was able to be boss. He issued orders in his chief's name. When the U.S.S. *Maine* was sunk in Havana harbor in February, 1898, Roosevelt became a jingo. He agitated for immediate war and when Congress declared hostilities he was in seventh heaven. In the absence of Secretary Long from his office, Roosevelt issued orders to the Navy personnel. He cabled Admiral George Dewey to "see that the Spanish fleet does not leave the Asiatic coast, and then begin offensive operations in the Philippines."

In May, 1898, Roosevelt resigned his post as Assistant Secretary of the Navy. He had met Captain Leonard Wood, an Army Medical Corps officer, who was also a Harvard graduate and who had a flare for military tactics. With Wood, Roosevelt organized the First Volunteer Cavalry, later to be known as the Rough Riders. They were not cavalry, however; they did not ride, and Roosevelt was not the commanding officer. Wood was the colonel of the regiment and Roosevelt, who was the lieutenant colonel, was to have less than two months actual military service in the war with Spain. His regiment was a part of Major William R. Shafter's army. The Rough Riders were dismounted and fought throughout the brief hostilities as an infantry unit. Roosevelt made the usual mistakes amateurs make in warfare, and it was General Joe Wheeler's regulars and the Negro troops who saved the day at El Caney and Kettle Hill. General Wheeler was desperately ill and had himself carried to the battlefield on a stretcher from which he directed the army to victory. But Lieutenant Colonel Roosevelt had found himself a horse, and he galloped up and down shouting orders. A regular army officer said afterward, "There were possibly 1,100 men in the Rough Riders, and I have personally known 15,000 of them."

Teddy Roosevelt returned from the wars to Montauk Point and was a signer of the famous round robin which scathingly denounced army conditions. He was not a regular army officer, he did not plan to remain in the service, and he had nothing to lose. The round robin provoked a mild scandal in the army but there had been so much inefficiency and bungling during the war that one more scandal did not create much stir.

The country was ripe for a hero, however, and Teddy was not reluctant to fill that role to the hilt. He had a good friend in Richard Harding Davis, who boosted and served him as his personal press agent with the end result that Teddy, with his campaign hat turned up at a rakish angle, soon became the hero the country demanded.

In the fall of 1898, he was a candidate for the New York governorship. Platt did not relish Teddy as the candidate, but the popular demand was so great that he gave way and Roosevelt, at forty, was elected governor and was now on his way as a national figure. His opponent in that race was Augustus Van Wyck, a former mayor of New York City, against whom Roosevelt campaigned with his characteristic dash. He stumped the state with his Rough Rider companions; he coined catch phrases by the score, and eventually he bested Van Wyck by a small margin.

A few days after his inauguration, Governor Roosevelt received a visit from Senator Platt. The two apparently patched up any differences between them.

There has been much debate over who was the real governor during Roosevelt's administration, and it would seem that there is room for argument. Platt was at all times a complacent boss, and if he did control Roosevelt it was not with any iron hand. He certainly made many "suggestions" to Roosevelt, and sometimes the governor was amenable and again he was not. But it would appear that Roosevelt was governor in fact, and that the elderly senator was a sort of friendly adviser. Between them they pushed through the legislature several important measures, particularly the tax on corporation franchises and the bill strengthening the government of New York City.

In 1900, it was definitely known that McKinley was to be renominated. The only question was over his running mate. Platt wanted Roosevelt as the Vice-Presidential nominee. He felt that the Vice-Presidency would be the safest place to put the "young" man and said that "he will do less damage there than any other place we could put him"—an apt comment on the nondescript character of that office. The President and Hanna did not want him as McKinley's running mate. They were frankly afraid of Roosevelt; they feared that he would steal the limelight from "Billy," and Hanna felt that he could not control the ebullient governor of New York.

Old Senator Matthew Quay of Pennsylvania was an ally of Platt's and between them they persuaded Hanna that the Vice-Presidency would be an ideal spot to shelve Roosevelt. That argument proved convincing in the end, and the ticket was eventually McKinley and Roosevelt, with the adroit though aging Hanna again the campaign manager. He elected McKinley and Roosevelt over Bryan and Stevenson.

The new President and Vice-President were inaugurated on March 5, 1901, and for five days only Roosevelt presided over the Senate as Vice-President. Before the Senate met again, President McKinley had died of an assassin's bullet, and Roosevelt was in the White House.

For the five days that Vice-President Roosevelt presided over the upper house, he conducted that body as though it were a high-school debating society. He was frankly partisan, he was nervous and irritable and even the kindly Chauncey Depew said that "he lacked the impartiality, equitable temper and knowledge of parliamentary law to be a good presiding officer." He appeared to treat every Republican motion as necessarily a sound motion because it was of Republican origin. He was a source of merriment to senators of a humorous turn of mind, but he was a worry and threat to the more sedate.

The Senate was in session from March 5 to March 9 for the purpose of passing on Presidential appointments, and it was only for those few days that Roosevelt presided. He had little experience in parliamentary law and none as a presiding officer over a deliberative body. He never had another opportunity.

Irrespective of what some biographers have written, McKinley did not like Roosevelt and, in turn, Roosevelt had a cordial dislike of the President. Roosevelt once said of McKinley that "he has a chocolate eclair for a backbone." For his part, McKinley is reported to have said of Roosevelt that he was "a smart aleck, a rough and uncouth person."

During the summer of 1901, Congress was not in session, and the Vice-President spent most of his time at Oyster Bay. In September he went to the Vermont woods as the guest of his friend, Governor Murray Crane of Massachusetts. President McKinley meanwhile paid a visit to the Centennial Exposition at Buffalo and on September 6, while attending a reception at the Temple of Music, he was shot by a Polish anarchist, Leon Czolgosz.

The Vice-President was quickly notified, and he prepared to go to Buffalo, but he was advised that there was no need for him to make the trip as it was believed that the President had not been seriously wounded. On September 13, however, the President became worse due to an infection, and on the next afternoon he died.

The Vice-President hurried to Buffalo and, while the nation mourned over the martyred McKinley, Theodore Roosevelt was sworn in as President of the United States. Soon afterward he promised to "continue, absolutely, the policies of President McKinley for the peace, the prosperity and the honor of our beloved country."

He retained McKinley's cabinet and, while President McKinley had had no definite policy, Roosevelt made an effort, for a time at least, to follow what John Hay believed would have been McKinley's policy had he lived. Hay had been Lincoln's private secretary; he had been ambassador to Great Britain; he was McKinley's Secretary of State, and he was a writer of reputation. He had known President Roosevelt's father, and he had known Teddy when he was a boy of ten; always, when he looked at the President, he saw not the man but a little weak-eyed, spindly and sniffling child of ten. The truth is that Hay could never take Roosevelt seriously.

For the years from 1901 to 1909, a rollicking, happy, rough-shod gentleman was President of the United States. It can fairly be said that Roosevelt was the only President who heartily enjoyed that grueling office. But he kept his eye on the main chance, and looked forward to 1904, when he hoped to be President in his own right. He promised, if elected, that he would not seek reelection, but would consider his seven years as two full terms. He lived to regret that commitment, and always felt that he had promised too much.

Under Roosevelt, the White House became a center of gaiety. The Roosevelt children were youngsters and it was a lively and interesting place in which to live. Roosevelt had a host of friends. He maintained close ties with his old Rough Riders. He gave them jobs and, when necessary, he got them out of jail. He entertained them in the White House as freely as he did ambassadors and other diplomats. They were invited to lunch rather than to dinner, since many of them were somewhat vague over the conventional use of knives and forks.

President Roosevelt played a good deal of tennis. He made close friends of the diplomatic corps, and he had what he called his "Tennis Cabinet." He was inclined toward snap decisions, and thus was guilty of a good many errors. His chief cronies were the British ambassador, Spring-Rice; the French ambassador, Jules Jusserand; and the German envoy, Speck von Sternberg, as well as the British historian, James Bryce. He made it a point to call the cabinet members by their first names, as did the later Roosevelt. He was at this time forty-three, and these cronies of his were mostly in their sixties, but he treated them as though they were young men, and they played up to the buoyant Teddy.

France had been struggling with the Panama Canal for twenty years. She had had her best engineers on the project and, while they could conquer the engineering problems involved, they could not overcome the weather conditions and the plague of mosquitoes.

For many years, the United States had been interested in a canal connecting the two oceans. No one will ever know exactly what happened. In any event, Panama staged a "revolution" on November 3, 1903, and thirty days later the United States recognized her independence from Colombia and offered Colombia, which had charged the United States with instigating the Panamanian revolt, the sum of $4,000,000 as an indemnity for her rights to the canal route. The offer was refused but nevertheless United States Army engineers went to work. Colonel William C. Gorgas cleared the canal strip of the pestilential mosquitoes, and the work went forward.

President Roosevelt had directed all of this without the consent of Congress. Roosevelt said that "I took the Canal Zone and let Congress debate and, while the debate goes on, the canal does also." Perhaps that was not accomplished under conventional rules, but the United States acquired a canal and, seventeen years later, Congress appropriated $25,000,000 to assuage Colombia's feelings. This was done in 1921, during the Harding administration, and in the meantime the canal had earned millions of dollars for the United States and had shortened the sea route to the West Coast from the Atlantic by more than 6,000 miles.

The United States intervention in Santo Domingo was another such incident as occurred in the construction of the Panama

Canal. President Roosevelt sent emissaries to take over the finances of the little republic without consulting Congress and, incidentally, Congress did not approve the move until 1907, three years after it had occurred.

Roosevelt had prepared carefully for the 1904 campaign. He had never been over friendly with the "Morgan crowd," and indeed had conducted his trust-busting campaign chiefly against them, but in 1904 he invited two leading Wall Street financiers, J. P. Morgan and E. H. Harriman, to the White House. The President had an amiable visit with them and the two men left Washington with kindly feelings toward the administration and a promise from the President of fair treatment in the future. The result was that money immediately was pumped into the Republican coffers, and George B. Cortelyou, the campaign manager, was able to report to the President that he was as good as nominated.

The convention met. Roosevelt was nominated on the first ballot. His running mate was Charles Fairbanks of Indiana, who had played some part in the campaign but who was to play little part in the administration which followed.

The Democrats nominated Judge Alton B. Parker, of New York, for the Presidency, and Henry G. Davis, a former West Virginia senator, for the Vice-Presidency. Senator Davis was eighty-one. Very wealthy, Davis had been expected to make a large contribution to the party treasury. But he refused to contribute and said he was too old to campaign. He was a bitter disappointment to the Democratic party at a time when its fortunes were at the lowest ebb in its history. (Davis, incidentally, was the oldest candidate to run for the Vice-Presidency.)

Roosevelt was elected by a large majority: now he was President not by act of God, but in his own right.

For eight years little attention was paid over the genesis of the campaign funds to elect Roosevelt, but in 1912 a senatorial investigating committee brought forth some interesting facts and figures regarding the contributors and the amounts they gave to keep Teddy in the White House in 1904. More than $2,000,000 was raised for the Republican campaign. Of that amount, 72.5 per cent came from big business leaders who could hope to receive favors from the government. Of the total funds collected, Wall Street raised $1,500,000. President Roosevelt said naïvely that he had not known who contributed to his campaign. Cortelyou, his manager, was an exceedingly forgetful witness, but finally acknowledged that the New York Life Insurance Company gave $48,000; the Mutual Life Insurance Company, the same amount; the Equitable Life Insurance Company, ditto; J. P. Morgan, $150,000; Edward T. Stotesbury, of Philadelphia, gave $165,000; George Gould, $100,000; C. S. Mellon, the Pittsburgh banker, $25,000; and the Standard Oil Company, $125,-000.

The day of March 5, 1905, was brisk and cold. The Rough Riders were out in force. They tied their horses to the hitching-posts of Washington's many saloons; they whooped and hollered, but they did not shoot up the town, as they would have liked, because the "Colonel" had pleaded that they refrain from boyish pranks.

President Roosevelt's second term began auspiciously. He had appointed Elihu Root as Secretary of State; William Howard Taft was Secretary of War; the Secretary of the Treasury was Leslie M. Shaw, to be followed by Cortelyou; the Attorney General was Charles J. Bonaparte. There were in succession five Secretaries of the Navy, William H. Moody being the first; Garfield was Secretary of the Interior; Commerce and Labor was headed by Cortelyou, the subsequent Secretary of the Treasury; and James Wilson was Secretary of Agriculture, a holdover from McKinley's administration.

During the first years of Roosevelt's second term, prosperity was more or less general throughout the nation. McKinley had been elected in 1897 on a "full dinner-pail" platform, and relatively good times continued for the first part of Roosevelt's term. Then the coal strike occurred and was long in settlement: it contributed to the panic of 1907.

There had been excessive speculation, like that to come in

1924-1929; life insurance companies had gambled unconscionably in land acquisitions, the financial structure generally had been stretched too thin, and the inevitable collapse came in the summer of that year. Banks in great number failed when runs on savings began, and the New York Stock Exchange closed temporarily; the farm-mortgage situation, particularly throughout the Middle West, grew acute with foreclosures a commonplace, gold payments were suspended and bank script was used in place of hard money. But two years later the panic was forgotten, with the characteristic American resiliency, and again prospects of renewed prosperity were in evidence.

President Roosevelt sent the Great White Fleet around the world. It left Norfolk in September of 1907 and returned in February of 1909. The long cruise was ordered by him without reference to Congress, and it was not Roosevelt's Congress but that of President Taft's which was eventually handed the bill for the purely Rooseveltian junket. Credit must be given him, however, for a daring and picturesque undertaking.

In 1908, Roosevelt was sorry he had rashly promised not to seek re-election. He was not yet fifty, and he was frankly worried what he would do when he ceased to be President. But he picked William Howard Taft as his successor. Taft possessed a fine judicial mind, he had little desire to be President, and he would have preferred an appointment to the Supreme Court, which, of course, he afterward received. But he bowed to Roosevelt's ostensible wishes and he was nominated at the convention which Roosevelt dominated.

For the third time, Bryan was nominated by the Democrats and again waged a losing fight—the perennial candidate. Taft was elected with "Sunny Jim" Sherman, of New York, as his running mate.

Roosevelt had hoped to be the power behind the throne during Taft's administration, a sort of President Emeritus. He was much surprised and pained when the big, good-natured President developed an astonishing amount of resistance and promptly rejected Roosevelt's "suggestions" as to cabinet appointments.

The former White House occupant soon had to realize that he was only a past President, and that he had to look elsewhere than to Washington to use his abundant energies. He had expectations that he might become president of Harvard, since President Eliot had resigned. He was disappointed, and made that disappointment plain, when he was passed by for Dr. Abbott L. Lowell. He looked into the senatorial situation but received little encouragement, and then thought seriously of becoming a candidate for mayor of New York City: party leaders were cool to that project.

Roosevelt was an active, energetic man, and he had to do something, if no job in the limelight was open or offered. He then decided on a hunting expedition to Africa, had a "bully time," and world-wide publicity in the course of it. In the nick of time, King Edward VII of Great Britain died while he was en route home, and President Taft appointed Roosevelt as a special ambassador to represent the United States at the funeral. The restless former President was made enormously happy at the appointment, and he had a joyous time hobnobbing with royalty at the fearsome obsequies.

When he returned to the United States the same year, in 1910, he had expectations of replacing Taft, and he began making preparations to that end. There was a hitch in his plans, however. He could not convince the Republican Old Guard that he was indispensable: they were well satisfied with Taft and leaders felt that the party owed him the renomination. Senator Lodge and Root, the Secretary of State, who had for long been Roosevelt's friends and supporters, turned a deaf ear to Roosevelt's arguments.

But Roosevelt was determined.

Lodge and Root, astute politicians, were prescient gentlemen. They easily stacked the convention against him to the point where his delegates bolted and formed the Progressive party, a third-party faction: an infallible method thus far to lose an election.

The Roosevelt-controlled Progressive Convention met in August, 1912. It nominated Roosevelt for President, of course, and Hiram Johnson for Vice-President. The Democrats picked Woodrow Wilson, a former president of Princeton University and governor of New Jersey, for the Presidency, and Thomas R. Marshall of Indiana, governor of Indiana, for Vice-President. Roosevelt may have had some small satisfaction of splitting the Republican vote, which he certainly did with overwhelming success. Wilson was elected; Roosevelt ran second; and Taft followed afterward.

Roosevelt had the congenital itch for action. He went back to Long Island, after writing three books and many magazine articles, and then laid plans for an expedition to South America and the then unexplored upper reaches of the Amazon. He was fifty-five. The expedition was overstrenuous for him. He had been blind in one eye, as a result in part of a friendly bout while President. His hearing was defective and rheumatism was another annoyance. His companions up the Amazon were fearful that he might not survive the expedition, but he discovered the ostensible headwaters of a River of Doubt. Several of his contemporaries made the obvious remark that they doubted the river existed and that, if so, they doubted Roosevelt had discovered it.

He returned home to be confronted with the appalling excitement, to him, of the World War. He was a national figure and, for all the physical handicaps with which he had begun life, Roosevelt was full of fire and ginger. He was strongly interventionist, and in April, 1917, when the United States entered the holocaust he promptly became an ardent and vocal patriot. He conceived the idea of recruiting another Rough Riders, consisting this time of artillery, cavalry, and infantry, with himself as the major general commanding. And why not? He was a mere fifty-nine.

He went to Washington and saw his distant cousin, another Roosevelt, who was Assistant Secretary of the Navy and who was married to his niece, Eleanor. Franklin Delano Roosevelt directed him to Newton D. Baker, the Secretary of War, who in turn led him to President Wilson.

President Wilson was full of admiration, but he declined the offer of a volunteer regiment raised by Roosevelt because he judged, correctly, that he was physically incapacitated, and General Pershing added that Roosevelt would be only a disrupting element: doubtless an accurate judgment.

Roosevelt was compelled to fret out his life as a bystander. He raised Liberty Loans and led parades throughout the country, but his health was failing. The dynamic Teddy one day sent for his Negro valet, and asked to be taken to his bed. On the night of January 6, he went to sleep, and a colorful and vigorous American, handicapped at birth, did not see the sun rise.

His was a complex character. Physically weak from birth, he built himself into a rugged, healthy, and energetic individual. He possessed intellect, which is sometimes called the art of thinking, and in his writing he had bounce and an eye on his audience. Aside from those highly rare qualities, he had enormous personal charm and magnetism.

It is another of the clowneries of American history that Theodore Roosevelt became one of the Heirs Apparent primarily because Senator Platt, the Republican boss, regarded him as too hot a potato in New York state politics, and as a man who endangered Platt's bossism. Platt was astute in the extreme and, to defeat Roosevelt's passion to succeed himself at Albany, he and Hanna decided to kick the gentleman upstairs into the limbo of the Vice-Presidency, if they could. They were successful in that immediate objective.

But the end result of that demotion was that Roosevelt, after taking the "Vice Presidential veil," as he told friends, and girding himself for the appalling boredom of that office, moved soon into the White House: he had suffered only a few days of ornamental impotency as the presiding officer of the Senate.

To a generation which has forgotten him, it should be said that Roosevelt was a man of unflagging vitality, of physical and moral courage, and of some thoughtfulness. He had the strength of his convictions, which by no means were always those of big business, and of a vivacity of manner and speech that alarmed conservatives, one of whom he undeniably was. He had a disarming but calculated passion for the limelight, and perhaps for the occupant of the White House, from whom leadership must be expected (it is so stipulated under the Constitution), just enough histrionics to appeal to the mass of the electorate.

In an era in which the United States, geographically and economically, was becoming a major world power, he fired the imagination of the country, doubtless immorally. In a later day, his Big Stick aphorisms were to sound puerile and unrealistic, if not suicidal. But he was incontestably head and shoulders above any of his Vice-Presidential predecessors, however briefly he served in that pigeonhole. The odds being what they are against any outstanding behavior of a Vice-President, it would seem a safe wager that he will keep that posthumous distinction. He had the rare luck of the Heir Apparent, and he arose to the occasion with excitement and dash.

CHAPTER XXVI

Charles Warren Fairbanks

IT HAS CERTAINLY BEEN SEEN that the office of the Vice-Presidency is usually tantamount to a one-way ticket to nowhere. That is true, of course, because of the Constitutional limitations placed upon it, and because of the necessary geographical considerations of national politics every four years. In the instance of the twenty-sixth Vice-President, that was made more fearfully evident because the incumbent of that restless office was driven completely out of sight by the pyrotechnics of

243

President Roosevelt. In the period 1904-1908, few of the tax-payers knew a Vice-President existed: Charles W. Fairbanks was almost the man nobody knows.

Fairbanks was the last of the log-cabin national nonentities. He was born in a one-room shack in Unionville Centre, Ohio, on May 11, 1852. He was a descendant of Johnathan Fayrebanks, who settled in New England in 1633. In early New England days, names were often spelled phonetically, and often members of the same family wrote their names in bibles, on wedding certificates and albums in any odd way they liked, or sounded most pleasant to their ears.

The father of the future Vice-President was one Loriston M. Fairbanks, whom his son describes as a "New Englander of good family," who went from there to Ohio "to become a sound Abolitionist." The son wrote that he could remember the shack as one stopping place for runaway slaves on their "underground" trip from the South to Canada.

Fairbanks was proud of his ancestry, he records, and he was mindful that he was a descendant of Puritan stock. All of his traits, manners, clothes, and thin smile were those of a Yankee.

He studied in the Unionville Centre schools and worked his way through Ohio Wesleyan University from which he escaped further punishment at the age of twenty. After his graduation, Fairbanks labored for several months for the Associated Press and studied law meanwhile, which will make most newspaper-men today wonder how it can be done ambidextrously, and reach the Heir Apparentcy.

In 1874, he was admitted to the Ohio bar. It appeared to the young barrister that Indiana was a more suitable climate to hang his shingle than Ohio, and he hurried to Indianapolis. He remained there for the next forty-four years. He became a well-to-do railroad attorney and, when only thirty-six, his corporation clients were so numerous he had to give business down the street.

Fairbanks was now showing an "interest" in politics although saying insistently he was not an office seeker. He managed the candidacy of Walter Gresham for the Presidential nomination on the Republican ticket. Harrison was nominated over Gresham and, despite that overwhelming defeat at the convention, Fairbanks supported the Republicans as long as he was a public figure.

For the next eight years, Fairbanks practiced law and became eminent in his field, and he made many friends among the Republican leaders. He was well acquainted with Hanna, who, in 1896, selected him as the keynote shouter at the St. Louis convention which nominated McKinley. The next year he was a candidate for the United States Senate, and was elected. In the following eight years he built such a well-oiled political machine that, next to Hanna, he was boss of the Republican party throughout the nation. He was the undisputed boss of the party in his own Indiana, of course and, because of his closeness to McKinley and Hanna, he controlled the political patronage of Indiana.

In the Senate, Fairbanks supported McKinley in both his foreign and domestic policies. He was a member of the Committee on Foreign Affairs. The President appointed him chairman of the Joint Committee to adjust the differences then existing between the United States and Canada. The work of the committee ended in failure because the disagreements over the Alaskan boundary were such that a decision could not be reached in the several months that the committee labored.

In 1902, Fairbanks was re-elected to the upper house, and two years later he was nominated for Vice-President as the running mate of Theodore Roosevelt. He was active in that campaign, speaking in thirty-two states, and traveling more than 25,000 miles on behalf of his party. Roosevelt was elected, and Fairbanks remained in the Senate as its presiding officer.

As Vice-President, Fairbanks was so overshadowed by the dramatic Teddy that he was little known outside the corridors of the Senate. Roosevelt did not believe he had much ability (which the President believed generally true of everyone but himself), and he had evidently little appreciation of Fairbanks' strenuous work during the campaign. For his part, Fairbanks was not overly enthusiastic about the capabilities of Roosevelt.

From 1909 until his death in 1918, Fairbanks held no political office. During 1909-1910 he took a trip around the world and was ceremoniously received as a former Vice-President.

In 1912, Roosevelt was a candidate for the Republican Presidential nomination. Fairbanks was chairman of the party's platform committee and, as such, a power in the convention. He was one of the drivers of the steam roller which efficiently crushed Roosevelt and his supporters. During the campaign he supported Taft and, when his friend Thomas R. Marshall was elected Vice-President, he returned to Indianapolis to resume his law practice.

He kept in contact with his political associates, however, and in 1916, when Justice Charles Evans Hughes was the candidate against Wilson, the Republican party nominated Fairbanks as his running mate.

With his defeat and that of Hughes by Wilson, Fairbanks lost interest in national politics. He had been an experienced campaigner, he had never been defeated for office until 1916, and he did not relish his defeat. He felt that had the campaign been conducted along the lines of Mark Hanna, he would have again been Vice-President.

In 1908, 1912, and 1916, Indiana had presented Fairbanks as its favorite son for President. Each time he had given way in the interests of party harmony. He lived to see the start of the first World War, but he was aging and his interest in public affairs was waning. He died at Indianapolis on June 4, 1918, at the age of sixty-six.

CHAPTER XXVII

James Schoolcraft Sherman

THE TWENTY-SEVENTH Vice-President presents the depressingly familiar picture of the machine-made politician elected to a post from which he may fall heir to crushing responsibilities far beyond his capabilities.

In 1908, Taft was the Republican nominee for the Presidency. He had been named by Theodore Roosevelt as his successor. That year, Roosevelt was the Republican party in himself, and his word was law. To placate some influential leaders of the Old Guard, the convention named James S. Sherman, of New York, as the Vice-Presidential candidate. Sherman, who had been a member of the House of Representatives for more than twenty years, and who was known as "Sunny Jim" to his associates, was to be promoted to the Vice-Presidency.

Despite his long service in the lower house, Sherman had not sponsored a single act of importance. A onetime mayor of Utica, he had been a member of several House committees, and he had been a loyal party worker. He was little known outside the congressional corridors and, when he was a candidate for Vice-President, many voters undoubtedly confused him with the Ohioan of the same name, then several years dead.

Sherman was born near Utica, New York, on October 24, 1855. His father was Richard Updike Sherman, and he was the seventh in descent from Philip Sherman, who had gone to the Massachusetts Colony in 1633 and who settled later in Portsmouth, Rhode Island. His father was a newspaper editor and a staunch Democrat. He had supported the Democratic ticket and had been a strong backer of Cleveland. He had held a number of appointive positions in the state and federal governments, and could not tolerate the humiliation that his son was a Republican.

Sherman's grandfather was Willard T. Sherman, a well-to-do glass manufacturer of upstate New York. He was graduated from Hamilton College in 1878. He studied law with his brother-in-law, H. J. Cookingham, with whom he practiced for many years. He specialized as a business adviser and did little trial work.

Sherman turned to politics early in his career and from 1884, when he was elected mayor of Utica, until his death in 1912 he was always in politics, most of the time as an officeholder. He was only twenty-nine when he became Mayor. He was popular in that post and, in 1887, the Republicans elected him to the House where he spent two terms. It was during these four years that Sherman associated himself with the Tom Platt machine and became a loyal run-of-the-mill Republican representative. He was defeated in 1890 but was returned to the House in 1892 and was continuously a member until 1909, when he became Vice-President.

In 1895, Richard Sherman died, and the son succeeded his father as president of the New Hartford Canning Company. In 1900, Sherman organized and became president of the Utica Trust Company. The financial enterprise prospered and with that interest, the canning concern and his membership in Congress, Sherman was Utica's leading citizen.

Sherman became strongly attached to Tom Reed, czar of the House of Representatives. Reed returned the friendship and, while he was Speaker of the House, he made it a rule to appoint Representative Sherman the Speaker pro tem when he was absent from the chair. Sherman later was a candidate for Speaker at one session of Congress, but was beaten by "Uncle Joe" Cannon.

In the House, the only movements he sponsored were the project to lay a cable to the Philippine Islands, an act to reform and rejuvenate the Revenue Cutter Service, and a bill providing for United States construction of the proposed Nicaragua Canal.

In 1906, Sherman served as chairman of the New York Republican Convention. He displayed ability as the presiding officer, and it was here that his boom for Vice-President was born. The party knew that unless the unforeseen occurred, Taft would be the Presidential nominee and, by right of precedent, the Vice-President should come from New York. Sherman had always been a regular party man, he was dependable, wealthy, and an untiring campaigner. When the time drew near for the national convention, Sherman was made chairman of its congressional committee and handled that assignment satisfactorily. During the Presidential campaign, however, charges were brought that Sherman had diverted certain campaign funds to his own benefit —that is, to his own congressional district; he was also charged with having been interested in a "dummy" oil company to exploit Indian lands. To these charges Sherman gave no answer— refusing, he said, to become party to any political mudslinging. Nothing came of the charges and when the convention met, the ticket was Taft and Sherman. The convention was a tame affair compared to that of the Democratic party, where William Jennings Bryan was again nominated.

Taft and Sherman were elected and "Sunny Jim" moved over from the House to the Senate. He was an excellent presiding officer—not so surprising perhaps since he had been trained by the master, Tom Reed. He knew parliamentary law as have few Vice-Presidents, and there have been few more able presiding officers of the Senate than the affable gentleman from Utica.

But Sherman did little of a constructive nature as Vice-President, even within the confinements of that office. It was evidently sufficient to be a regular Republican. He had supported the ticket from Hayes to Taft, and "Sunny Jim" remained the same wheel-horse Republican while Vice-President. He was well liked by the senators and he was a favorite in Washington society.

In 1912, President Taft was renominated at the historic Chicago convention after Roosevelt was beaten off, and Sherman was again Taft's running mate. The campaign was hectic. There were three major tickets in the field. Roosevelt made a lively campaign as the Bull Moose standard-bearer, and it soon became evident that the Republican party was split so that there was no hope of victory for either. The realization grew that the reign of the Republican party was over and that once more the Democrats would ride to victory. From 1860 to 1912 there had been only one Democratic President: Grover Cleveland had been elected twice, but for forty-four years the Republican party had been in control of the nation. For eleven terms of four years each, there had been a Republican President backed by a Republican Congress. At times the majority had been small but always when it came to a vital issue the party could control Congress.

The long Republican reign ended in 1912. Woodrow Wilson was elected.

Sherman did not live to see his own defeat. He died on October 12, 1912, only a few days before the election at the age of fifty-seven.

Sherman was a product of the Republican machine of New York. He was a follower of Roscoe Conkling and later of Tom Platt. He was prosperous, clever, and ingratiating. He was never a great lawyer and by no means an outstanding man, but it is just to say that he was a better than average parliamentarian. He was the last Vice-President as of this writing to come from New York, "Mother State of Vice-Presidents."

CHAPTER XXVIII

Thomas Riley Marshall

FOR MORE THAN EIGHTY years, no man was re-elected Vice-President of the United States. From John C. Calhoun to Thomas R. Marshall, there were twenty Vice-Presidents, each of whom served only a single term. Early in the history of the nation there had been four Vice-Presidents who were re-elected—Adams, Clinton, Tompkins, and Calhoun—but for the next eighty-four years no man had been successful in being returned to that office.

Marshall, who served as the twenty-eighth Vice-President under Woodrow Wilson from 1913 to 1921, was not only particularly successful in that post, but he was unquestionably the most popular man who ever sat in the chair. He violated all the orthodox rules governing a political career. He had held no public office before his election to the governorship of Indiana. He had had no experience as a presiding officer, yet he was a most successful parliamentarian. But Marshall displayed good sense when elected Vice-President. He went to the secretary of the Senate and had him designate the parliamentary clerk as his assistant until he became accustomed to his duties as presiding officer.

Because of that precaution, Marshall avoided the mistakes most Vice-Presidents have committed when first discharging their duties as President of the Senate, and he avoided the pitfalls into which most presiding officers are led by scheming senators who delight in embarrassing the novice.

Marshall was born on March 14, 1854, at North Manchester, Indiana. His father was a country doctor. When the son was two, his father moved to Illinois where he practiced medicine for six years, and from there the family moved again, this time to Kansas.

In Illinois, Marshall wrote he was taken to hear the Lincoln-Douglas debates and he added that he was "informed" that he sat on both Lincoln's and Douglas's knee, sitting on one orator's knee while the other spoke. Marshall became a great admirer of the Little Giant and later of Samuel J. Tilden and, following in the footsteps of his father, he was at all times a staunch Democrat. While in Kansas, Dr. Marshall became too outspoken in his criticism of lawless elements, and he was forced to flee the state. He moved this time to Lagrange, Missouri, and thence back to his native Indiana. He settled at Crawfordsville where the son first attended the town schools and later went to Wabash College.

Marshall was graduated from Wabash in 1873 and he wrote that he received his diploma but "I have never seen it since." When he had but two weeks to go before graduation, he was threatened with expulsion as the leader of student strike. When brought to trial as the spokesman for the "strikers," he dared the faculty to expel him and his followers. The faculty took no action.

He studied law with Judge Walter Olds, of Fort Wayne, and on his twenty-third birthday he was admitted to the bar and began his practice at Columbia City; there he practiced law for thirty-four years. Marshall spent many happy and contented years in the little city, became its outstanding citizen, a member of the Presbyterian church, a Sunday-school teacher and a thirty-third degree Mason. He wrote that as far as he knew he was the only lawyer in the United States whose name was Marshall and who did not claim descent from the celebrated Chief Justice.

Marshall made many influential friends throughout Indiana. He was a leading Democrat in the northern part of the state and was once sought as the party's nominee for the House of Representatives. He refused to be a candidate and, when asked to give the reason for his refusal, he answered, "I am afraid I might be elected, and I don't want to be a Congressman."

Marshall had cast his first vote for Tilden, the New Yorker who ran against Hayes in 1876. The young man took the defeat of Tilden to heart and thought, as did many people throughout the land, that Tilden had lost the election because of unfair tactics by the Republican party.

In 1908, the Democrats of Indiana sought a candidate who had a chance of beating Governor Hanly. Thomas Marshall had said that he "would like to be Governor," so they nominated him and more important, succeeded in electing the little bushy-haired lawyer at a time when Democratic victories were the exception. Marshall later said that the reason for his nomination came "through the inability of the leading candidates to obtain a majority of the votes in the Convention, and so they nominated me." Marshall stumped the state tirelessly. He delivered 169 speeches and he remarked, Mrs. Marshall insisted that "I did not make 169 speeches but one speech 169 times, and that she could say it backward and forward."

In the 1908 Presidential year, Taft carried Indiana but Marshall was elected governor with only two or three other Democrats to state offices. He had campaigned on the platform of city option as against county option on the liquor issue, and on the need of a new state constitution.

Marshall was an able governor of Indiana. He treated both capital and labor fairly. He refused to order out the militia to protect the quarry owners in a strike, and gave as his reason that "no strike breaker, brought from Chicago, could prove that he was a quarry man" and that he "would not protect thugs and hoodlums from decent citizens of the state who were striking for what they thought was right." He did call out the militia, however, to drive out bookies and the race-track touts who had swarmed into Indiana from Chicago.

In 1912, Wilson was nominated for President at the Democratic Convention held at Baltimore. Champ Clark, of Missouri, Speaker of the House of Representatives, at one time had a majority of the votes for the nomination but could not muster sufficient strength for the necessary two-thirds majority. William Randolph Hearst had been a strong supporter of Clark and much bitterness resulted from Bryan's final speech in the convention in which he bitterly attacked Clark and his association with Hearst. This was Bryan's last bid for power in the Democratic party.

When the time came to nominate a Vice-President, the convention spent little time deciding on Governor Marshall.

The Republican party was hopelessly split and, in consequence, Wilson and Marshall were elected by a large majority in the Electoral College. The poll showed 435 electoral votes for Wilson and Marshall, eighty-eight for Roosevelt and Johnson, and eight votes only for Taft and Sherman. The combined popular vote of Roosevelt and Taft was larger than that polled by Wilson, but they were so scattered that Wilson received the majority in the Electoral College.

Marshall went from Indianapolis and the governor's chair to sit in the seat of the Vice-President at Washington. He had seldom been in Washington; he had never been in the Senate chamber; and he knew few members of the Senate other than those from his native state.

In his *Recollections*, Marshall told many amusing incidents of his life as Vice-President. He told of being guarded by the Secret Service and of telling its men, "No one would ever take the trouble to shoot a Vice-President." He referred to himself as "His Superfluous Excellency" and laughed over the innocuous life he led.

Despite the fun he poked at his post, Marshall made an excellent Vice-President and an able presiding officer over the Senate. He overcame the natural animosity which the members of the Senate have for a stranger in their midst. With the aid of the parliamentary clerk, he was soon proficient at his duties. He came to know and like the members of the Senate personally. He sincerely wanted to be a conscientious Vice-President, and he was. The Senate came to like and admire the diminutive gentleman from Indiana. Its members knew that he was fair, that he bore no animosities and that, being an able lawyer, he carried no ill feeling off the floor.

Marshall felt a sincere friendship for President Wilson. He knew that Wilson was a cold and analytical individual, that "he was more brains than heart," yet for eight years he consulted with and followed the advice of his chief. He also was friendly with Secretary of War Newton D. Baker and William G. McAdoo, Secretary of the Treasury. He admired many of the senators who were his political opponents and in his *Recollections* he paid tribute to many of them.

In 1913, Marshall predicted that within five years the nations of the world would be engaged in deadly war. Many senators scoffed at that prediction and asked him what kind of liquor he had been drinking.

During President Wilson's first administration, the country had been kept out of the World War and it was on that platform that he campaigned for re-election. Charles Evans Hughes, a former governor of New York and Justice of the Supreme Court, who afterward was to be Secretary of State and Chief Justice of the Supreme Court, made an active but inept campaign for the Presidency. The Republican party very nearly carried the country but, due to Hughes's lack of political adroitness, the Republicans lost.

Vice-President Marshall devoted all of his energies to the war effort, once the United States was involved. He was an able assistant to President Wilson and did everything in his power to keep the Senate in line. He did not approve of President Wilson's appeal to the country for a Democratic Congress. Marshall would have preferred an appeal only to patriotism and he so told the Chief Executive, but when the President made that plea he went along with him, as he always had.

When President Wilson suffered a physical and nervous breakdown, Vice-President Marshall might have been appointed Acting President had he insisted on the letter of the Constitution. He was loyal to Wilson, however, and refused to entertain the suggestion when it was advanced by members of the Senate. He had followed the President through all of his trials and he could not be a party to any semblance of disloyalty in his last great fight.

In 1920, Governor James M. Cox of Ohio was nominated by the Democrats for the Presidency and a thirty-eight-year-old New Yorker, Franklin Delano Roosevelt, was his running mate. The Republicans nominated Senator Warren Gamaliel Harding of Ohio for President and the dour-faced governor of Massachusetts, Calvin Coolidge, for Vice-President. Vice-President Marshall had known Senator Harding as a member of the Senate but made no mention of him in his *Recollections*.

The Republicans returned to power. Woodrow Wilson left the White House to spend a few short years as an invalid and to die an embittered idealist. Marshall went back to Indiana, a little grayer and not quite so straight as he had been eight years before, but the same dapper, blue-eyed, well-groomed gentleman who had been a Washington social favorite, the friend and crony of diplomats and senators, and the best-liked man official Washington could remember.

He returned to his law practice and he wrote his *Recollections* —entirely from memory; he spent some time on the lecture platform; he was a popular and amusing speaker and he wrote that he even "made some money." He had led a busy life and in later life he made it a point to keep busy. In 1925, he made a trip to Washington, and on June 1 of that year he died.

Marshall's entire philosophy is summarized in the foreword to his *Recollections*. He wrote that "this book is not intended to turn the tide of history nor change the opinions of men as to the great things which took place when I was in public life. It has been written in the hope that the tired businessman, the unsuccessful golfer and the lonely husband, whose wife is out reforming the world, may find therein a half hour's surcease from sorrow." *

He was a refreshing character in American public life.

Of all his quaint and amusing observations, perhaps the best remembered is that made when, wearying of a flatulent debate in the Senate, he turned to the clerk at his side and said out of the corner of his mouth, "What this country needs is a good five-cent cigar."

CHAPTER XXIX

Calvin Coolidge

CALVIN COOLIDGE, SHREWD Yankee who became the thirtieth President by the accident of death and who climbed to the twenty-ninth Vice-Presidency by playing unbelievably astute politics for thirty years, was born in Plymouth, Vermont, on July 4, 1872. He was a typical down-East son of a down-East family although history has little to say of the Coolidges. They were respectable farmers, storekeepers, selectmen, council members and state legislators. George Washington wrote of a "Widow Coolidge" who ran a tavern at which he spent a night during his "grand tour," and he reported in his diary that it was a "dirty place." However, no family connection can be established, and the tavern is mentioned here only as evidence that there were Coolidges in the New England colonies in Revolutionary times.

John Coolidge, father of Calvin, kept store in Plymouth. He had been a member of the Vermont legislature and at one time was a state senator. He became well-to-do and a leader in his little community. There was a daughter, Abbie, who died in early childhood. These two children were John's only family; his wife died when Calvin was six. After the death of Abbie, the father and son kept house with the aid of a hired girl. Calvin attended the village schools and later Black River Academy in Ludlow. Here he spent four years and his only outstanding achievement was his regular attendance. He took the Amherst College entrance examinations but failed them and returned to prep school, this time to an academy at St. Honsbury. The next year he passed the entrance exams and the then nineteen-**year-**

old, red-haired, slender, sour-visaged, and somewhat prissy youth became a student at Amherst, together with some four hundred other young men from New England.

"Red Cal" Coolidge was not popular at Amherst; for one thing, he was not an athlete. He was not a particularly good student. He was lonely, made few friends and had few interests other than his school work. He paid $3.50 a week for his board, at a private home, since he was not a member of a club.

There were many fraternities at Amherst. Coolidge did not make one of them until his senior year. For three years he was an "Ouder," sometimes called a "Barb," but in his last year at Amherst he received a "bid" for Phi Gamma Delta, a new fraternity which had lately established a chapter at Amherst. Asked if he would like to become a member, he simply said "yes" and the chapter elected him; he had waited three years to be asked. He was always a patient waiter.

During his last year at Amherst, he carried five subjects: debating, English, philosophy, history, and Italian. One wonders why he took up Italian. He made a "C" in Italian and history and a "B" in the other three subjects. His philosophy instructor was Professor Charles A. Garman whose influence was to be a lasting one.

John Coolidge had remarried while Calvin was in college. The father wanted Cal to be a merchant, perhaps a druggist, but the youth shrewdly asked his Congregationalist father, "Would you like for me to sell rum, Father?" Cal was not to become a druggist.

A classmate at Amherst was Dwight Morrow, later a Morgan partner, ambassador to Mexico and father-in-law of Charles A. Lindbergh. Morrow was an outstanding student at Amherst and was said by his fellow students to have been the brains of the class. Somewhat oddly, he was friendly with Coolidge and that intimacy lasted throughout their lives.

When he was graduated from Amherst in 1895, Coolidge talked over his future with young Morrow, and when Morrow bluntly asked him where he planned to study law, he said

"Northampton is the nearest Court House." Coolidge crossed the state line to Massachusetts and began his law studies in the office of Hammond and Field. There he was as uncommunicative as ever; he sat in silence while the partners discussed their cases—the average cases in the average town, cases which a none too prosperous lawyer would have in a town of 30,000. In time he was admitted to the bar, obtained a room in the second ward of Northampton, which was strongly Republican, and opened a law office. He became a member of the Republican Committee and promptly began running for office, since a public career offered less hazards financially than did private practice.

Coolidge was to be an inveterate office seeker. He ran for office twenty times in his sixty years of life and was defeated only once. His batting average was .950, which is very high in any league.

Coolidge was to become a city councilman, city solicitor, mayor, state representative, state senator, court clerk, lieutenant governor, governor, Vice-President, and President. He was defeated only for the post on the school board of Northampton. His few friends protested that his defeat was due to his having no children in school at the time. William Allen White, who wrote an excellent life of Coolidge, *A Puritan in Babylon*, reported that his defeat resulted because, in Northampton, Coolidge was known as a politician, and Yankee voters did not relish the idea of a political school board.

At this time Coolidge practiced a little law. He became counsel to the local brewer and he got other brewers out of jail when they were in trouble. He was abstemious; he drank one glass of beer a month, he smoked five-cent cigars, and he was known to be an honest and thrifty young man; and for the rest he consistently played at politics. Coolidge was a dyed-in-the-wool Republican. He could never see anything but evil in the Democratic party and, when President, he refused to appoint Democratic judges, even though so urged by Chief Justice Taft. He maintained that equally able Republicans could always be found.

As city solicitor of Northampton, Coolidge attended to the

business of the municipality in a painstaking manner. He had a comfortable salary as court clerk. He made a good mayor of the city and he was a wheel-horse Republican in the state legislature. In that body he was not a member of any major committees; he looked after Northampton's interests, and he rode the day coach to Boston, commuting home over the week ends. He had a room in a second-rate hotel. When possible he took his lunch with him to the legislature and patronized the restaurants only when that was unavoidable. He kept a bottle of whiskey in a drawer and doled it out sparingly: he did not drink it himself.

As a state senator, Coolidge moved into a higher legislative bracket. But he kept the same room in the hotel and frequented Lucey's Shoe Shop, as he had for many years; he patronized the same barber; he continued to drink his monthly glass of beer in the same saloon; and after a period of this routine he considered himself ready to run for lieutenant governor.

Massachusetts politics were then divided not only as between Republicans and Democrats, but the Republican party was divided between Murray Crane as the leader of the Western faction, and Senator Henry Cabot Lodge as the leader of the Eastern wing.

Early in his political life, Coolidge had become a follower of Senator Crane. The Senator was a millionaire paper manufacturer, a man of considerable ability who saw possibilities in the tight-lipped, noncommittal, sandy-haired Northampton lawyer. He assisted Coolidge in his lieutenant governorship campaign, and the Coolidge luck held.

In 1917, the United States entered the war against Germany and the now forty-five-year-old senator from Northampton stepped up another bracket and was elected lieutenant governor of the Commonwealth of Massachusetts.

At this time the governor of Massachusetts was Samuel McCall, a learned and able man who was eager to become a member of the United States Senate. He encouraged Coolidge to run for governor and, with the aid of Murray Crane, Tom White, an astute politician, and the Boston merchant, Frank W. Stearns,

Coolidge became governor of the state in 1919. In that year came the Boston police strike. It was this event which made Governor Coolidge a national figure. Before that strike he had simply been one of forty-eight governors in the Union. He had been mentioned as a possible Vice-Presidential candidate and, some say, even as a Presidential candidate in 1916. When Senator Lodge heard of this he said, "Coolidge—my God!" The same senator remarked in 1920, "I have only known Calvin Coolidge as long as I have had to." Three years later Coolidge was President and Lodge was an old and embittered man.

Coolidge was governor for two terms. He handled the policemen's strike in a manner that won him much admiration and publicity. He wrote Samuel Gompers the famous letter in which he told the President of the American Federation of Labor that "there is no right to strike against the public safety by any body, anywhere, anytime." The handling of that delicate situation brought Coolidge national acclaim and in 1920, when the Republican National Convention met in Chicago, Coolidge was a dark-horse candidate for the Presidency.

The two leading candidates were Major General Leonard Wood and Governor Frank Lowden of Illinois, with Hiram Johnson of California always a threat. Harding, United States senator from Ohio and a politician of the McKinley stripe, was Ohio's favorite son, with Harry M. Daugherty as his manager. Harding was a weak and vacillating individual, who had been a small-town newspaper publisher. Only Daugherty believed that he had a chance for the nomination but he was playing a shrewd game. He reasoned that General Wood and Governor Lowden would wear themselves out and that Harding could eventually step in and grab the prize. Precisely that occurred, and a weary convention stampeded to Harding. At one time, Coolidge had polled thirty-four votes for the nomination. His strength waned until he polled only five votes at which time the stampede to Harding began.

The convention was worn out and many delegates had left the hall when nominations were called for Vice-President. Senator

Medill McCormick of Illinois took the floor and nominated Senator Lenroot of Wisconsin for Vice-President. McCormick made a perfunctory, two-minute speech which was seconded by four of the Old Guard and it looked as though it was all over. But suddenly the convention chairman recognized the delegate from Oregon, and Wallace McCamant, in a speech which took less than half a minute and in which he used 108 words, placed Coolidge in nomination for Vice-President. What was left of the convention went wild, and "Silent Cal" was on his way to the seats of the mighty. The Convention was so nearly empty of delegates that the majority of the Massachusetts delegation did not know of Coolidge's nomination until they read it next day in the newspapers.

The Democratic Convention at San Francisco nominated Governor James Cox of Ohio for President and Franklin Delano Roosevelt for Vice-President.

Grace Goodhue had been a teacher in a deaf and dumb institute in Vermont. She had married Coolidge in November, 1905, when he was thirty-two years of age, a mediocre lawyer, and an office-thirsty politician. They had lived in a two-family house in Northampton where Mrs. Coolidge did her own housework.

The Harding administration was a tragedy and a scandal. The Ohio crowd literally expropriated the White House and the Capitol. Daugherty was appointed Attorney General and brought with him his henchmen and his sycophants, both male and female. Offices were sold to the highest bidder; the Teapot Dome oil scandal and the affairs of the Veterans Administration were more than malodorous.

Coolidge, as Vice-President, must have known of this rottenness. He sat with the cabinet as an ex-officio member. He presided over the Senate. He knew Edwin Denby, who was Secretary of the Navy and of whom he later had to rid himself. He was well acquainted with Albert Fall, who had been a senator from New Mexico and Secretary of the Interior in the Harding Cabinet, and who was to be sent to the penitentiary for accepting a $100,000 bribe. He knew and for some time retained Daugherty as his own Attorney General. He could not plead ignorance of any knowledge of what was taking place; he regarded it as none of his business, however, and he continued calmly to preside over the Senate.

By 1923, the situation had reached the boiling point. Scandal was openly charged. The President's morals were attacked; the oil swindles were creating a furor and the Veterans Administration mess had been disclosed. An amiable but weak President realized finally that he had been betrayed by his friends. He decided to leave Washington while in the hope the storm would blow over. He and his party journeyed to Alaska on an "inspection trip." He returned by way of Seattle and San Francisco, where he became seriously ill. It was announced that he had been poisoned by crab meat but the luncheon menu showed that crab meat had not been served at the meal. One day encouraging news came from the sick room at the Palace Hotel in San Francisco; the next, he died. Harding, whose only distinction perhaps was that he looked a little like George Washington, was gone. The date was August 2, 1923.

Calvin Coolidge was President.

Coolidge was vacationing in Vermont when the news was flashed of the President's death. He was at Plymouth with his father and had, as usual, gone early to bed. Shortly after 2 A.M., a messenger clattered up in an old car and informed John Coolidge that the President had died in San Francisco. They awakened the Vice-President at 2:30 A.M. and, in the light of a coal-oil lamp, the father administered the oath of office to his son as President of the United States. Old John Coolidge was a justice of the peace and thus empowered to administer oaths.

A hundred years before another New England father had lived to see his son become President. Old John Adams, who had been the second President, saw his son, John Quincy Adams, become the sixth Chief Executive.

President Coolidge returned to Washington and for five years carried on in his penny-pinching Yankee manner. He retained Harding's cabinet until he was forced to rid himself of Denby,

Secretary of the Navy, Fall of the Interior, and Daugherty, the Attorney General. President Coolidge soon "realized" that there had been much criminality in the Harding administration. It is difficult to believe that he did not have some knowledge of the venal conditions before he became President.

He did nothing for a time, but eventually cleaned house thoroughly. He appointed his friend Harlan Stone, an Amherst graduate, as Attorney General; Curtis Wilbur, an able public servant from California, as Secretary of the Navy, and Hubert Work as Secretary of the Interior. Fall went to jail, Denby into obscurity, and Daugherty back to Ohio where he proclaimed that he had been the "goat of the entire scandal."

President Coolidge kept Andrew Mellon as Secretary of the Treasury. He listened closely to the shrewd Pittsburgh banker; and if any one individual influenced Coolidge, it was the frail, soft-spoken "Andy" Mellon. Coolidge worshiped power and, particularly, the power of money. He had once been a poor boy. He had always saved a good portion of the money he earned. He could never conquer his fear and admiration of money and the moneyed classes. Secretary Mellon represented to the parsimonious little Yankee all that he worshiped, and Mellon just about ran the administration himself.

The Coolidge administration was marked by far too much parsimony to suit many people. He vetoed the Soldiers' Bonus Bill and he vetoed the Soldiers' Insurance Act; the insurance measure was passed over his veto. Lodge voted to override the President, and he and the President came to a definite parting of the ways. Coolidge asserted that Lodge should have supported him on the veto, not as a personal matter but as the Republican leader of the Senate.

In 1924, Coolidge laid plans for his nomination as President in the same methodical manner he had always prepared his campaigns. Bascom Slemp, a Virginia Republican, a former representative and the son of a lower house member, was his secretary. Slemp lined up the Southern delegates; Frank Stearns, the Boston merchant, saw to the New England states; Mellon collected the campaign funds; and James Watson of Indiana lined up the Midwestern senators. Coolidge was nominated without serious opposition. Charles Gates Dawes, a former brigadier general of the Army, a native of Ohio, who had practiced law in Lincoln, Nebraska, and who was a Chicago banker, was the Vice-Presidential nominee.

Senator William E. Borah, of Idaho, had been approached by President Coolidge to be his running mate, but the Idaho senator had dryly replied by asking Coolidge at which end of the ticket.

The Democrats met in New York and for days the convention battle raged between Al Smith, governor of New York, and Senator McAdoo, who had been Wilson's Secretary of the Treasury. The deadlock was finally broken when the weary delegates nominated John W. Davis. Charles Bryan, governor of Nebraska and a brother of William Jennings Bryan, was the Democratic nominee for Vice-President. Senator Robert M. LaFollette advanced the forlorn hopes of the Progressive party, with Burton Wheeler as candidate for Vice-President.

The campaign was a runaway for the Republicans. Coolidge polled 15,718,789 votes; Davis 8,878,912 and LaFollette 4,822,-319. In the Electoral College the vote was even more one-sided. Coolidge and Dawes received 383 votes, Davis and Bryan 136, and LaFollette and Wheeler thirteen. The Republicans had even won some of the border states which had been conceded to the Democrats.

President Coolidge was inaugurated on a cold, sunny day in March 1925. He delivered a forty-seven-minute inaugural address and went to the Senate chamber to see Dawes inducted into office. The Vice-President stole the show with a vociferous speech. He waved his arms and lectured the Senate in a manner which that body had not heard since old John Adams lectured it one hundred and thirty-three years before.

Coolidge had invited the members of his cabinet and their wives, as well as other guests, to the White House. He had neglected to order lunch for his guests and they went without food while waiting for President and Mrs. Coolidge to receive them. It was a typical Coolidge omission. He would have had to pay for the food and, furthermore, "they didn't need any lunch"—in his own words. He had a couple of sandwiches brought to him in midafternoon.

The President suffered two sorrows about this time. His youngest son, Calvin, died from an infected foot and his own father passed away at the family home in Plymouth. Coolidge was genuinely fond of these two people, the old man and the fourteen-year-old boy.

Now President in his own right, Coolidge revised his cabinet. Dwight F. Davis was made Secretary of War; Harlan Stone went to the Supreme Court; and John Sargent, a fellow Vermonter, was made Attorney General. Herbert Hoover remained as Secretary of Commerce, although President Coolidge did not like him. He afterward said of Hoover that "the man has been giving me advice for five years, and all of it was wrong." James Davis, of Pennsylvania, a former coal miner who had been Secretary of Labor under Harding, was retained.

Coolidge's administration can be characterized by two words —economy and prosperity. He reduced the public debt by more than two billion. He reduced taxes, especially those of rich corporations and wealthy individuals.

Hughes went back to the Supreme Court as Chief Justice and President Coolidge brought former Senator Frank B. Kellogg back from London, where he had been ambassador, and put him in the State Department as Secretary. "Crying Nellie" Kellogg negotiated some of the disarmament treaties with the European powers and Japan; the Navy was not given the appropriation for which it asked; the Army was allowed to stagnate, and the Air Corps was a stunted stepchild. Prosperity was seemingly everywhere, and speculation rampant. It was easier to float a loan than to pay debts. Later, when the debacle came, Coolidge's name was found on J. P. Morgan's preferred list; he had bought shares at thirty and thirty-two when the market price was at forty. That was not particularly dishonest, according to the ethics of "Roaring Twenties," but certainly open to criticism.

The President clashed with the Senate occasionally and lost one battle which irked him considerably. He had named Charles B. Warren, of Michigan, to be Attorney General. This was before the appointment of Sargent. The Senate, by a narrow vote, refused to ratify the nomination, and Coolidge did more talking than usual—all of it critical of the senators who crossed him.

Wages were high and most of the people of the country believed that the era of good times would continue forever. But when 1927 came, Coolidge issued his famous edict, "I do not choose to run." He had hoped, however, that the party would draft him, and he pulled every string possible to bring that about.

There was a new day coming. Hoover was riding a wave of popularity (the two-cars-in-every-garage and a-chicken-in-every-pot fiction), and the rank-and-file of the Republican party would not rally to the cry of "Draft Coolidge!" He had been somewhat too friendly with "Mellon, Morgan, and the Money Lords," it was charged. Senators felt that he was out of touch with the country and Republican leaders argued that the 1924 victory had been more of a Democratic debacle than a Republican landslide. They were afraid of "Silent Cal" for 1928, and Hoover led the field among the Republican candidates.

The convention nominated Hoover and Senator Charles Curtis of Kansas, while the Democrats convened at Houston where the personal magnetism of Franklin Delano Roosevelt carried the day for Al Smith. But Governor Smith and Senator Joseph Robinson of Arkansas went down to overwhelming defeat, and the stodgy Quaker, who called California his home but who had been born in Iowa, and who had spent most of his adult life abroad, was President.

Coolidge returned to Northampton and for a time lived in the same old duplex for which he paid $36 a month. Times were good and rents had risen since he had first gone to Washington. He purchased a large home outside Northampton and tried to live in the grand manner. He was a rich man. He had always saved more than half of his salary. He had turned over every penny he could, and one United States senator said that "Cal Coolidge has $1.65 of the first dollar he ever earned." Coolidge wrote his *Autobiography;* he loafed around town; he had a dingy little law office; he sat on his front porch and watched the cars go by "The Beeches"—cars filled with curiosity seekers. He signed autographs and charged a dollar for his signature—or so some of them asserted. He kept a record of his household expenses and made out his own income-tax returns.

But he was at loose ends. He had been in public service for more than thirty years. He had lived in an era of prosperity and, when the depression came, he worried more than his wife and his friends knew. He gave a little to charity and saw his townspeople lose their jobs and go hungry. He sold his memoirs for a reputed $75,000 and deposited the money in a safe bank. He became a director in a life insurance company and attended board meetings regularly, for which he was paid the customary fee. The little graying Yankee could still turn a penny.

Coolidge was bothered with a slight heart ailment, but although he was said to be good for many years, he found that he tired easily, and Mrs. Coolidge noticed that he was taking two naps daily in place of his usual one.

The Presidential election of 1932 interested the former President a great deal. He showed some activity and, at the request of the Republican Speakers Bureau, he went to New York and made one speech at Madison Square Garden. Mrs. Coolidge listened to the speech over the radio, and realized that her husband was speaking under stress.

He voted for Hoover and saw Hoover humiliatingly defeated at the hands of Roosevelt.

On January 5, 1933, Mrs. Coolidge left her home to do her shopping. Her husband was preparing to shave. Mrs. Coolidge came home to find him dead on the bathroom floor.

From 1872 to 1933, a little more than sixty years, Calvin Coolidge was active in politics. From the little town of Plymouth, which then was without electric lights, a railroad or modern improvements, to the White House in Washington, was a long journey for the sour-faced antisocial Yankee to travel, but he made it.

Calvin Coolidge was a product of the bleak hills of New England. He looked and acted the part. He never stepped out of character. "Ike" Hoover, head usher of the White House, wrote that Coolidge would run around the second floor of the Executive Mansion in an old-fashioned nightshirt, checking up on household affairs, and that he once found him counting the apples in a barrel sent by Vermont friends.

When he started for the little academy in Vermont, he had as capital one calf. He ran that capital to $400,000. He had no charm, no affability, no friendly handclasp. He was as inspiring as a dead codfish and yet he was elected to office in his home town, his home state, and in the nation nineteen times.

Calvin Coolidge will not go down in history as a great man. Thrift can become parsimony and caution grows sometimes into suspiciousness. The lack of breadth of view and worry over trivialities keep men from greatness. The New England states have produced many great men, but it is just such qualities as Coolidge possessed, which are sometimes classed as virtues, that keep many men mediocre. Coolidge possessed all of the Yankee "virtues" and yet he was not above the average in ability.

CHAPTER XXX

Charles Gates Dawes

PERHAPS THE EXCEPTION that proves the political rule that the Vice-President must be a cipher is best exemplified by the figure of Charles Gates Dawes. He violated almost all the senatorial traditions, and did so with a good deal of refreshing bounce and fire; and he had a magnificent indifference and contempt of Vice-Presidential precedent.

The thirtieth Vice-President was born at Marietta, Ohio, on August 27, 1865. His father was Brigadier General Rufus Dawes, who had commanded a Wisconsin regiment during the Civil War and who had been brevetted for gallantry in action. General Dawes had also been a member of Congress and was, for that period, a man of considerable means. In the panic of 1873, he lost most of his fortune but he soon re-established himself.

The Dawes family have been Americans since the days of the Pilgrims. William Dawes arrived from England in 1635, and Charles G. Dawes is the eighth generation of the family to have been born on American soil. It was a William Dawes who made the historic ride from Boston to Concord on the memorable night of April 18, 1775. Longfellow gave credit for that feat to a silversmith named Paul Revere, but history records that Revere was captured near Lexington and that it was Dawes who galloped his horse from Boston, alerting the colonists to the danger of the British advance.

Mary Gates Dawes, mother of the Vice-President, bore six children of whom Charles was the oldest. He attended the Marietta schools and later entered Marietta College, where he was an uneven scholar. He learned to play the flute and also became something of a pianist.

Dawes had been an engineering student at Marietta College and he decided to study law as well. He entered the Cincinnati Law School at nineteen. He was graduated in 1886 and passed the bar examinations. He was then twenty-one.

Dawes looked about for a city in which to hang his shingle. He finally selected Lincoln, Nebraska, which he decided offered opportunities. He opened an office in a building which had as another tenant a young attorney named William Jennings Bryan. Bryan and Dawes, although temperamentally poles apart and belonging to opposed political parties, soon became friendly. Dawes once remarked, however, that he doubted Bryan's sincerity because the orator had once offered to debate any issue with him, taking either side.

There were two other young men in Lincoln who came to be cronies of Dawes and who repeatedly crossed his path in later life. One was the younger brother of William J. Bryan, Charles Bryan, who was to be governor of Nebraska and, in 1924, the Democratic candidate for Vice-President against Dawes. The other friendship which Dawes made at that time was with a second lieutenant in the United States Army, one John J. Pershing. Pershing, a Missourian and a West Point graduate, was an instructor in military affairs at the University of Nebraska.

Dawes was a successful attorney in Lincoln. He specialized in finance and financial reorganizations. He began taking over run-down and semibankrupt gas companies, reorganizing them and then selling them. In that way, the young man, who had estimated that he could not marry until he was earning $80 a month, soon became fairly well off.

He moved to Illinois, settled at Evanston outside Chicago, and became an active worker in the Republican party.

Young Dawes had met Mark Hanna and William McKinley. He attached himself to the Hanna machine and, although only thirty-one and a resident of Illinois for only two years, he volunteered to manage McKinley's campaign in that state. He promised Hanna that he would see to it that the four delegates-at-large were McKinley men. That was as much as Hanna could hope for. Through shrewd manipulation, Dawes was able to deliver the delegates-at-large to McKinley, as he had promised, and McKinley was duly nominated for President. Dawes's friend from Lincoln, William J. Bryan, made his famous "Cross of Gold" speech at the St. Louis convention. But in the end, McKinley was elected and young Dawes, who had "delivered," was appointed comptroller of the currency.

Dawes's interest in politics widened. He looked with a longing eye to the United States Senate. He felt that with the help of the administration, with the assistance he could expect from federal officeholders, and with the personal friendship of Hanna, he could be elected. Hanna and the President saw eye to eye with Dawes's ambitions.

The death of President McKinley changed the political picture. Theodore Roosevelt was not friendly with Hanna, and Dawes saw his hopes go a glimmering. He returned to Illinois and, with a brother, his cousins and a few business associates, he founded the Central Trust Company, a state bank capitalized at $4,000,000. It was well managed and after a succession of mergers became one of the largest banks of the country. The bank has been a Dawes organization since its inception. There was a time during the depression of the thirties when the sledding was hard, and Dawes had to ask help from the Reconstruction Finance Corporation, but the bank weathered the storm.

Dawes's one act as a banker which needed an explanation was his loan to Senator William Lorimer of $1,250,000 in order that the senator might show it to the Illinois State Bank Examiner, and thus obtain a charter to open a bank. Dawes made the loan; Lorimer obtained the charter, and the next day repaid the loan. In a subsequent investigation, Dawes contended that it was a common enough transaction, that the loan had been repaid, that no one suffered any loss, and that he had merely assisted a fellow banker. He added, in further extenuation, that Senator Lorimer had sufficient collateral in the form of stocks and bonds to have covered the loan but that by means of the loan Lorimer avoided the alternative of selling his securities to obtain ready cash.

Lorimer's bank failed, however, and he was indicted for criminal conspiracy. The Central Trust Company was sued by the receiver for the Lorimer bank and, in 1924, ten years after the failure, the Dawes institution settled the case by paying the receiver damages in the amount of $75,000.

From 1912 to 1917, Dawes was a successful banker, the builder of a large fortune, an amateur musician of note, and he was interested in politics only as a side-line spectator. In 1917, when the country declared war on Germany and her Allies, he was fifty-two, in excellent health, intellectually at his prime, and a financier and engineer of wide repute. His friend Pershing was the commander of the A.E.F., and Dawes saw no reason why he, too, should not see active service. He made an application for a commission and, after a hard fight, was commissioned a major in the Engineer Corps.

Hoover had tried to shunt him to the Belgian Relief Commission and, even after Dawes received his commission as a major, Hoover made a vain effort to get the Army to assign him to his department as his assistant. But Major Dawes insisted that as an engineer he was entitled to army duty. He persuaded General Pershing to ask for his assignment to the A.E.F. and, with the general's backing, he was detailed to the purchasing department on the staff of the A.E.F. commander.

Major Dawes was soon promoted to a colonelcy and in 1918 he became a brigadier general in charge of army purchasing. A dynamic personality and a hard worker, he was unaccustomed to and impatient with army red tape. He acted as would the purchasing agent of a large corporation. He had the ear of the general in command of all the American forces in France. General Pershing gave Dawes more leeway than he could have given a regular army officer, and the Chicago banker became one of his most valued assistants. General Dawes had his headquarters with "Black Jack" Pershing, and they were more nearly business associates than senior and junior army officers.

Many tales are told of General Dawes's methods as the Army's top purchasing officer. He demanded results and did not inquire into methods; the end deserved the means. He smuggled mules into France from Spain, when the Army was in desperate straits for artillery animals. He used the telephone first and made the formal request later. He lightened the load for Pershing at a time when the burden was heaviest.

General Dawes was afterward called as a witness before a Congressional committee because of his highhanded action in the purchase and resale of army equipment. The hearing soon turned into a battle of wits, with Dawes getting much the better of the committee members. It was during that hearing that General

Dawes made his famous "Hell-and-Maria" speech. In the end, the committee found that it could allocate no blame to Dawes.

The brigadier general returned from France in 1919 and hung up his uniform. He had met Harding, and the President in 1921 appointed him as director of the budget. Dawes did his usual efficient job. He organized the department and made the post mean what its creators had intended. He was continually badgered by members of both houses of Congress who said they believed in holding down the budget—that is, for everyone except themselves. It should be stressed that he was not a party to any of the widespread corruption that prevailed during the Harding regime.

In July 1922, Dawes resigned as director of the budget and the next year, at the request of the Reparations Commission, he was appointed president of the expert commission on German finances. He and Owen D. Young, his associate, went to work in earnest. Out of their combined efforts came the so-called Dawes Plan, which the general insisted should have been named the Young Plan.

The Republican National Convention met in June, 1924. Coolidge was entitled to the nomination and he had little opposition. The contest thus was over the Vice-Presidential nominee. There were several senatorial aspirants, the strongest of them Senator Charles Curtis of Kansas. But the lower house faction dominated the convention. Lodge and the Old Guard senators were brushed aside, and Dawes was nominated. Former Governor Frank Lowden of Illinois could have had the nomination but he refused it, and the convention stampeded to the Chicago banker who had been a proficient comptroller of the currency, a successful banker, an able purchasing agent for the A.E.F. in France, an outstanding success as the first director of the budget, and president of the expert commission on German finances.

The Democrats held their convention in New York and, for more than a hundred ballots, the battle raged between Al Smith and the "wets" against William G. McAdoo and the "drys." The convention finally compromised on John W. Davis, an able but colorless candidate, for President, and Governor Bryan of Nebraska for Vice-President. The Progressives again nominated Robert LaFollette, the senior senator from Wisconsin, with Burton K. Wheeler of Montana as his running mate.

General Dawes was a forceful campaigner and he carried the oratorical burden for his party in 1924. The Democrats showed little enthusiasm for the fight; there was too much bitterness left as an aftermath of the hectic days at the Madison Square Garden Convention. Their cause was hopeless and Coolidge and Dawes were elected, polling 382 votes in the Electoral College as against 136 for Davis and Bryan. LaFollette polled thirteen.

If Coolidge's inaugural address was colorless, Dawes made up for it after he was given the oath of office by Albert Cummins, the senior senator from Iowa and the President pro tem of the Senate. The new Vice-President broke every precedent that distinguished body had established in its more than one hundred and thirty-five years of existence. He pounded the desk and demanded that all the new senators take the oath of office simultaneously rather than in the old established method of four at a time. He delivered a scathing attack on the Senate rules, on unlimited debate, on the cloture rule, on outmoded procedure. The most "exclusive club in the world" was outraged. No man since the days of crotchety John Adams had dared to assault the Senate's members as had the sixty-year-old banker who had never before presided over a deliberative body.

The dour-faced Coolidge saw the limelight stolen from him. As a result of that diatribe, the Vice-President was an unpopular presiding officer of the Senate. Thomas Marshall had been the most popular man to sit in the big chair. Coolidge had not been personally popular but at least he had been a respected Vice-President. Dawes fought the Senate for four years and, while he could never persuade its members to change the rules, they in turn could never upset his rulings. He studied parliamentary law thoroughly and he went to the people in his fight against what he regarded as an archaic Senate.

Coolidge was never friendly with his Vice-President. They appeared friendly in public, but "Silent Cal" never forgot that Dawes was taking a nap in his suite at the new Willard Hotel while the Senate rejected the nomination of Charles Warren for Attorney General. There had been much opposition to Warren's appointment. He had been an attorney for the sugar interests and he was connected with corporations which had business with the government. The Democrats were solidly opposed to him and they rallied the support of liberal Republicans and a few Progressive senators. The Vice-President knew that the vote on the confirmation would be close, and he had discussed the possibility of a roll call with the Republican leaders. Senator Curtis, the Republican floor leader, believed that the vote would not come for several hours at least, and the Vice-President went to his hotel to rest. During his absence from the Senate, Senator Tom Walsh of Montana and Senator James Reed of Missouri attacked Warren so bitterly that Senator Curtis feared too many votes might be lost if the roll call were postponed. He called for a vote and sent frantic messages to Dawes to return to his post. The Vice-President grabbed a taxi and raced to the Senate Chamber, only to arrive after the vote was cast.

That was the only major setback Coolidge suffered as President. Dawes's napping has never been satisfactorily explained. Some observers felt that the Senate had voted against Warren merely to get even with an unpopular presiding officer. Others held that Dawes had a political grudge against Warren because of the opposition of the corporation lawyer to Dawes's political ambitions. Whatever the motives, Coolidge held the Vice-President to blame. Add this incident to that of the inaugural address, when Dawes stole the spotlight from Coolidge, and there is ample evidence that the closemouthed New Englander could not abide the highly articulate Vice-President.

Four years passed and another election was held. Coolidge had issued his famous "I do not choose to run" pronouncement. The Republicans nominated Hoover and Curtis of Kansas. Vice-President Dawes polled only four votes in the Convention for

President, one from Illinois, one from Ohio, and two from Missouri. He was not even nominated for Vice-President.

There were three factors which prevented Dawes from consideration for the Presidency or even for renomination as Vice-President. First, he had been Vice-President, which had long since come to miligate against a man's chances of getting into the White House. Only once in more than one hundred and twenty years has a Vice-President been advanced to the Presidency—Van Buren, alone since Jefferson, was elected without first succeeding to the Presidency by the death of the incumbent. Second, Dawes did not have the support of the Senate, which he had antagonized. Third, Coolidge was opposed to Dawes and he had passed on the word that his Vice-President must not be nominated.

It is interesting to note that the Vice-Presidential nominee on the Republican ticket in 1928 did not like his running mate. Before the convention, Senator Curtis had asked, "Why should we nominate a man for whom we will have to apologize throughout the campaign?" Hoover was nominated and elected as a Republican, yet as late as 1920 he was not certain whether he was a Republican or a Democrat.

Shortly after retiring from the office of Vice-President, Dawes accepted an invitation from the President of the Dominican Republic to form an economic commission to study and revise the finances of that small Republic.

In the meantime, President Hoover had selected Dawes as ambassador to Great Britain. Dawes agreed to the appointment, but said that he must first discharge the Dominican undertaking, which he did, assisted by a commission of American experts.

The Dawes economic committee finished its duties within a month, and Dawes returned to Washington and from there went to London.

As ambassador to Great Britain, Dawes was a source of amusement and astonishment to diplomatic, social, and political circles in London. King George V liked him immensely; Prime Minister J. Ramsay MacDonald became his friend; and his breezy manner appealed to the restrained Britishers. Dawes was now sixty-five, but he had not lost the enthusiasm of youth. In London he went places and did things that often offended protocol. In all, he was a popular and successful ambassador. In 1930, he was the American representative at the London Disarmament Conference.

In the election of 1932, Hoover was soundly beaten in his attempt at re-election, and Franklin D. Roosevelt returned to Washington as President. Dawes returned to Chicago and saw his pet, the 1933 Chicago World's Fair, become a success.

CHAPTER XXXI

Charles Curtis

NO MAN WITH THE BLOOD in his veins of the original Americans, the Indians, has yet been President of the United States. John Randolph, a senator from Virginia in the nation's early history, was a descendant of Pocahontas. Matthew Quay, a Pennsylvania senator, had some Seneca blood in his veins. Senator Owen of Oklahoma was part Cherokee, and Charles Curtis, of Kansas, the thirty-first Vice-President, who served during the administration of Herbert Hoover, was a quarter-breed Kaw.

His mother was a half-breed and his great grandfather had been one "White Hair," the head chief of the Osages. His cousins were Indians who lived in tepees, and he was himself a member of the tribe. He often attended the councils of the Kaws and took part in their councils. For several years he lived with his mother's people in various Indian villages and he learned to ride horseback as the Indian boys rode, with only a rope for a bridle. He became an excellent rider and he was a jockey, riding at tracks in Kansas until he was sixteen, when he grew too heavy to remain a professional.

Curtis was born in North Topeka, Kansas, on January 25, 1860. Kansas was then in the throes of the pre-Civil War disturbances. John Brown and his giant sons had gone to Harpers Ferry, Virginia, from Kansas. They had captured the fort and had all been killed while fighting the Regulars under Colonel Robert E. Lee, or had been hanged later for treason with their leader.

Curtis' father was Oren Curtis, the son of William Curtis. William was born in 1800, and was the father of fourteen children, most of whom lived to advanced age. Don Seitz, in his life of Charles Curtis, wrote that as late as 1928 there were five of them living. Oren Curtis died in 1898, his wife, Charles's mother, had died in 1863 and the son did not remember her. Oren Curtis had been in the Union Army during the closing part of the Civil War. He did not join the Army until after the death of his wife. Oren married a second time and raised a family, and one of his daughters was Mrs. Dolly Curtis Gans, who acted as Curtis' hostess during his term as Vice-President.

Young Curtis was educated in the Topeka schools. He led the normal life of a Kansas boy in the post-Civil War period. He spent three years with the Indians, he rode and hunted with them and he even learned to use a bow and arrow. He saw the last of the great buffalo herds and he witnessed the flight of wood pigeons where there were millions of them in the air, obscuring the sun.

Charles Curtis worked before and after school; he shined shoes; he sold papers and peanuts at the races and the county fairs. Later he drove a hack around Topeka. He acted as a sort of leg man for the Topeka *Times* and contributed such items of news as he picked up in his jaunts around town in his hack.

Curtis was small of stature with black hair which he parted in the middle and wore long in Indian fashion. The boys of Topeka called him Indian and old Tom Reed, Speaker of the House of Representatives, always addressed him as "Indian" while he was in Congress.

The youth was graduated from high school in 1879. He had

been a good student, he had worked hard, he had met the girl whom he was to marry and he was his class orator at his graduation.

Young Curtis' ambition was to be a lawyer. He studied law for two years in the office of A. H. Chase and in 1881 he was admitted to practice. That year he married Annie Baird with whom he had gone to high school. He was at first a junior partner with Chase but soon afterward formed a partnership with David Overmyer and, for the rest of his life, Curtis had law offices in Topeka.

In 1881, Kansas voted state-wide prohibition. The state had been overrun with outlawry in every form and the people determined to rid themselves of the liquor traffic. The saloon element defied the edict of the people, and Shawnee County, of which Topeka is the seat, was honeycombed with dives and a strongly organized political association. The organization thought of electing Curtis, the twenty-four-year-old Methodist lawyer, as prosecuting attorney. Curtis was willing to run but he told the machine leaders who approached him that if elected he would enforce the law and that they might be sorry that they had elected him. The gang had heard such threats before but this time they had picked a tartar. They elected Curtis and he promptly closed the dives. He prosecuted the big boys as well as the small fry.

He had been elected for a term of two years and, when his term expired, he ran for re-election. This time the church element went to the polls to keep him in office, and he won by a large majority. During the four years he was prosecuting attorney of Shawnee County, he closed eighty-eight bootleg dives and convicted 103 of their operators—a good record for a young man who was only twenty-eight when he finished his second term and whom old-timers remembered as a shoeshine boy around town. Soon after his second term expired, Curtis and Overmyer became one of the most prosperous law firms of Topeka.

In 1889, Curtis was a candidate for the House of Representatives. A vacancy had occurred and the twenty-nine-year-old attorney was almost elected. The next year the Republican party again offered him the nomination, but he surveyed the situation and refused to enter the race. He used good judgment, or had good advice, for Kansas was in the throes of one of her political upheavals and the Farmers Alliance candidate was elected.

By 1892, when Curtis was thirty-two, he was regarded one of the leading citizens of Shawnee County, most of which represented the Fourth Kansas Congressional District. He felt that he stood a good chance of election to Congress even though the Populist party was strong in Kansas. General Weaver, the Populist candidate, carried Kansas; Grover Cleveland was elected President; and Curtis went to the House of Representatives. He was appointed to the Indian Affairs Committee and was always spokesman for the Indians, both as representative and later as a senator. He was a member of the Fifty-third, Fifty-fourth, and Fifty-fifth Congresses. He was popular with the electors of his district but did not get along with the state house coterie. That clique had "gerrymandered" the district so that Curtis was no longer in the Fourth District but in the First, with Leavenworth and Atchison the controlling towns. Nevertheless he became as popular in the First Kansas District as he had been in the Fourth, and he represented his new constituents in the lower house for ten years.

In 1907, Representative Curtis, who had been the Republican whip during his last two years, was elected to the Senate, where he served one term of six years but was defeated in 1912 when Kansas followed Theodore Roosevelt into the Progressive fold. In 1914, the Seventeenth Amendment went into effect and, in the popular election, Curtis went back to the Senate where he remained until he moved into the Vice-Presidential chair on March 4, 1929. In the Senate Curtis was, as he had always been in Congress, a regular Republican. He followed the party program without question.

During the years of World War I, Senator Curtis supported the war effort but he was opposed to President Wilson's domestic policies and, since he was Senator Henry Cabot Lodge's assistant floor leader, he was an opponent of Wilson's League of Nations program.

Curtis had had hopes of being nominated Vice-President in 1924, but the shrewd banker from Chicago, Charles G. Dawes, was nominated and elected with Coolidge. Senator Curtis, however, bided his time. He was by now one of the senior members of the Senate. He had been in the House and the Senate almost continuously for thirty years, he had served his party faithfully, and he felt that he should be rewarded in 1928 by the nomination for President. In 1928, Kansas sent him to the Chicago convention as her favorite-son candidate, but his name did not arouse any enthusiasm outside of his own state. Herbert Clark Hoover, for whom Curtis had no particular admiration, was nominated. Curtis was openly opposed to the nomination and had worked actively against him in the party caucus and even in the convention.

With the Presidential nomination out of the way, a spontaneous demand arose for the nomination of Curtis as Vice-President. The Party leaders recognized that some consideration should be shown the sixty-eight-year-old war horse. Little opposition developed and the quarter-breed Kaw was duly nominated. In November, Hoover and Curtis were overwhelmingly elected over Al Smith and Senator Joe Robinson of Arkansas.

Vice-President Curtis was a relief to the Senate after the table-pounding and dictatorial Dawes. He had been a member of the "world's most exclusive club" for many years; he had presided over its deliberations on numerous occasions; he knew and observed the rules of the Senate; and he proved to be an efficient presiding officer over the upper house.

Curtis was Vice-President during the worst depression the nation had ever known. He had virtually no part in the Hoover administration, his advice and counsel were seldom sought and he had little of either to offer to a Chief Executive with whom he was never on intimate terms.

From a number of standpoints, the Hoover administration was a failure and in 1932, when the Republican convention met, the delegates were on the defensive. The party had little to offer in the way of a constructive record and its entire campaign was defeatist. Hoover was renominated and again his running mate was Curtis. The Democrats nominated the vigorous Franklin D. Roosevelt and named as his running mate John Nance Garner of Texas, the Speaker of the House. Roosevelt and Garner polled 472 electoral votes while Hoover and Curtis polled only fifty-nine.

The Republican party had been in power for twelve years. There had been Harding and the Ohio gang. There had been the era of spurious Coolidge prosperity and the four years under Hoover which had led to the economic debacle.

Charles Curtis went back to Topeka. He was once more a private citizen and was now seventy-three. He died three years later on February 12, 1936.

Charles Curtis was far from a brilliant statesman and, indeed, only a cut above the mediocre. Perhaps it is not an unfair estimate to say of him that he had the qualities necessary to a wheel-horse Republican as well as those usually required to win the Vice-Presidency.

CHAPTER XXXII

John Nance Garner

THE THIRTY-SECOND VICE-PRESIDENT, one of only six to be re-elected to that office, was also one of the few Heirs Apparent to escape the strait jacket of that post. By no means was he a nonentity, a dummy presiding over the Senate. Considered in the light of the dynamic personality of Roosevelt, under whom he served, the fact that for two terms he wielded a great deal of power remains an unprecedented feat.

Garner was the fourth John Garner of that family. His father, grandfather and great-grandfather were all named John. The family dates from Revolutionary days. The Garners and the Nances were of sturdy English ancestry, who had come to the colonies in the early eighteenth century. They had made their way to Tennessee and, in 1842, one "Widow Garner" drove a two-horse team to the Republic of Texas, bringing with her six fatherless children. She established herself near the little town of Blossom Prairie and she built for her brood a home in a wild country, only ten miles from the Indian territory. The territory was a no man's land. When men faced the consequences of crime, and had to disappear, they fled to the territory.

In 1845, Texas entered the Union, the country became more tranquil, and such towns as Detroit, Clarksville, and Paris grew into small cities. But little Blossom Prairie remained a small community in Northeast Texas.

In 1864, John Garner III rode off to the Civil War. He was a member of Joe Wheeler's cavalry and was a good soldier for the Confederacy. He returned to Blossom Prairie to marry Sarah Guest, a girl whom he had known before riding off to the wars. On November 29, 1869, Sarah Garner gave birth to a son who was named John Nance Garner. Later, there were five brothers and sisters.

John Garner led the life of the average country boy in a sparsely settled country. He walked three miles to school which he attended only three or four months each year. But he studied also with a maiden aunt, Kitty Garner, who exerted a powerful influence on the puny boy who was threatened with lung trouble. Through her aid, the lad gained more knowledge than the neighborhood boys and girls, and accordingly he was able to enter Vanderbilt University at Nashville, Tennessee. He spent only one week at Vanderbilt, however, because he did not possess sufficient credits. He returned to Prairie Blossom and began the study of law in the neighboring town of Clarksville. He studied with a Captain Simms, a former Confederate officer, and he boarded with another onetime Confederate soldier, a Dr. Lane.

He was a good student and, shortly before he was twenty-one, he was admitted to practice in the district court. The court waived the fact that the applicant was under the legal age to practice. He hung out his shingle in the little county seat of Clarksville for two years; there he ran for city attorney but was defeated.

In 1892, he moved to the southwestern part of the state. He was now twenty-three years. But his lungs were still weak, he was not doing well with his law practice in Clarksville, and at this time he was offered a junior partnership with a firm in Uvalde. He arrived there one night in December, 1892, and there he was to remain for more than half a century. He had $150 which eventually he ran up to more than a million.

Garner practiced law throughout nine counties; he drove a buckboard over a county larger than many states of the Union. He was the junior partner in the firm of Clark, Fuller and Garner and court wits made sport of the firm name. It came to be a stock joke throughout the cow countries, where every man drank his whiskey straight, that "Clark's Fullern Garner." The young lawyer was a good drinker, and an excellent poker player, prime qualifications for a successful legal career in Texas fifty years ago.

Garner was elected a judge of Uvalde County in 1895. He was only twenty-six years but he had made substantial progress during three years in the little town. He now married Marietta Rheiner, the orphaned daughter of a wealthy cattleman and, with her capital, the partnership of Etta and John soon became one of the well-to-do families of Uvalde. Garner was county judge for four years; he learned more law; he developed a good legal mind; and, more important to a thirty-year-old attorney, he learned to play politics. In 1899, Judge Garner was elected to the state legislature. He was at this time of medium height, slender, blue-eyed and sandy-haired, and he wore a derby: Etta thought that he looked both "funny and terrible."

Garner served two years in the state legislature at Austin. He soon became the spokesman for the Rio Grande counties and when the census of 1900 showed that Texas was entitled to another representative, he had himself appointed to the committee which delimited the boundaries of the new district. He "cut himself" a Congressional district and, with his intimate knowledge of men and local conditions, he had himself elected from it. Garner was to represent the Fifteenth District for thirty years. He went to Washington a thirty-four-year-old novice; he remained there as a representative, and later as Vice-President, for thirty-eight years. He was never defeated for office after he failed to become city attorney of Clarksville, as a youngster of twenty-three.

When Garner went to Washington, he brought Etta with him, who had studied stenography. She became his secretary. She was not only an efficient assistant but a shrewd judge of people. She saw to her husband's correspondence with his constituency; she handled his callers; she was ambitious for her husband and much of the credit for his political success must go to the efficient Marietta Rheiner Garner.

In 1903, when Theodore Roosevelt was President and the Republicans were in power—and were to retain power for nine years—Garner was forced to accept minor committee assignments. He was no orator but he was an earnest worker and he never overlooked the interests of the Fifteenth District, which covered an area greater than all of Pennsylvania. He made friends at Washington with the leaders of both political parties. He became a crony of the young Nicholas Longworth and played poker with old Joe Cannon, the Speaker of the House, and his clique. Its members soon realized that the representative from the Rio Grande country was shrewd, a sound student of the Constitution and particularly of finance—in all, a dependable young man who did not talk too much.

Garner was elected and re-elected. He climbed the House committee ladder until he became a power. He led the fight to strip the Speaker of his dictatorial powers and, after many setbacks, he won that fight.

Representative Garner introduced few bills. He seldom made

speeches, fewer than any man who ever came to the leadership of the House of Representatives. It was in behind-the-scenes committee work that he exercised his power. He was punctual and a hard worker. He was an early advocate of a graduated income tax and fought for enabling legislation for eight years before he convinced his colleagues that a revenue-raising method was both sound and equitable.

Garner became a friend of Champ Clark of Missouri and, when Clark became Speaker of the House, Garner, then a veteran of ten years' service, was again advanced in committee assignment. He became the watchdog of appropriations. He opposed what he regarded as wasteful expenditures; he thoroughly analyzed expense accounts and was a thorn in the side of "junket-takers" who padded expense accounts. He once said, "I have no confidence in anybody who figures it will cost $350 to go to St. Louis for one day."

With the election of Wilson in 1912, the Democratic party was in complete power for the first time since the era of Grover Cleveland. The drought had been a long one and "deserving" Democrats lined up at the political trough. Garner, however, was opposed to any indiscriminate distribution of patronage. Inevitably he became unpopular with some powerful members of the House but he was able to retain his friendship with Champ Clark and other leading members in the lower branch of Congress.

Garner was entitled by this time to the chairmanship of the House Committee on Foreign Affairs, but he gave way and asked to be appointed to a lower place on the all-powerful Ways and Means Committee. He was given that assignment and for twenty years he was a member and eventually chairman of that important revenue-raising committee.

Champ Clark and President Wilson were not on friendly terms. Clark had never forgotten that he had come so near winning the Presidential nomination at Baltimore. It rankled that at one time in the balloting he had had more than a majority vote and, had it not been for Bryan and Wilson, he would have been President. Thus, Clark was more or less *persona non grata* at the

White House. But in looking for someone to be his personal representative on the floor of the House, President Wilson picked Garner, and during Wilson's eight years in office, the two men spent many evenings in the White House. The bushy-browed and now graying man from the Southwest came to know intimately the studious, long-faced Wilson. Garner was never a "yes man" to the President and Wilson's secretary Joe Tumulty, testified that they had many hot arguments. In 1917, Garner voted for the War Declaration and was a consistent supporter of all war measures during the next two trying years.

Garner was a man of pronounced views. He opposed Prohibition when Texas went dry, he opposed the Eighteenth Amendment to the Constitution (women's suffrage), and he was an active opponent of the Ku Klux Klan at a time when it enjoyed its greatest popularity in the South. There was never a day when his constituents did not know where he stood and the voters of the Fifteenth District supported him even though they did not always agree with him.

While Garner was never a speechmaker, he kept in touch with the voters by personal contact. He invited them to his famous barbecues in the yard of the big brick house in Uvalde; he religiously answered their letters; and he listened sympathetically to their requests. He was unbeatable. His fight for a graduated income tax caused perturbation to rich men of the district but Garner pointed out that he, too, was wealthy and that if he could afford to pay the tax, so could others in the same brackets.

Garner had become a national figure even during the lean Democratic years of Harding and Coolidge. He fought the losing fight for Governor Cox, for John W. Davis and Al Smith. In 1932, when the country repudiated Hoover, and Roosevelt was nominated for President, John Nance Garner, who had been an able Speaker of the House for one session of Congress, was named as his running mate.

Roosevelt and Garner were overwhelmingly elected. Hoover suffered one of the worst defeats ever inflicted on a President running for re-election. His electoral vote was fifty-nine while

Roosevelt and Garner received 472. In the 1932 campaign, Garner made only one campaign speech. When asked by Roosevelt why he had not spoken more often, he explained that "Hoover is making speeches—and that's enough for us."

Garner moved over to the Senate chamber and for eight years was an efficient presiding officer. He knew parliamentary law; he was a consummate politician; and he knew men. Many of the members of the Senate had been fellow members of the House with him during his long office in the lower branch. They respected him and he, in turn, respected the cumbersome Senate rules.

In 1936, the Republicans nominated Governor Alf Landon of Kansas for President and again the Democrats nominated Roosevelt and Garner. The election was even more of a walkaway for the Democrats than that in 1932. Landon carried only two states, Vermont and Maine. This was an all-time low for the candidate of a major political party. The defeat administered Governor Landon was the most severe in a hundred years.

Garner was sixty-six when he was inaugurated for his second term. But he was hale and hearty, and he retained all of his mental faculties.

Vice-President Garner soon began to disagree with President Roosevelt's New Deal principles and, during the last four years of his incumbency, there was not the close relationship between the two which had existed during their first four years. Garner was opposed to the President's Supreme Court reorganization plan; he differed with Roosevelt on labor legislation; and he was opposed to the subsidy policies adopted by the President. By 1940, the breach had widened until Garner was at the breaking point with "The Chief." He was not seriously considered by the party as a running mate with Roosevelt for a third term. In company with James A. Farley, Al Smith, and other onetime intimates of Roosevelt, he opposed a third term, but Roosevelt was again nominated and he requested that the convention name, as his running mate, Henry Agard Wallace, who had been Secretary of Agriculture for eight years.

Wendell Willkie, a corporation lawyer who called Indiana his home but maintained a residence in New York, was the Republican nominee. Roosevelt was again overwhelmingly elected and Garner, then seventy-one, and his partner Etta, returned to Uvalde to rub shoulders with cattlemen and citrus farmers, to talk crops, the weather, and politics with the goat raisers and the beemen. There he is John to the townspeople.

John Garner is a Texan of the old Southwest where there are few of his breed left. He traveled far from the Blossom Prairie farm to the Vice-Presidency. He is a millionaire cattleman and banker, a good poker player, a shrewd politician and a devout member of the Methodist church. The finger of suspicion has never been pointed at him. He learned early in life to do two things superlatively well—to keep his word and to keep his mouth shut.

CHAPTER XXXIII

Henry Agard Wallace

IN THE SPRING OF 1948, Henry Agard Wallace, the thirty-third Vice-President, was the highly articulate spokesman of a number of those dissatisfied with the foreign policies of President Truman. As the national conventions approached, his influence had to be appraised carefully by the top strategists of the two major parties.

The Wallaces came to Iowa from Pennsylvania. Wallace's grandfather founded *The Western Farmer*. He was well liked by farmers throughout the Middle West and was "Uncle Henry" to thousands of men and women who subscribed to his magazine. His son took over *The Western Farmer* and edited it until 1921, when he went to Washington as Secretary of Agriculture under

President Harding. He had supported the Republican ticket and received the appointment to the Department of Agriculture as a reward for his political activities and as the Midwest representative in Harding's official family. Henry Wallace was an able cabinet member and a friend of the farmer, and he was not a party to any of the corruption of the Harding administration. He once told intimates that during his term of office he wore himself out arguing with Hoover over jurisdictional disputes.

The subject of this chapter became the associate editor of the family journal, now called *The Wallace Farmer,* and was appointed its editor in 1924. He was an earnest student of farming, an authority on the culture of corn, Iowa's staple crop, and he is still considered both a careful and progressive farmer.

The Wallaces had been Republicans both in Pennsylvania and later in Iowa. They had been leaders in the party ranks.

Henry A. Wallace first voted in a national election in 1912 when he cast his ballot for Taft. For the next sixteen years he was a regular Republican, voting for Hughes, Harding, and Coolidge. As remarked before, his father had disagreed consistently with Hoover when they were fellow cabinet members and when, in 1928, Hoover was a candidate for President, the son, then forty-two, bolted the Republican party and voted for Al Smith.

In 1932, Wallace again supported the cause of the Democratic candidate and made an active campaign on behalf of Roosevelt. He carried Iowa for Roosevelt against Hoover, who was a native of that state. Wallace campaigned for Smith and Roosevelt as an enrolled Republican. He did not enroll as a Democrat until 1936 and, during his first four years as Secretary of Agriculture, he occupied the anomalous position of being a Republican cabinet member in a Democratic administration. Wallace brought the secretaryship of the Department of Agriculture to the fore as a cabinet position of importance. From its inception it had been looked upon as a secondary post to be given to a Midwesterner as a reward for party effort, or to appease a populous state which had aided the party.

When he went to Washington as Secretary of Agriculture,

Wallace was forty-five. He had been in the capital while his father was Secretary and thus he did not have to learn his way around. Washington thought that he looked like a farmer's boy in Sunday clothes, but it was soon apparent that he was a close student of men and of economic conditions.

Wallace became a trusted friend and adviser of President Roosevelt; and in 1940, when the President came to the parting of the ways with Garner, he picked Wallace as the Democratic candidate for Vice-President. At that time, Speaker H. T. Rainey of the House and former Governor Paul V. McNutt of Indiana were active seekers after the nomination. Both had strong support but when the President signified his desire for Wallace, the convention fell in line.

Wallace resigned his post as Secretary of Agriculture and made an active campaign. He spoke throughout the Middle West. Roosevelt was elected President for the third time, defeating Wendell Willkie, the New York corporation lawyer and a former Democrat. Wallace moved over to the Senate chamber where he was a quiet if inexperienced presiding officer. As Vice-President he was the same earnest public official that he had been as Secretary of Agriculture.

Roosevelt made him an active assistant, again breaking with the long-established precedent that a Vice-President must be seen but not heard. He appointed him chairman of various commissions and made him an ex-officio member of the cabinet. He also appointed him as a sort of ambassador at large to represent the administration through the world. He sent Wallace as an envoy of good will to Mexico. Wallace's visit to the southern republic was well timed and he left a favorable impression with the Mexican people—one salient reason being that he had prepared himself by learning to speak Spanish with considerable fluency. Wallace also made a trip to Russia and China as the personal representative of the President. He speaks Russian almost as well as Spanish.

Aside from his friendship for the farmer, the Vice-President showed a marked sympathy for labor.

As an ex-officio member of the cabinet, Wallace frequently

clashed with members of that body. They looked upon him as merely another Vice-President, and begrudged him the privileges and responsibility which had been given him by the President. This was particularly true of the Secretary of Commerce, Jesse Jones, who was jealous of his prerogatives as a cabinet member. On several occasions the President was compelled to interfere to bring peace among his official family.

In the spring of 1944, it became evident that Roosevelt would be nominated for a fourth term, and attention was once more centered on his running mate.

As far back as 1937, Stanley High had written that "a good many people believe Henry Wallace to be Mr. Roosevelt's Heir Apparent." This opinion had prevailed through his term as Vice-President and Wallace, not without reason, felt he was entitled to renomination. He was not, however, a friend of the city political leaders. He was not acceptable to the Southern Democrats and, while he had great strength in the Middle West and in the Pacific states, it was felt he could not swing sufficient strength from the South and East to win him the nomination.

The Democratic Convention met in Chicago where Roosevelt was nominated for a fourth term with little opposition. Numerous candidates for Vice-President were advanced, the outstanding ones being Wallace and Senator Harry S. Truman of Missouri.

Senator Truman had been a member of the Pendergast machine in Missouri politics but was not tarred with the brush of corruption. He had been the hard-working chairman of the Committee to Investigate War Expenditures, his record in the first World War was good, and the chairman of the Democratic National Committee, Steve Hannegan, knew him to be acceptable to the President. Roosevelt had written Vice-President Wallace a letter endorsing his candidacy—a mild sort of pat on the back—but Hannegan knew that the President would accept either Truman or Supreme Court Justice William O. Douglas.

Wallace went to the convention as the incumbent of the Vice-Presidency; he had the support of the West; he had the written endorsement of the President, and he had the solid backing of all factions of labor, which in recent years is normally strongly Democratic. He was the one man labor considered as its friend at court. At one time during the convention, the only thing that saved the Truman cause was an overnight adjournment. Could the Wallace supporters have staved off that adjournment and forced a vote, it is quite likely that Wallace would have been nominated, as a count of noses at the time showed more than 450 votes for him. On the first ballot after the adjournment, Wallace received 427 votes with Senator Truman running second and various favorites trailing. On the second ballot, the tide swung to Truman and, in the landslide which followed, he was nominated with slightly more than one thousand delegates voting for him.

Some bitterness developed during the convention but soon afterward the Democratic party presented a solid front in its effort to elect Roosevelt for a fourth term. Despite his defeat, Wallace took an active part in the campaign. He barnstormed throughout the Middle West and the Eastern states. He was an energetic campaigner, and he also demonstrated to the public that he was a good loser and a "good sport."

On November 7, 1944, President Roosevelt was re-elected, this time with a slightly smaller popular majority but with an electoral vote of landslide proportions. The Electoral College vote was 432 for Roosevelt and ninety-nine votes for Governor Thomas E. Dewey of New York.

The "dispensable" Wallace was one of the first to congratulate President Roosevelt on his victory. He had been an untiring worker for the President and he had paid his own expenses during the campaign, refusing to accept compensation from the Democratic Campaign Committee.

Soon after the inauguration of Roosevelt for his fourth term, he requested the resignation of Jesse Jones, his Secretary of Commerce. The President wrote Jones that he was appreciative of his past services but that nonetheless Wallace was entitled to a cabinet post because of his long record of service for the Democratic party. The Chief Executive was roundly assailed by the opposition for his reputed ingratitude, and the ousted Secretary of Commerce was frank in his reply that Wallace was totally unfitted to hold the Commerce portfolio. Jones, however, had no alternative but to resign.

Roosevelt thereupon appointed Wallace as Secretary of Commerce. Senate opposition was considerable, however, and Wallace did not have a comfortable time when asked to appear before an upper-house committee to answer questions as to his qualification for the office. He was ultimately confirmed but not before the Roosevelt administration agreed to remove the Reconstruction Finance Corporation from the jurisdiction of the Department of Commerce.

If Jesse Jones was ousted, Wallace in 1946 was to find himself accorded the same treatment. On September 12 of that year, in an address at Madison Square Garden in New York, Wallace called for a pro-Soviet policy by the United States. Secretary of State James F. Byrnes, then attending the Conference of Paris, was apparently left out on a limb by this move on the part of a cabinet member, and in transatlantic talks with the White House he protested that the Wallace talk had enormously complicated his efforts to adhere to a stronger line where Russia was concerned. He insisted that Wallace be ousted.

President Truman further complicated the situation by first saying that he had read and approved the Madison Square Garden address by Wallace before it was delivered, and then reversing himself to say that he had only approved the right of his Secretary of Commerce to express any view he desired. The upshot of the affair was that the White House asked and, of course, obtained Wallace's resignation a week after the controversial address, and he was soon thereafter appointed to the editorship of *The New Republic*, the liberal weekly.

In 1947, Wallace was fifty-nine. He had already had a distinguished career in government service. A man of pronounced talents in economic, agrarian and political fields, his career is by no means ended, even though he is no longer in the administration. As to his one term as Vice-President, it would appear a fair appraisal to say that in that usually nondescript office he displayed more intelligence, thoughtfulness and vigor than almost any of his predecessors. On December 29, 1947, he announced that he would run as independent candidate for President.

CHAPTER XXXIV

Harry S. Truman

SEVEN PRESIDENTS HAVE died in office. Seven men, elected as Vice-Presidents, have realized their "Heir Apparentship." The latest of these is Harry S. Truman of Missouri, who succeeded to the office of President on April 12, 1945.

The only President to be elected three and four times, Franklin Delano Roosevelt died at Warm Springs, Georgia, on the afternoon of that day. He had served only a little more than three months of what would have been his fourth term. When the news of his passing was flashed to the world, men turned to one another and asked, in effect, "What about this man Truman? Can he make the grade?"

Like so many men before him, President Truman was an unknown quantity when he was tossed into the maelstrom of world affairs on a scale never before known to history. He was sixty, a small-town Missourian, the son of a Confederate soldier. He had been raised on a farm. He was not a college graduate nor a lawyer, and he was serving his second term as the junior senator from his state when he was offered to the Democratic party as its candidate for the Vice-Presidential nomination.

Mr. Truman had been active in the state militia before World War I. He had enlisted in the Army at the outbreak of that conflict. He served in the artillery where he made a creditable record. His battalion saw much active service, and Truman returned to the little Missouri town of Independence as an artillery major and something in the way of a town hero.

For a time he was a haberdasher but failed at it. He and his partner lost their shirts, but the young Truman did not go through bankruptcy. He made a long and successful effort to pay off his debts. In 1922, he entered politics to the extent that he became the "machine" candidate for circuit judge in his home county. In Missouri the circuit judge is not a magistrate but is the county commissioner or what is called, elsewhere, the county supervisor. He is a county executive, serving as one of a board which governs the county and handles its fiscal affairs. Mr. Truman was elected in that first political venture, and he has never been defeated for office since.

Politics was more to Mr. Truman's bent than business. He had been a good farmer, a good company commander, and a good soldier. He had shown little aptitude for business. But when he entered politics, the somewhat phlegmatic, pleasant, piano-playing, thirty-seven-year-old Truman found that which suited him down to the ground.

Many men who have left their mark on the world of politics have started life similarly. Lincoln was also a business failure. Grant failed miserably at every undertaking up to the time he became the most successful general in the Union Army. Theodore Roosevelt was "totally irresponsible when it came to money matters," and William McKinley thought seriously of going into bankruptcy before he became a candidate for President.

Truman made a fair record as circuit judge of Shelby County. He kept a watchful eye on appropriations; he looked after the welfare of his constituents in the district he represented; and he was an efficient vote getter. What was more important in Pendergast-controlled Shelby County, he readily took orders.

Senator James A. Reed of Missouri had been a firebrand senator for many years. Champ Clark was a steady workhorse Democrat from the eastern part of the state but a successor was needed for "Fireman Jim" Reed. In looking over the field, Pendergast picked Circuit Judge Harry Truman as a likely candidate. His record was uncontroversial, he was an active Legionnaire, a Mason, and he came of an old established family in the state. No one could impugn his honesty or his war record, and his connection with the corrupt Pendergast machine had been of short duration. The wily Tom Pendergast, who had made millions illicitly and who afterward went to the penitentiary for an insurance fraud, who was dictator of Kansas City and western Missouri, picked the fifty-year-old Shelby County "boy" to be his candidate to succeed the aging Reed.

Mr. Truman was highly flattered. His political experience had been limited. He had been elected to one office only in his life, and to land in the United States Senate in one jump was almost too much to expect. But again he proved himself a good vote getter. He attended Legion meetings, circulated among his lodge brothers, good-naturedly played the piano at rallies, and was elected as junior senator.

Truman was a hard-working senator if not a brilliant one or a good speaker. He was regular in his upper-house attendance and "regular" in his voting. He worked better in committee than on the floor. He supported President Roosevelt's policies and, when the war began, the administration came to depend on him as a workhorse with leadership possibilities. Vice-President Wallace appointed him to the chairmanship of the Committee to Investigate War Expenditures. This committee was outstanding in the amount of work it accomplished.

Senator Truman and his committee showed neither fear nor favor in their treatment of those who had been careless or corrupt in their handling of war contracts. As chairman of the committee, Senator Truman reaped the usual amount of favorable publicity for a job well done. When, in 1944, Roosevelt was assured of renomination for a fourth term, he was approached as to his choice of a running mate. There were a number of names mentioned. As the incumbent, Wallace was looked upon as the likely nominee but many of the Southern and Eastern leaders preferred a candidate more favorable to their policies. Wallace was regarded by many as visionary, impractical, and unpredictable.

Hannegan, chairman of the Democratic National Committee, suggested three names to the President—Wallace, Justice Douglas of the Supreme Court, and Senator Truman. The President was willing to accept any of them, and Hannegan went forth to nominate his fellow Missourian. He played Wallace against Douglas and used the oft-quoted statement, "Gentlemen, we are not only going to nominate a Vice-President, we are likely to nominate another President as well."

The South and East showed a solid front against Wallace or Douglas and out of that solidity came the Truman nomination for Vice-President.

During the campaign of 1944, Mr. Truman showed himself a better speaker than had been expected. He conducted an active campaign throughout the country and on November 6, 1944, he was elected. Roosevelt and Truman polled 432 electoral votes while Dewey and Bricker polled ninety-nine.

Mr. Truman was Vice-President for three months and twelve days. He had been a United States senator for ten years. He was a "Senator's Vice-President," one of their own. He would have been a popular presiding officer, even in the absence of any training in law.

The Democrats had increased their majority in both houses of Congress and a continuation of the President's policies was assured. The war had been in progress for more than three years and was fast drawing to a victorious close when, on April 12, 1945, the Vice-President found himself President of the United States. A country boy, a soldier, an unsuccessful small-town merchant, a county commissioner, a United States senator, a Vice-President—and then the White House.

There is, of course, no indispensable man. Roosevelt was colorful and dramatic. He had been President for a longer period than any predecessor. He had been a hero to millions and his name had been anathema to others. No fair appraisal of a man's place in history may be drawn until every individual who knew him has passed on. Men wondered what would happen to the young nation when George Washington ceased to be President. Americans have similarly worried after Jackson, Lincoln, and Roosevelt.

President Truman retained the members of Mr. Roosevelt's cabinet until he had time to orient himself. He kept the leadership of the Army and Navy intact; he continued to conduct the war along the lines planned by Roosevelt and the General Staff; and he followed the New Deal policies. He had never met Winston Churchill or Marshal Stalin, but he adopted a middle-of-the-road course. He listened to advice from men who knew, and he made a minimum of mistakes in his first weeks in office; moreover he had the good will of the nation.

Gradually the new President drew into his official family men with whom he had served. He sent Secretary of State Edward R. Stettinius Jr. to represent him at the first United Nations Conference at San Francisco. President Truman attended the closing meeting of the conference and made a fair impression on the delegates. Mr. Stettinius was appointed Chief United States delegate to the United Nations and the President selected in his stead, at the State Department, his friend and former colleague in the Senate, James F. Byrnes. Byrnes had been a member of the Supreme Court and a sort of "Assistant President" to Roosevelt, and proved himself invaluable to President Truman. Henry Morgenthau Jr. resigned as Secretary of the Treasury and the President appointed Judge Fred M. Vinson to that position. Representative Clinton P. Anderson of New Mexico was made Secretary of Agriculture and Judge Lewis B. Schwellenbach of Washington, a former senator, was given the Labor portfolio. Assistant Secretary of War Robert P. Patterson succeeded Henry L. Stimson when that official, who had served in three cabinets, resigned. He momentarily retained Secretary of Interior Harold L. Ickes, the sole remaining member of Roosevelt's original cabinet; and Wallace as Secretary of Commerce.

Mr. Truman created a favorable impression upon the country by a proposal he launched scarcely two months after he fell heir to the Presidency. This was a message sent to Congress on June 19, 1945, dealing with the Presidential succession and suggesting that, except in one extremity, the Speaker of the House of Representatives become Vice-President when that office becomes vacant.

The President reasoned cogently in this message, which was referred to the Committee on the Judiciary, and it is worth reading, at least in part:

> I think that this is an appropriate time for the Congress [Mr. Truman wrote] to re-examine the question of the Presidential succession.
>
> The question is of great importance now because there will be no elected Vice-President for almost four years.
>
> The existing statute governing the succession to the office of President was inacted in 1886. Under it, in the event of the death of the elected President and Vice-President, members of the cabinet successively fill the office.
>
> Each of these cabinet members is appointed by the President, with the advice and consent of the Senate. In effect, therefore, by reason of the tragic death of the late President, it now lies within my power to nominate the person who would be my immediate successor in the event of my own death or inability to act.
>
> I do not believe that in a democracy this power should rest with the Chief Executive. . . . There is no officer in our system of government, besides the President and Vice-President, who has been elected by all the voters of the country.
>
> The Speaker of the House of Representatives, who is elected in his own district, is also elected to be the presiding officer of the House by a vote of all the representatives of all the people of the country. As a result, I believe that the Speaker is the official in the Federal Government whose selection, next to that of the President and the Vice-President, can be most accurately said to stem from the people themselves. . . .
>
> I recommend, therefore, that the Congress enact legislation placing the Speaker of the House of Repre-

sentatives first in order of succession in case of the removal, death, resignation, or inability to act of the President and Vice-President. Of course, the Speaker should resign as a representative in the Congress as well as Speaker of the House before he assumes the office of President.

If there is no qualified Speaker, or if the Speaker fails to qualify, then I recommend that the succession pass to the President pro tempore of the Senate, who should hold office until a duly elected Speaker is elected.

If there be neither Speaker nor President pro tempore qualified to succeed on the creation of the vacancy, then the succession might pass to the members of the cabinet, as now provided, until a duly qualified President is elected. [As the Presidential succession stood until 1947, the first cabinet member to succeed was the Secretary of State.]

In the interest of orderly, democratic government, I urge the Congress to give its early consideration to this most important subject.

Congress did not draft any such enabling legislation as President Truman wanted in either 1945 or 1946 but, after the off-year elections and the overwhelming Republican victory at the polls, an act to that effect was adopted by the House in July, 1947, and also approved by the Senate the same month. The President signed it.

For all the favorable comment that this proposed measure provoked, Mr. Truman's White House honeymoon was short-lived. Inevitably, it should be admitted, he suffered by contrast with Roosevelt who, whatever else he was, was dynamic and forceful and ready at the drop of a hat to go to the people with a controversial issue. Roosevelt, in addition, had a commanding voice; Mr. Truman's is reedy and treble, unfortunately, and although on several occasions he has had magnificent texts to read (as at the opening of the United Nations General Assembly at New York, late in 1946), he has no talent for the spoken word.

Mr. Truman soon appeared reluctant to assume strong leadership, although, as the Chief Executive in the accumulating stresses and strains that followed the end of hostilities in Europe and the Pacific, leadership was desperately needed. He had a fair measure of the good will of Congress, of which he had been a member, but he manifestly preferred to be subservient to the national legislature rather than to lead it. He made some mediocre appointments in high places: in 1946 he discharged Secretary Ickes, an unquestionably able administrator, because of that cabinet officer's opposition to one of Mr. Truman's preferences for the post of Assistant Secretary of the Navy; and after blowing hot and cold, he expelled Secretary Wallace in the same year. His policy on price control did not contribute to his popularity and unquestionably did contribute to the rout of his party in 1946.

In foreign policy, the outstanding events were the so-called Truman Doctrine and the European Recovery Program, which bears the name of Secretary of State George C. Marshall.

In March of 1947, President Truman addressed a message to Congress asking for financial aid to Greece, in the amount of $350 million, and $100 million to Turkey. Mr. Truman asked that sum to "relieve the gravity of the present situation which confronts the world today." He remarked that "assistance is imperative if Greece is to survive as a free nation," and added that "Greece's neighbor, Turkey, also deserves our attention. The future of Turkey as an independent and economically sound state is clearly no less important to the freedom-loving peoples of the world than that of Greece. . . . Turkey now needs our support. Great responsibilities have been placed upon us by the swift movement of events."

This was a drastic reorientation of United States foreign policy, in the sense that it implied our further involvement abroad. Its design was to stave off further inroads in the Balkans by the Soviet Union. The Truman Doctrine gave rise to attacks in some circles of public opinion that the United States was imperialist. Two special economic and military missions were sent to each country.

The same criticism, much more vocal among Communists

overseas, was leveled in 1947 at President Truman's Secretary of State, Gen. George C. Marshall. On June 5, 1947, General Marshall made an address to Harvard University in which he suggested that the United States might aid those European nations which would co-operate among themselves. The sequel was a meeting at Paris of 16 nations; the Soviet Union and its satellite nations declined. Discussion of the plan, which as stated by President Truman, required 17 billions, began as the Congress met in 1948.

Bibliography

The following list of sources on the Vice-Presidents of the United States is by no means exhaustive. The reader interested in learning more in detail about one man or more of the Heirs Apparent, however, will find these volumes rewarding:

Works (10 vols) by John Adams.

The Writings of Thomas Jefferson (10 vols) edited by P. L. Ford, and Jefferson's *Autobiography*.

Memoirs of Aaron Burr (2 vols), and *Reports of the Trials of Col. Aaron Burr* (2 vols), David Robertson.

The Public Papers of George Clinton (10 vols).

The Life of Elbridge Gerry (two vols), James T. Austin (his son-in-law).

Public Papers of Daniel D. Tompkins (three vols).

Life of John C. Calhoun (written by himself, although attributed to R. M. T. Hunter).

Martin Van Buren to the End of His Public Career, George Bancroft. (There is voluminous material, including correspondence, in the Library of Congress, and not available elsewhere.)

The Life and Times of Col. Richard M. Johnson of Ky., L. R. Meyer.

The Letters of the Tylers (3 vols), Lyon G. Tyler (his son).

Diary of George Mifflin Dallas (edited by Susan Dallas).

Millard Fillmore, W. E. Griffis.

Dictionary of Alabama Biography (vol III, for William R. King). *Sketches of Hon. John C. Breckinridge, Democratic Nominee for President* (among the Breckinridge manuscripts in the Library of Congress).

The Life and Times of Hannibal Hamlin, C. E. Hamlin (his grandson).

The Life and Public Services of President Andrew Johnson, John Savage.

Life of Schuyler Colfax, O. J. Holister.

The Life and Public Services of Henry Wilson, Elias Nason and Thomas Russell.

Life and Public Services of Thos. A. Hendricks, J. W. Holcombe and H. M. Skinner.

Levi Parson Morton: Banker, Diplomat and Statesman, Robert McElroy.

The Life and Labors of Hon. Adlai Ewing Stevenson, J. W. Cook (in Journal of the Illinois State Historical Society, July 1915).

Life of Garret Augustus Hobart, David Magio.

Theodore Roosevelt and His Times, Shown by His Own Letters. J. B. Bishop, editor.

Senator Fairbanks—The Boy and Man, E. J. Lewis.

Recollections of Thomas R. Marshall, Vice President and Hoosier Philosopher—A Hoosier Salad (autobiography).

Puritan in Babylon: the Story of Calvin Coolidge. William Allen White.

Essay and Speeches (Charles Gates Dawes).

Democracy Reborn; Selected from the Public Papers of Henry Agard Wallace.

Missouri Compromise, Tristram Coffin (for Harry S. Truman).

Index

310

political positions held by, 225
vice-president:
  nomination for and election as, 225-226
  Spanish War, part played in, 227

Jefferson, Thomas:
Aaron Burr and, 30-31
Alien and Sedition Act and, 29
ancestry, 16
as governor of Virginia, 22
as Minister to France, 24-25
as President:
  accomplishments as, 30 ff.
  election as, 30-31
  re-election as, 32
as Secretary of State, 25 ff.
as student and scholar, 24, 33
charges of ineffectual resistance against
  enemy, 22
Committee of Correspondence, influence in, 19
Continental Congresses, activities in, 20
Declaration of Independence, part
  played in, 21
education:
  early, 16
  college, 17
  law, 18
French Revolution and, 27
House of Burgesses, election to, 19
life and work, estimate of, 16, 33-34
Marquis de Lafayette and, 34
marriage and children, 18, 24
Monticello, building of, 20
negotiation of peace with England, part
  played in, 24
slavery and:
  as slave owner, 17, 18
  legislation for freeing slaves, introduction of, 28
University of Virginia, part played in
  founding of, 32 ff.
vice-president, election as, 28 ff.
Virginia House of Delegates, work
  in, 21, 23

Johnson, Andrew:
Abraham Lincoln and, 168, 169
ancestry, 161
as President of the United States:

Alaska, purchase of, 173
cabinet, clashes with, 170-171
General Amnesty Proclamation, issuance of, 173
impeachment procedures against, 171-173
political amnesty for the South, advocacy of, 170, 171
Presidential Succession Act, passage of, 173
unconstitutional attacks on, 171
as tailor, 161
Constitution, sponsorship of changes in, 165
education, 162
Homestead Act, sponsorship of, 165, 166-167
Know-Nothings and, 166
life and work, estimate of, 161, 174-175
love life, 161-162
marriage and children, 162
migration to the West, 162
military service in Civil War, 168
political positions held by, 163-164, 165, 166, 174
pro-Union convictions of, 167-168
tariffs, attitudoe toward, 164
vice-president:
  election as, 168-169
  public disgrace as, 169
Johnson, Richard Mentor:
ancestry, 112
as chairman of the Military Affairs
  Committee, 114-115
as United States senator, 115 ff.
Bank Bill, opposition to, 116
Congressional Compensation Bill, sponsorship of, 115
education, 113
financial difficulties of, 115
life and works, estimate of, 112, 120
political offices held by, 113
presidential ambitions of, 118-120
Tecumseh, debates concerning death of, 114
vice-president:
  election as, 117-118
  record as, 118
War of 1812:
  active military service during, 113-114
  attitude toward, 113